A FAIR DAY'S WAGE FOR A FAIR DAY'S WORK?

A Fair Day's Wage for a Fair Day's Work?

Sweated Labour and the Origins of
Minimum Wage Legislation in Britain

SHEILA BLACKBURN
University of Liverpool, UK

ASHGATE

Published by
Ashgate Publishing Limited
Gower House
Croft Road
Aldershot
Hampshire GU11 3HR
England

Ashgate Publishing Company
Suite 420
101 Cherry Street
Burlington, VT 05401-4405
USA

Ashgate website: http://www.ashgate.com

British Library Cataloguing in Publication Data
Blackburn, Sheila
  A fair day's wage for a fair day's work? : sweated labour and the origins of minimum wage legislation in Britain. – (Studies in labour history)
  1. Minimum wage – Great Britain – History 2. Minimum wage – Law and legislation – Great   Britain – History 3. Sweatshops – Great Britain – History
  I. Title
  331.2'3'0941

Library of Congress Cataloging-in-Publication Data
Blackburn, Sheila, 1949–
  A fair day's wage for a fair day's work? : sweated labour and the origins of minimum wage legislation in Britain / By Sheila Blackburn.
    p. cm. — (Studies in labour history)
  Includes index.
  ISBN 978-0-7546-3264-1 (alk. paper)
  1. Minimum wage—Law and legislation—Great Britain—History. 2. Sweatshops—Great Britain—History. 3. Labor policy—Great Britain—History. I. Title.

  KD3118.B53 2007
  344.41012'3—dc22

2007021975

ISBN 978-0-7546-3264-1

Printed and bound in Great Britain by MPG Books Ltd, Bodmin, Cornwall.

Contents

List of Figures

Studies in Labour History
General Editor's Preface

This series of books provides reassessments of broad themes in labour history, along with more detailed studies arising from the latest research in the field. Most books are single-authored but there are also volumes of essays, centred on key themes and issues, usually emerging from major conferences organised by the British Society for the Study of Labour History. Every author approaches their task with the needs of both specialist and non-specialist readerships in mind, for labour history is a fertile area of historical scholarship, stimulating wide-ranging interest, debate and further research, within both social and political history and beyond.

When this series was first launched (with Chris Wrigley as its general editor) in 1998, labour history was emerging, reinvigorated, from a period of considerable introspection and external criticism. The assumptions and ideologies underpinning much labour history had been challenged by postmodernist, anti-Marxist and, especially, feminist thinking. There was also a strong feeling that often it had emphasised institutional histories of organised labour, at the expense of histories of work generally, and of workers' social relations beyond their workplaces – especially gender and wider familial relationships. The Society for the Study of Labour History was concerned to consolidate and build upon this process of review and renewal through the publication of more substantial works than its journal *Labour History Review* could accommodate, and also to emphasise that though it was a British body, its focus and remit extended to international, transnational and comparative perspectives.

Arguably, the extent to which labour history was narrowly institutionalised has been exaggerated. This series therefore includes studies of labour organisations, including international ones, where there is a need for modern reassessment. However, it is also its objective to maintain the breadth of labour history's gaze beyond conventionally organised workers, sometimes to workplace experiences in general, sometimes to industrial relations, and naturally to workers' lives beyond the immediate realm of work.

Malcolm Chase
Society for the Study of Labour History
University of Leeds

Abbreviations

ACAS	Advisory, Conciliation and Arbitration Service
ASE	Amalgamated Society of Engineers
AST	Amalgamated Society of Tailors
BJIR	*British Journal of Industrial Relations*
BLPES	British Library of Political and Economic Science
CA	*County Advertiser for Staffordshire and Worcestershire*
CBI	Confederation of British Industry
CE	*County Express for Worcestershire and Staffordshire*
CIR	Commission on Industrial Relations
CMA	Chain Manufacturers' Association
COS	Charity Organisation Society
CTB	Chain Trade Board
CTC	Child Tax Credit
EHR	*Economic History Review*
FES	Family Expenditure Survey
FIS	Family Income Supplement
HSIR	*Historical Studies in Industrial Relations*
ILP	Independent Labour Party
IPM	Institute of Personnel Management
IRSH	*International Review of Social History*
JBG	Jewish Board of Guardians
JIC	Joint Industrial Council
LCC	London County Council
LPC	Low Pay Commission
LPU	Low Pay Unit
LSE	London School of Economics
MC	*Morning Chronicle*
NA	National Archives
NASL	National Anti-Sweating League
NBPI	National Board for Prices and Incomes
NCPD	National Committee for the Prevention of Destitution
NFWW	National Federation of Women Workers
NHWL	National Home Workers' League
NIC	National Industrial Conference
NMW	National Minimum Wage
NUPE	National Union of Public Employees
NES	New Earnings Survey
OED	*Oxford English Dictionary*
PJC	Provisional Joint Committee
PP	Parliamentary Papers

RCHW	Royal Commission on the Housing of the Working Classes
RCL	Royal Commission on Labour
SCH	Select Committee on Homework
SCSS	Select Committee on the Sweating System
SDF	Social Democratic Federation
SDP	Social Democratic Party
SJIC	Statutory Joint Industrial Council
TBI	Trade Boards Inspectorate
TELCO	The East London Communities Organisation
TGWU	Transport and General Workers' Union
TP	Tuckwell Papers
TUC	Trades Union Congress
UGWTU	United Garment Workers' Trade Union
WFTC	Working Families Tax Credit
WIC	Women's Industrial Council
WIN	*Women's Industrial News*
WLL	Women's Labour League
WTA	Working Tailor's Association
WTC	Working Tax Credit
WTUL	Women's Trade Union League
WTUR	*Women's Trade Union Review*

Currency Conversion Table

The British system of currency before February 1971 involved pounds (£), shillings (s) and pence (d). Until 1971, one pound (£1) contained twenty shillings (20s) or 240 pence (240d). Following that date British currency was decimalised so that one pound (£1) contained 100 new pence (100p). Sums in the old system and their modern decimal equivalent values are as follows:

Old system	Decimal system
¼d (farthing)	0.1p
½d (half-penny)	0.2p
1d (penny)	0.4p
3d (three-penny)	1.25p
6d (sixpence)	2.5p
1s (one shilling)	5p
2s (two shillings)	10p
3s (three shillings)	15p
4s (four shillings)	20p
5s (five shillings)	25p
10s (ten shillings)	50p
£1 (twenty shillings)	100p

Acknowledgements

This book has had a long gestation, and I am indebted to many people. My special thanks are due to Professor Tony Mason of De Montfort University who first suggested the topic to me, and to Dr Eric Taylor of Wolverhampton University who helped me in the early stages of my research. I am particularly indebted to Swansea University for awarding me a Welsh Tinplate Trust research fellowship to investigate industrial change, and to the Economic and Social Research Council for awarding me a Senior Research Fellowship, (Award number H52427506594). I am grateful to Michael Rose, Emeritus Professor in the University of Manchester for his generous assistance. I also wish to thank Professor John Belchem of the University of Liverpool for supporting my study-leave application, and Professor Michael Hughes, also of the University of Liverpool, for lightening my teaching load during a crucial stage of research.

My special thanks are due to Professor Chris Wrigley of Nottingham University, the first editor of the series in which this book appears, for his faith in the project, and to his successor, Dr Malcolm Chase of Leeds University, for his patience and consistent encouragement. I would also like to thank Emily Yates of Ashgate Publishing for seeing the book through to its final stages. I am grateful to Ian Qualtrough of Liverpool University for his technical assistance with the illustrations.

My brothers Baden and Barrie Blackburn as well as my good friend Ray McEntegart have reminded me that there is a real world beyond academe. Finally, I am indebted to Dr Alan Campbell of Liverpool University. He has been a good friend, colleague and more besides.

Acknowledgements

Introduction

Following the abandonment of paternalistic wage-fixing in the late eighteenth and early nineteenth centuries, the 1909 Trade Boards Act was the state's first attempt in nearly a hundred years to regulate pay in Britain. Initially applied to tailoring, paper boxmaking, lace and chainmaking, the legislation encompassed some 250,000 sweated workers and established a minimum rate that the individual industry could bear.[1] Although Parliament had previously sanctioned the legal control of hours and working conditions, it was only with the greatest trepidation that it assented to trade boards. Economic philosophers had steadfastly held that intervention in the wages contract would be disastrous for Britain. According to R.H. Tawney, the measure's inception marked a critical turning point in British economic and social thought.[2] To *The Times*, it was 'a remedy of an exceptional kind' designed to curb one 'of the worst reproaches against our modern type of industrial civilisation ... the "sweating system"'.[3]

Despite the widespread interest, the meaning and utility of this former slang word remained controversial. On the Second Reading of the Trade Boards Bill, Lord Hamilton of Dalzell, Lord-in-Waiting to the King, commented: 'I do not suppose that during the last twenty years there is any feature of our social system which has been so much inquired into, so much spoken about, and so much written about as the evil of sweating...'.[4] When recommending trade boards as a solution to a painfully notorious problem, he proclaimed: 'Every one knows what sweating is...'.[5] Similarly, the Labour MP, J.R. Clynes, insisted that sweating was 'easy' to define.[6] But practical investigators were more circumspect. Writing in 1899, the factory expert, R.W. Cooke-Taylor, considered that it was 'a very unfortunate term ... and were better perhaps discarded altogether where scientific accuracy is aimed at'.[7] In 1907, the Fabian socialist, Barbara Hutchins, remarked that the

---

[1]   At their peak, just before the Second World War, there were forty-seven boards covering approximately 1,136,000 employees. In 1945, in order to rid the system of the old stigma associated with sweating, trade boards were re-named wages councils: D. Sells, *British Wages Boards* (Washington, D.C., 1939), p. 366. Young workers were removed from wages council protection in 1986, and the councils were abolished in 1993. Britain enacted a national minimum wage in 1999.

[2]   R.H. Tawney, 'Fixing minimum wages: the historical aspects of the subject', in League of Nations Union, *Towards Industrial Peace* (London, 1927), p. 19.

[3]   *The Times*, 31 August 1909.

[4]   *Hansard* (Lords), 30 August 1909, col. 975.

[5]   *Ibid.*

[6]   *Hansard* (Commons), 28 April 1909, col. 410.

[7]   R.W. Cooke-Taylor, 'Sweating', in R.H. Inglis Palgrave (ed.), *Dictionary of Political Economy, Volume 3* (London, 1899), p. 503.

expression 'sweating' was misleading.[8] That same year, the social investigators, Edward Cadbury and George Shann, observed that, although the idiom had become commonplace, 'its precise meaning is … rather vague ….'[9] Modern historians' views have reflected these contemporary divisions of opinion. While Duncan Bythell finds the phrase very useful, Jenny Morris judges 'sweating' to be an unsatisfactory analytical concept since: 'It is not a precise tool for the historian ….'[10] The upshot is that, despite the recent appearance of a number of scholarly books and articles on the subject, historians still remain uncertain as to what specific forms sweating took, which forces governed its growth, where it was primarily located and how many sweated labourers there were.[11]

A major problem in 'opening up' the sweating issue in both the past and the present has been the over-riding interest of some investigators to associate it with the so-called 'antiquated' domestic workshop sector as distinct from the 'progressive' factory system. Another weakness has been the tendency to concentrate on women homeworkers locked into exploitative, labour-intensive industries as a result of a rigid gender division of work. It is argued here that sweating cannot be analysed within a static framework – it was a dynamic phenomenon and formed an integral part of a developing capitalism. Nor was it identical with outwork or women's employment. Responses, attitudes and definitions of sweating evolved and adjusted according to changes taking place in the British economy. If initially loosely identified with small-scale production, by the opening decade of the twentieth century, sweating was associated with a wide range of occupations unconnected with industrial homeworking or a sexual division of labour. The issue became linked to low pay – wherever this occurred.

In 1908, Leo Chiozza Money declared: 'In view of the conditions which exist amongst some factory workers, and especially amongst female factory workers, it is simply absurd to regard sweating as an evil confined to "home work".'[12] The system of dual employment whereby articles were taken home by factory girls to be finished out of hours belies the notion that sweated workers were a separate and identifiable group who only worked at home.[13] The problem of sweating – if defined

---

[8]   B. Hutchins, 'Homework and sweating', *Fabian Tract*, 130 (1907), p. 3.

[9]   E. Cadbury and G. Shann, *Sweating* (London, 1907), p. 1.

[10]   D. Bythell, *The Sweated Trades: Outwork in Nineteenth Century Britain* (London, 1978), p. 11; J. Morris, 'The characteristics of sweating: the late nineteenth-century London and Leeds tailoring trade', in A.V. John (ed.), *Unequal Opportunities: Women's Employment in England, 1800–1918* (Oxford, 1986), p. 96.

[11]   For details of recent literature on sweating, see note 37 below.

[12]   *Christian Commonwealth*, 2 September 1908. See also, C. Smith, *The Case for Wages Boards* (London, 1908), p. 4. Clementina Black thought that the most wretched looking girl worker was not a homeworker, but a *factory* cocoa packer: C. Black, *Sweated Industry and the Minimum Wage* (London, 1907), pp. 25–6. Wages were also further reduced in factories by deductions for power, the provision of hot water for tea, the supplying of materials such as thread and glue, as well as fines for spoilt work and bad-time keeping: E. Cadbury, M.C. Matheson and G. Shann, *Women's Work and Wages* (London, 1906), pp. 93, 193, 200; A. Anderson, *Women in the Factory* (London, 1922), p. 60.

[13]   Anderson, *Women in the Factory*, p. 60.

as inadequate wages – also embraced some practically all-male activities such as agriculture, fishing, dock work, transport and the Sheffield cutlery trades.[14] As the staunch opponent of minimum wage legislation, Sir Frederick Banbury, declared on the Second Reading of the Trade Boards Bill:

> A great number of people say that the agricultural labourer who receives only 12s. or 15s. a week is sweated ... So far as I know the only standard fixed by hon. Members ... is the wage standard – a wage on which the person who receives it can live comfortably ... but that opens the door practically to all trades.[15]

Even branches of well-organised crafts like marine engineering were susceptible to sweating.[16]

This book suggests that, if we are to identify which factors generated and underpinned sweating, then the focus needs to shift to a new emphasis on how notions of sweating varied at different junctures, and how they varied according to breadwinning patterns and the specificities of place. In particular, a greater awareness of the structure, performance and complexities of local labour markets is essential. Two inter-related elements were necessary preconditions for sweating to develop: an over-supply of labour and a lack of trade union organisation amongst the work force. These were both linked to unregulated labour markets. The main reason for the first problem was ease of entry into a trade and lack of *bona fide* apprenticeship requirements. The sweated were not necessarily devoid of dexterity or inbred talent. But many of the processes that the low waged were engaged upon could be acquired in the district or region where sweating occurred. This caused a surplus of labour, a 'reserve army' competing for work, and barely adequate rates for the workers. In nail and chainmaking, for example, children were literally born and reared in the chain shop and learnt their trade at their mother's block.[17] Similarly, boxmaking was started young and ran in families.[18]

Before 1870 and the more rigorous enforcement of the Education Acts, children constituted a significant source of sweated labour. Even after 1870, reliable evidence

---

[14]   Black, *Sweated Industry*, ch. 4.

[15]   *Hansard* (Commons), 28 April 1909, col. 406. The Labour MP, J.R. Clynes, retorted that long hours, bad conditions and poor pay: 'exist in connection with ... thousands of the workers of our railway systems': *ibid.*, col. 410. On this basis, many municipal workers, despite fair wages resolutions, could also be classed as sweated. The House of Commons adopted fair wages resolutions in 1891, 1909 and 1946. The Fair Wages Resolution of 1946 was rescinded in 1983 on the grounds that it was a relic from the days of sweated labour. Fair wages resolutions specified that government contractors should pay rates commonly recognised as current for a competent workman in his trade and that contracts should not be sub-let. Although the resolutions applied to central government contracts, they were customarily adopted in local government contracts as well. They were rarely effective. See B. Bercusson, *Fair Wages Resolutions* (London, 1978), chs 1–6.

[16]   G.D.H. Cole, 'Living wages: the case for a new minimum wage act', *New Fabian Research Bureau*, 42 (1938), p. 32.

[17]   *Reynolds's Newspaper*, 4 September 1910.

[18]   M. Bulkley, *The Establishment of Minimum Rates in the Boxmaking Industry, Under the Trade Boards Act of 1909* (London, 1915), p. 66.

indicates that the education laws were widely flouted. The inter-departmental committee on the employment of school children in 1901 found at least 200,000 of the latter in paid employment. Although these occupations included homework, they also encompassed drudgery in brickfields, bakery factories, and shops (as errand boys).[19] As Clementina Black, the social investigator, observed:

> Even in establishments visited by the factory inspector this evil of child labour exists, and a case is known where a boy of twelve was employed for twenty-four hours with only one break of an hour. In another case a baker's boy was found before six o'clock in the morning cleaning the ashes from the oven. He was twelve years old, and for three years previously had been employed in delivering loaves and running errands .... Several children of 13 and under were found working full-time in brickfields.[20]

Added to this was the misuse of the half-time system – even in the well-organised textile districts.[21]

A further factor was the over-supply of adult workers. Many women were sweated due to the sexually segregated labour market. Married women were doubly disadvantaged because their family obligations constricted their employment to an even narrower range of jobs. But it should also be remembered that the sweating of women workers was frequently associated with the low pay or under-employment of males.[22] In the eastern counties of England women were exploited because they were forced to take in tailoring to augment the meagre earnings of the male breadwinner engaged in fishing or agriculture. Tawney cites the case of the wife of an undertaker compelled to toil at tailoring because 'people aren't dying half fast enough'.[23] The same applied to East London where the irregular wages of dockworkers necessitated sweated tailoring on the part of their wives.[24] In chainmaking the

---

[19]   National Anti-Sweating League (NASL), *Report of Conference on a Minimum Wage* (London, 1907), p. 43. See also, E. Hogg, 'School children as wage earners', *Nineteenth Century*, 42 (1897), pp. 235–44. Olive Malvery's sensational survey, *Baby Toilers* (London, 1907), outlined how sweating imposed special constraints on the young.

[20]   NASL, *Report of Conference*, pp. 43–4.

[21]   Adler considered that, despite the incompleteness of returns, there were more than 82,000 half-timers in England. These were chiefly engaged in northern textile factories: N. Adler, 'Child employment and juvenile delinquency', in G. Tuckwell *et al.*, *Women in Industry From Seven Points of View* (London, 1908), p. 126. Half-timers, including textile workers, were frequently dismissed at sixteen to enter blind-alley occupations. See N. Adler and R.H. Tawney, *Boy and Girl Labour* (London, 1909), p. 8. The post office and the railways also dismissed errand boys when they reached eighteen or twenty: see A. Freeman, *Boy Life and Labour: The Manufacture of Inefficiency* (London, 1914), p. 201.

[22]   Horrell and Humphries suggest that women were inclined to work when their children were young and family resources most straitened: S. Horrell and J. Humphries, 'The origins and expansion of the male breadwinner family: the case of nineteenth-century Britain', *International Review of Social History (IRSH)*, 42, Supplement 5 (1997), pp. 25–64.

[23]   R.H. Tawney, *The Establishment of Minimum Rates in the Tailoring Industry, Under the Trade Boards Act of 1909* (London, 1915), p. 191.

[24]   Tawney estimated that there were 20,000 sweated dockers in East London alone: Tawney, *Minimum Rates in Tailoring*, p. 112. See also, Select Committee on the Sweating

sweated circumstances of women were frequently linked to those of their husbands. The majority of women chainmakers were married to casually employed workers and, in view of the fluctuations in their partners' wages, these women would often discontinue work when the male breadwinner was fully employed, and recommence during periods of low earnings for their spouses. John Burnett pinpointed this issue when he stated of the male chainmakers in 1888:

> On the one hand they seem to feel that the cheaper labour of their wives and daughters is forcing them to lower and lower wages, while on the other their earnings are so miserably low, and their state so bad, that they fear to give up the few shillings which the female workers add to the family income. *They are between the devil of cheap labour competition and the deep sea of family poverty.* (Emphasis added)[25]

In effect, women were often exploited because they were married to sweated males.

It is therefore erroneous to view females and, in particular, women homeworkers, as the sole victims of sweating. Age, lack of skill, a temporary personal misfortune such as ill health or alcoholism, could also cast many adult males into the sweated labour market.[26] The social reformer, Constance Smith, highlighted this specifically when she commented: 'In individual cases, the illness of the breadwinner, or the failure of an employing firm is often sufficient to bring a whole family within the grip of the sweating system.'[27] That sweating could not be combated without extending

---

System (SCSS), *First Report* (PP 1888, X), QQ. 1,617–19, 1,693–700.

[25]   *Report as to the Condition of Nailmakers and Small Chainmakers in South Staffordshire and East Worcestershire* (PP 1888, XCI), p. 502.

[26]   Money, following Booth and Rowntree, stressed the implications of the life cycle for sweating. While Booth and Rowntree had emphasised that poverty was experienced early in life, Money's statistics indicated that, from middle age, good wages were exceedingly difficult to obtain. He considered that: 'After 50–55 the age factor ... begins to tell, and the workman trembles at thought of the future. Each grey hair is a deadly enemy to his livelihood': L. G. C. Money, *Riches and Poverty* (London, 1905), pp. 259–64, 271. Booth neglected elderly workers due to his dependence on school board records. He rectified this in his *The Aged Poor in England and Wales* (London, 1894), p. 420. Rowntree ignored the residents of workhouses and infirmaries, and maintained that only five per cent of primary poverty was the consequence of old age or infirmity of the main breadwinner: B.S. Rowntree, *Poverty: A Study of Town Life* (London, 1901), p. 379. More recently, Macnicol has shown how jobs for the older worker began to disappear in the 1890s as employers increasingly viewed the shedding of the ageing as a means of improving efficiency: J. Macnicol, *The Politics of Retirement in Britain, 1878–1948* (Cambridge, 1998), esp. pp. 44–8. Even the very skilled, if they lived too long, might also end their days eking out a barely subsistence society pension, where one existed, with sweated production. Royal Commission on Labour (RCL), *Fifth and Final Report (Minority)* (PP 1894, XXXV), pp. 127–8. The chainmakers were particularly vociferous concerning the entry into their trade of worn-out miners and quarrymen who, in better days, had been classed among the skilled or semi-skilled: *County Express for Worcestershire and Staffordshire (CE)*, 22 September 1910, 11 December 1911.

[27]   Smith, *Case For Wages Boards*, p. 40. More has suggested that between 1890 and 1940 employment stabilised and lasted longer than previously thought. But, as Gospel notes, job insecurity was probably pervasive: C. More, 'Reskilling and labour markets in Britain

protection to males was clearly demonstrated by the attempted legal solution to sweating, the 1909 Trades Boards Act. This piece of legislation initially embraced approximately a quarter of a million workers, at least ten per cent of whom were men. By 1921, when the Act had been widely extended, over a million workers, of whom one third were males, had their wages legally regulated by trade boards.[28] Sweating, in effect, was akin to a form of outdoor relief. Together with the pawnshop, it was a way of avoiding outright destitution.

The second vital factor contributing to sweating was the absence of trade union organisation. Combination was not unknown amongst the sweated but it was seldom permanent. Sweated workers were never strong enough to negotiate standard rates of pay. Collective action only occurred when prices were forced down to near starvation levels. Once the workers had won an advance of wages, the trade society would typically fall into abeyance. Only when the rates reached a low point again would another strike be declared. Poverty meant that workers could only exert intermittent demands on their employers. The constant pressure required to maintain wage rates and conditions was beyond their financial ability. As one union official told the sweating committee, speaking particularly of the chainmakers:

> They cannot afford the 3d per week [to the union] simply because their condition is such that 3d means a loaf of bread to them; and a loaf of bread short a week means a piece for each child or a meal short ... I have told them it would be better to suffer a bit longer to make the union much stronger, but they said they could not really do it, they thought they were suffering enough as it was.[29]

Mary Macarthur of the Women's Trade Union League (WTUL) put the same case, but more succinctly. Sweated workers, she informed the Select Committee on Homework (SCH) in 1907, were unorganised because they were low paid and poorly paid because they were unorganised.[30] She also made it very plain to the SCH that low rates of wages were not confined to homeworkers. Organisation was equally difficult amongst low-waged factory labourers. Indeed, even in the factory, the rate for the same job was frequently not only different in the same district, but even in the same establishment.[31] Black made a similar point to the SCH regarding an East London shirt factory:

> When we came to take a register of the wages we found that in the two workrooms in that same firm where the women were actually working upon the very same sort of shirts cut out by the same people from the same bale of material there was a difference in wages of between 45 and 50 per cent.[32]

---

*c.*1890–1940', *Historical Studies in Industrial Relations* (*HSIR*), 2 (1996), pp. 93–110; H. Gospel, 'Labour markets and skill formation in theory and practice: a reply to Charles More', *HSIR*, 4 (1997), pp. 113–29.

[28]   S. and B. Webb, *English Local Government: English Poor Law History, Part II: The Last Hundred Years, Volume 9* (London, 1929), p. 559.

[29]   SCSS, *Third Report* (PP 1889, XIII), Q. 19,342.

[30]   SCH, *Report* (PP 1907, VI), QQ. 2,693–5.

[31]   *Ibid.*, QQ. 2,704–7; 2,712–14.

[32]   *Ibid.*, Q. 2,856.

In addition to the two principal elements of an excess of labour competing for work and the individual haggling over wages, several secondary factors intensified the sweating problem. These included trade swings, seasonality of demand for a product and lack of good management. Those employers who were guilty of sweating frequently engaged in cut-throat competition. As Smith remarked, 'the typical sweating employer ... rarely takes a long view: his aim is the immediate gain to be snatched out of the competitive struggle.'[33] During a recession, when wages were depressed, these unscrupulous employers would habitually stockpile merchandise and sell it at a greatly enhanced price when business improved. This haphazard and speculative method of management resulted in a deficiency of investment, innovation and training. It also contributed to trade fluctuations, much short-time working and product market instability. But it also included factories as well as the outwork sector.[34] Indeed, Tawney viewed many small Jewish-tailoring workshops as highly efficient.[35] On the other hand, some large clothing factories, like Barran's of Leeds, were notorious for their employment of workers at sweated rates.[36]

Unquestionably, an accurate assessment of sweating is vital to our understanding of the dynamics of nineteenth and twentieth century capitalism. This book contends that, if we are ever to fully comprehend the complex mechanism of sweating, we need a broader analytical framework than one which identifies it, intrinsically, with women's paid work in the home. It also maintains that we need to take a longer view than has hitherto been the case, starting in the 1840s and ending with the implementation of Britain's national minimum wage in 1999. The overwhelming focus of previous studies has been tailoring in the metropolis and occasionally in Leeds and Glasgow.[37] Only Bythell has attempted a more extensive survey of various

---

[33] Smith, *Case for Wages Boards*, p. 7.

[34] In 1913, when the Trade Boards Act was extended, it incorporated three entirely factory trades: hollowware, confectionery and laundries: Women's Industrial Council (WIC), *Women's Industrial News (WIN)*, July 1913, p. 136. The Kenrick hollowware firm employed nearly 1,000, some seventy per cent of whom were males: W. and C. Staples, *Power, Profits and Patriarchy: The Social Organization of Work at a British Metal Firm, 1791–1922* (Lanham, MD, 2001), p. 58.

[35] Tawney, *Minimum Rates in Tailoring*, p. 135.

[36] J. Morris, *Women Workers and the Sweated Trades* (Aldershot, 1986), p. 57; Morris, 'The characteristics of sweating', p. 116. In 1904, Barran's employed between two and three thousand workers: K. Honeyman, *Well Suited: A History of the Leeds Clothing Industry, 1850–1990* (Oxford, 2000), p. 261. The rival firm of Messrs Arthur and Co. were also castigated in the local press for their low average earnings: J. Hannam, *Isabella Ford* (Oxford, 1989), pp. 37–8.

[37] Stedman Jones, Schmiechen and Thom see sweating (as did Booth) as intrinsically a metropolitan issue. Additionally, Schmiechen and Thom, together with Bythell, Gilbert, Pennington and Westover, identify it with outwork afflicting mainly female homeworkers. This leads Bythell and Schmiechen to assume that, when homeworking declined at the beginning of the twentieth century, sweating disappeared: see G.S. Jones, *Outcast London* (Oxford, 1971); Bythell, *Sweated Trades*; J. Schmiechen, *Sweated Industries and Sweated Labor: The London Clothing Trades, 1860–1914* (London, 1984); A. Gilbert, 'Fit work for women: sweated homeworkers in Glasgow, c.1875–1914', in E. Gordon (ed.), *The World is Ill-Divided: Women's Work in Scotland in the Nineteenth and Early Twentieth Centuries* (Edinburgh, 1990),

sweated trades. But even this is limited to England, concentrates on handloom weavers and clothing workers, and omits detailed treatment of such notoriously sweated sectors as the West Midland metal trades. Moreover, his study, concerned as it is with the Victorian period, stops short of considering the Trade Boards Act of 1909. As a result, he scarcely touches on the most important and interesting aspect of sweating – the vigorous campaign to achieve minimum wage legislation. He modestly points out that his book is 'no more than a superficial introduction to a large and complex ... subject' and adds: 'The introduction of trade boards heralded a far bolder break with the past than many of the other Liberal reforms; and it is time some energetic young historian did fuller justice to the great campaign against "sweating" than has been possible within the confines of the present study.'[38]

Similarly, James Schmiechen deals only fleetingly with minimum wage law. Even then, following the traditional school of thought, he perceives the 1880s as a major watershed for anti-sweating legislation. Guided by the early works of Tawney, he is overly optimistic regarding the impact of the first boards. He neither examines the shortcomings of the 1909 Act nor analyses the responses of the various pressure groups to it. As he concedes: 'Perhaps we need to take a better look at the impact of the Trade Boards Act of 1909.'[39] Morris is probably the most perceptive historian of trade boards, but even she dismisses them as the outcome of the conscious desire of large employers for social control.[40] Vivien Hart, whilst similarly blaming big business for the feebleness of minimum wage legislation, also castigates male trade unionists for being indifferent towards the legal control of low pay.[41] Nor are studies on the role of civil servants in the creation of social policy very enlightening. Roger Davidson attributes the narrowness of the 1909 Act solely to the lukewarm attitude of Board of Trade officials and largely ignores evidence, which minimises the role of civil servants in its passage.[42]

---

pp. 158–77; S. Pennington and B. Westover, *A Hidden Workforce: Homeworkers in England, 1850–1985* (Basingstoke, 1989); D. Thom, 'Free from chains? The image of women's labour in London, 1900–20', in D. Feldman and G.S. Jones (eds), *Metropolis London: Histories and Representations since 1800* (London, 1989), pp. 85–99. See also D. Feldman, *Englishmen and Jews: Social Relations and Political Culture, 1840–1914* (New Haven, CT, 1994), esp. ch. 8. Although Feldman (following Schmiechen) considers that sweating formed part of dynamic capitalism, he still associates it with home and domestic workshops. K. James has furthered the study of garment outworkers by reviewing them in the context of inter-regional wage competition: K. James, '"Unregulated and suicidal competition": Irish rural industrial labour and Scottish anti-sweating campaigns in the early twentieth century', *Labour History Review*, 70 (2005), pp. 215–29.

[38] Bythell, *Sweated Trades*, p. 247.

[39] Schmiechen, *Sweated Industries*, p. 305.

[40] Morris, *Women Workers*, pp. 218–27.

[41] V. Hart, *Bound By Our Constitution: Women Workers and the Minimum Wage* (Princeton, N.J., 1994), pp. x, 22. See also Morris, *Women Workers*, p. 131; B.C. Roberts, *The Trades Union Congress, 1868–1921* (London, 1958), pp. 215–17; J. Rickard, 'The anti-sweating movement in Britain and Victoria: the politics of empire and social reform', *Historical Studies*, 18 (1979), pp. 587–8.

[42] R. Davidson, *Whitehall and the Labour Problem in Late-Victorian and Edwardian Britain* (London, 1985), pp. 269–73.

In contrast to such restricted approaches, this book explores what constitutes sweating and what generates sweating and low pay; what strategies have been advocated and implemented to combat these problems; how images of sweated workers have changed over time; and how successful reforms have been. The study also maintains that, if we are fully to grasp the origins of the Trade Boards Act, we must address two further issues. First, we have to evaluate the Act in a more general framework, in a setting which embraces trends in economic and social theory, which were rooted in the 1890s. Peter Hennock tentatively suggested such an approach almost three decades ago, but his concepts have never been rigorously developed.[43] If we expand and develop Hennock's thesis, we discover that a significant break with laissez-faire ideology concerning wages occurred, not in the 1880s as is commonly assumed, but rather from 1896.

The initial challenge came with the publication of Hobson's article 'A living wage' in that year.[44] In 1897, the Fabian socialists Sidney and Beatrice Webb in their *Industrial Democracy* advocated a national minimum wage as the solution to sweating.[45] At the same time, the Liberal politician, Sir Charles Dilke, drew attention to the wages boards of Victoria, Australia, with their industry-based minimum for a few, selected sweated industries.[46] Yet, broadly speaking, British society remained immune to the arguments of trade board enthusiasts until 1906.

Second, we need to investigate more fully the limited character of trade boards. In doing so, it is essential to refute the assertions that this was due variously to the antipathy of the labour movement, employers' desire for social control or that civil servants deliberately restricted low pay legislation. As Roy Hay rightly cautions, we should be wary of exaggerating the role of civil servants in social policy formation.[47] The concept of social control is also of doubtful utility.[48] The book will argue that the organised labour movement should be given much more credit in the long struggle against sweating and that it is far too simplistic to blame male workers for the persistence of low pay. The study will draw attention to the constraining role of the National Anti-Sweating League (NASL) – a broad coalition of all religious creeds and social philosophies – and, in particular, will focus on the motives of leading anti-sweating activists such as Tawney.

Tawney opposed the Webbs' concept of a national minimum wage on the ground that it was subsistence based. He also dismissed a more generous minimum if it was considered to be above what an individual trade could bear. He lauded trade boards for permitting rates to be decided by those who had a personal interest in preserving the efficiency of the industry. In order to prove the boards a success, he exaggerated

---

[43] P. Hennock, 'Poverty and social theory in England: the experience of the eighteen eighties', *Social History*, 1 (1976), pp. 67–91.

[44] J.A. Hobson, 'A living wage', *Commonwealth*, I (1896), pp. 128–9, 165–7.

[45] S. and B. Webb, *Industrial Democracy* (London, 1897), pp. 766–84.

[46] See E.H. Phelps Brown, *The Growth of British Industrial Relations* (London, 1959), p. 208.

[47] J.R. Hay, *The Development of the British Welfare State, 1880–1975* (London, 1978), pp. 7–8.

[48] J.R. Hay, 'Employers' attitudes to social policy and the concept of social control, 1890–1920', in P. Thane (ed.), *The Origins of British Social Policy* (London, 1978), pp. 107–25.

their advantages. These opinions were so well received by contemporaries that they dominated propagandist literature for the subsequent decades. As a result, when many western European countries adopted a statutory national minimum wage following the Second World War, the British government, bolstered by the knowledge that such eminent social reformers as Tawney supported trade boards, merely expanded the old board system in the new guise of wages councils. Our contention is that Britain, by supporting trade boards and later wages councils, missed a valuable opportunity to end low pay. The final chapter will demonstrate that wages councils, like the old boards, never clearly defined the concept of reasonable or adequate pay levels, and even the most generous awards frequently fell well below decency thresholds. Underpayment also continued to be rife. Moreover, since the councils only applied to twenty-six trades in the private sector, and some two and a half million workers (ten per cent of the workforce), an unsympathetic Conservative government in 1993 easily abolished them. Ironically, the book concludes, the abolition of wages councils by free market Conservatives released Britain from the narrow Edwardian origins of its pay regulating machinery and finally opened the door to the enactment of a national minimum wage by the Labour government.

Although concerned with these broad themes, the book is organised chronologically so that the rich empirical and theoretical literature of particular periods can be explored and assessed. Chapter one examines how the mid-century writings of Thomas Hood, Henry Mayhew and Charles Kingsley initially provoked public discussion on the sweating issue. But their disturbing disclosures proposed little by way of remedies to the problem. Hood's seamstress in *The Song of the Shirt* was brushed aside as an isolated instance of distress. His poem also served to focus attention on London and away from other centres of sweating. Mayhew and Kingsley, on the other hand, by concentrating on the oppressed, male artisan, especially in metropolitan tailoring, were misled into believing that sweating was a separate industrial order revolving around small-scale employment, domestic piecework and subletting of contracts. Yet the most extreme instances of sweating, such as shirtmaking, had no necessary connection with these. And where Mayhew had portrayed the middleman as victim as well as villain, Kingsley typecast the so-called 'sweater' as a manipulative and sinister Jew.

Chapter two traces how, when the outcry against sweating was renewed in the 1870s and 1880s, it was Kingsley's overblown rendition, not Mayhew's more nuanced approach, that was recalled. The influx of poor Jews into East London heightened the mistaken belief held by a large section of British society that the Jews were simultaneously both avaricious moneymen and also impoverished under-cutters of indigenous wage earners. Private and government reports alike depicted the Jew as anti-social, a danger to public health, upwardly mobile 'princes of the sweating system', and deficient in scruples. Although Jewish immigrants possibly made a bad situation worse, there was little evidence that they displaced native labour to any significant extent. Sweating had existed in the 1840s prior to the arrival of the most significant wave of immigration and it prevailed in trades unaffected by any foreign element. Nevertheless, the alarm generated by such respected journals as the *Lancet* and the reports of John Burnett, Labour Correspondent to the Board of Trade, led directly to the hysterical clamour for a select committee urgently to investigate sweating.

This chapter demonstrates that, prior to the Select Committee on the Sweating System, 1888–1890 (SCSS) sweating had been viewed, and still is by historians such as Gareth Stedman Jones, as an East London issue. But after five months, the committee was forced to admit that the problem was a national one and that it touched the manufacture of a large range of goods. However, the 1880s were far from being a watershed for anti-sweating reform. Working-class witnesses were intimidated and unwilling to appear. The popular journalist and eugenicist, Arnold White, produced witnesses of doubtful provenance who were only prepared to testify against the iniquities of alien labour. Even pioneering investigators such as Charles Booth and Beatrice Potter (later Webb), although they dismissed the emotive explanations for sweating dating back to Kingsley and the 1840s, only suggested more stringent homeworking regulation.

Chapter three focuses on how stricter inspection of domestic workshops as a possible solution to sweating became common currency throughout the 1890s. Yet it was this decade (rather than the 1880s) that witnessed a substantial break with laissez-faire attitudes towards the legal control of low pay. Hobson's 1896 treatise on a living wage was quickly followed by the Webbs' theory, which cogently argued for a national minimum wage. The latter stressed that the sweated sectors of industry were 'parasitic' and characterised by the lack of a 'responsible' or 'good' employer. The Webbs have frequently been dismissed as empiricists concerned only with the organised working class. This chapter indicates that their highly selective theory was explicitly formulated to appeal to the self-interest of large and prosperous business-owners and was intended as a direct attack on the 'little master'. But orthodox Victorian economists still held that state intervention in the wages contract would be ruinous for Britain. Even Sir Charles Dilke's proposed wages boards were rejected as unworkable. Despite the new social theories, reformers bickered over the most desirable course of action and this, combined with a lessening of interest with social questions as a result of the Boer War (1899–1902), meant that sweating persisted.

Chapter four surveys how a renewed assault on sweating and the acceptance of a limited legal minimum wage came only after 1906. As Hennock remarks, periods of theoretical innovation and times of maximum public interest do not always correspond. The shift in popular opinion had a good deal to do with the election of a Liberal government and the dramatic staging in London's West End of a sweated industries exhibition. The exhibition brought the privileged into close proximity with the sweated for the first time and demonstrated that even lavishly priced items were not immune from the problem. It also raised the implications of sweating for alleged racial degeneration. More importantly, the exhibition revealed that sweating was not an issue of females working at home. It affected male workers, too, and was part of a wider problem of poverty. The powerful, visual impact of the exhibition, sponsored by the *Daily News*, was sustained when it was mounted in the provinces. The awareness aroused by the spectacle led directly to the establishment of a powerful, all-party pressure group, the NASL, and to the SCH. Both of these proposed that only the legal regulation of wages would curb sweating. Bythell has questioned the significance of the NASL for the minimum wage movement in Britain.

This chapter demonstrates that the activities of the NASL were vital in securing trade board legislation. Furthermore, the organised pressure of the labour movement was not as unimportant as historians such as Morris have supposed.

Chapter five examines the first trade board industry, chainmaking, through a case study of the small community of Cradley Heath, South Staffordshire, centre of the world's chain trade. Recent years have witnessed a welcome number of articles on employers' attitudes to social policy. But where writers such as Morris touch on this subject with regard to trade boards, they dismiss employers' concern as merely connected with considerations of social control. This chapter demonstrates that employers' motives were a good deal more sophisticated and ambivalent than this. Initially, large chain manufacturers favoured trade board protection. They looked to the boards to improve industrial efficiency. More significantly, they wished to be viewed as 'good' employers rather than as unscrupulous sweaters. Yet when they sensed that increased rates of pay arising from the legal minimum wage might conflict with maximising their profits, they schemed to topple the board by conniving with middlemen to abuse the six months waiting period laid down by the legislation. The ensuing strike in 1910 became a significant test case for the successful application of the Act and Cradley Heath became the focal point of international attention. The success of the strike ensured that the 1909 Act was applied not only to chainmaking but extended to other industries – rather than remaining a dead letter. In addition, this chapter places the Webbs' theory of the 'good' employer in a local context and corrects the inaccurate assumption that only 'bad' middlemen, not 'responsible' employers, refused to pay the increased rates.

Chapter six provides the first detailed account of the practical operation of trade boards. It stresses how Tawney, although viewed as one of the most important contributors to British socialist thought in the twentieth century, was surprisingly traditional in his analysis of poverty wages. His two studies of chainmaking and tailoring, funded by the Ratan Tata Foundation and carried out at the London School of Economics (LSE), show him to be preoccupied with expedient reforms rather than radical ideas. In order to affirm the boards as an overwhelming success, Tawney ignored their failings. It can be argued that what was necessary to eradicate low pay was not industry-based trade boards but a national minimum wage based on an agreed living income. While Tawney rejected Beatrice and Sidney Webb's subsistence minimum wage as misguided, he also rejected a higher minimum on the grounds that it might ruin the industry. Despite being well received by contemporaries, Tawney's surveys prove an unreliable guide to the problems of low pay in the twentieth century.

Chapter seven explores why, despite repeated shifts in the attitudes of supporters and opponents alike, trade boards and later wages councils survived, albeit in a modified form, until 1993. It assesses the merits and defects of wages councils and the attitudes of the state, the labour movement and employers towards them and their abolition. The chapter examines why Britain rejected demands for a national minimum wage after the Second World War. Finally, it reviews the recent arguments, which have led to the enactment of a national minimum wage and questions whether, on its own, such legislation is sufficient to eradicate Britain's long and historical tradition of being a low-paying economy.

PART I
Sweating Revealed, 1843–1890

Chapter 1

The 'Discovery' of Sweated Labour, 1843–1850

Although a concept of sweating was not unknown in pre-industrial Britain, it was not until the mid-nineteenth century that it became recognised as a serious social issue.[1] Richard Dugard Grainger, in his 1843 report for the Children's Employment Commission, uncovered the especially gross exploitation of girl apprentices in millinery and dressmaking.[2] He calculated that these trades employed 15,000 in London alone, of whom the vast majority were less than twenty-five years old. While outdoor learners were expected to work at no expense to their employer, indoor apprentices paid a premium and were given a room and board, often in overcrowded lodgings.[3] Some of the residential learners complained that they were denied meals and heating, and that they were cast outdoors to roam the streets on their Sundays off. When apprentices gave evidence regarding long hours, they were dismissed or threatened by their employers. Even the wages of journeywomen with considerable skill were found to be excessively low.

Consumption, heart palpitations, spinal disorders, ocular problems, emaciation and pulmonary disease formed a few items in the long catalogue of maladies complained of by the principal victims, which were verified by expert medical witnesses.[4] The latter included Sir James Clerk, physician to the Queen. Grainger's

---

[1] Schwarz traces the origins of sweating to Tudor and Stuart times: L.D. Schwarz, *London in the Age of Industrialisation: Entrepreneurs, Labour Force and Living Conditions, 1700–1850* (Cambridge, 1992), pp. 179–83. Neff points to sweating in the sixteenth century: W. Neff, *Victorian Working Women* (London, 1966; first published 1929), p. 115. George refers to 'garret masters' and 'chamber masters' in the shoe and watch trades: D. George, *London Life in the Eighteenth Century* (Harmondsworth, 1966), pp. 174–5.

[2] R.D. Grainger, 'Report on the manufactures and trades of Nottingham, Derby, Leicester, Birmingham and London', *Second Report of Commissioners, Children's Employment, Trades and Manufactures* (PP 1843, XIV). The Children's Employment Commission had been set up following Ashley's overtures for Parliament to inquire into the working of the 1833 Act, and into those industries not covered by legal controls. The 1833 legislation restricted the hours of young people (13–18) to twelve per day and prohibited night working for those under eighteen. It applied to virtually all textile factories. It excluded lace making. Silk mills were exempted from the Act's provision for children under nine. It also instituted a salaried inspectorate to administer it: B.L. Hutchins and A. Harrison, *A History of Factory Legislation* (London, 1966; first published 1903), pp. 40–41.

[3] Grainger, 'Report on the manufactures and trades of Nottingham, Derby, Leicester, Birmingham and London', p. 555.

[4] *Ibid.*, pp. 800–805.

investigations provided positive evidence that fashionable junkets and other 'high' society functions such as weddings and funerals, resulted in young girls having to sew through the night to meet the last minute rush of orders. Mr Tyrell, surgeon to the London Ophthalmic Hospital, gave evidence concerning a fair, delicate girl aged seventeen and apprenticed as a dressmaker. She had completely lost her sight through overwork. He stated:

> She had been compelled to remain without changing her dress for nine days and nights consecutively ... during this period she had been permitted only occasionally to rest on a mattress placed on the floor for an hour or two at a time ... her meals were placed at her side, cut up, so that as little time as possible should be spent in their consumption ....[5]

One milliner and dressmaker, Harriet Baker, declared she received no more than four hour's rest in twenty during one three month period. On the occasion of the national mourning for William IV, she toiled without sleep from early on Thursday until ten thirty on the Sunday morning – a total of sixty-eight and half-hours.[6] Grainger concluded: 'there is no class of persons in this country, living by their labour, whose happiness, health, and lives are so unscrupulously sacrificed as those of the young dress-makers.'[7]

Grainger's report was much discussed in the press. The *Pictorial Times* quoted extensively from it in a sensational leading article, 'Slaves of the needle'. The feature also carried dramatic illustrations contrasting the sufferings of the needlewomen with the pampered lives of their female customers.[8] *The Times*, in a less melodramatic vein, congratulated Grainger and his associates for garnering information on 'this painful subject' from 'the mouths of the employers and of the employed', for:

> Hitherto these sufferings have been considered mere matters of rumour, incapable of being substantiated by direct and tangible proof; now we have them placed before us in a statistical form, of which the authenticity is vouched for by the Factory Commissioners ....[9]

Referring to milliners as 'young blossoms' being forced 'to perish prematurely on their stem', the paper urged 'fair countrywomen' to oppose 'the inhuman system' by the boycotting of unscrupulous employers' goods.[10]

---

[5]   *Ibid.*, p. 802.

[6]   *Ibid.*, p. 772.

[7]   *Ibid.*, p. 558.

[8]   *Pictorial Times*, 20 May 1843.

[9]   *The Times*, 21 April 1843. Prior to the ending of Stamp Duty in 1855, *The Times'* daily circulation was 50,000. It was one of the most powerful, most profitable and most widely read newspapers in England and one of the most influential newspapers in the world: J. Black, *The English Press, 1621–1861* (Stroud, 2001), p. 188.

[10]   Earlier, Cruickshank's *Awful Sacrifice* (1842), had blamed unthinking females looking for a bargain for the sufferings of needlewomen. McWilliam suggests that many establishments were owned or managed by females and that the pattern of exploitation was rendered in a gendered manner: R. McWilliam 'The melodramatic seamstress: interpreting a Victorian penny dreadful,' in B. Harris (ed.), *Famine and Fashion: Needlewomen in the Nineteenth Century* (Aldershot, 2005), p. 107.

While stories of such hardship were widely circulated, the conscience of the nation, as the distinguished medical journal, the *Lancet*, pointed out, was only fully awakened by the publication of Thomas Hood's, *Song of the Shirt*.[11] The poem appeared anonymously in the 1843 Christmas edition of the satirical magazine, *Punch*.[12] Three publishers had rejected the poem in rapid succession. Hood apologetically submitted it to the editor, Mark Lemon, because he believed it was too painful for a comic journal. Lemon published it despite opposition from his staff.[13] Hood described a lone, Christian female clothed in 'unwomanly rags' whom, despite labouring day and night in a barely furnished and leaky garret, earned insufficient wages to keep body and soul together. To while away the lonely monotony of her long hours (her only company is her shadow), she sings in a 'dolorous pitch', the *Song of the Shirt*. Pathetically, she utters her longing to evade her misfortune, to stroll in the countryside for 'only one short hour'. But, no 'blessed leisure for love or hope' is possible. Even weeping would impede her stitching. Death, she laments, would be a welcome release from her tribulations. Hood poignantly pointed out that this unfortunate creature was sewing her own shroud as well as a shirt.

As with nearly all of Hood's social protest writings, the poem was based on a real incident – the case of a Lambeth widow named Biddell who, desperate to buy 'dry bread' for her two starving infants, pawned the garments she had been sewing. Having been forced to leave a deposit of two pounds for the safe return of the materials entrusted to her, the woman had been plunged into debt. Engels commented on the 'shameful barbarism' of this custom whereby impoverished women had no option but to pawn the garments only to redeem them at a loss.[14] Biddell (her first name was not given) was subsequently prosecuted by her employer, Henry Moses of Tower Hill.[15] She blamed overwork and near starvation for not fulfilling her contact.[16] Moses' foreman caused a furore when he insisted that at seven pence a pair and supplying her own needle and thread, the widow, could make a 'good' living had she been honest and industrious. When pressed, he replied that she could earn seven shillings a week. As the widow pointed out, this would mean working day and night including Sundays.[17]

---

[11]   *Lancet*, 19 December 1908, p. 1826.

[12]   *Punch*, 16 December 1843.

[13]   A.A. Adrian, *Mark Lemon: First Editor of Punch* (London, 1966), p. 53; J. Clubbe, *Victorian Forerunner: The Later Career of Thomas Hood* (Durham, N.C., 1968), p. 149.

[14]   F. Engels, *The Condition of the Working Class in England* (Harmondsworth, 1987; first published 1845), p. 221. *The Times*, 7 November 1843, also condemned the practice of requiring sureties.

[15]   The police case on which Hood based his poem concerned trousers rather than shirts. It is probable that he considered that a shirt maker would gain more sympathy. Whilst trouser finishing was at the bottom of the unskilled social scale, the unskilled woman at the top finished shirts. The latter were widely considered to be impoverished gentlewomen worthy of assistance. Trouser making was also sexually suggestive: S. Casteras, '"The gulf of destitution on whose brink they hang": images of life on the streets in Victorian art', in J. Treuherz (ed.), *Hard Times: Social Realism in Victorian Art* (London, 1987), p. 19.

[16]   *The Times*, 26 October 1843.

[17]   *Ibid*.

In court it was claimed that she lived in one room, which was 'the very picture of wretchedness'. It was devoid of furniture and quite unfit for human habitation.[18] Biddell was spared the house of correction. But when she and her children were despatched to the workhouse, her employer was publicly excoriated and subjected to a great deal of racial stereotyping. Branding Moses worse than a cannibal who '*slays his victim before he commences his revolting feast*', *Punch* fulminated:

> Seven shillings a week! One penny – not the value of the pestiferous cigar which Moses' man puffs in the faces of passers' by, from the threshold of his master's door – one penny only, for an hour's ceaseless labour at tasks that if long pursued will shut out the blessed light of heaven, and make the sweet air a torture to the ulcerated lungs of the poor living wretch who devotes herself to such self-sacrifice … and yet this jackanapes … dares to call such a pittance a good living for a mother and her two infants. We would that Moses and his class were doomed to walk the streets of London arrayed in their choicest 'slops' (blood-stained as the shirt of Nessus, but without its avenging qualities,) branded SEVEN PENCE, that men might know how they gained their sleekness![19]

The Times commented that Henry Moses 'like SHYLOCK, "will have his bond"…', and that: 'The … Jews are revenging on the poor of a professedly Christian country the wrongs which their forefathers sustained at the hands of ours ….'[20]

Moses complained about being 'intemperately singled out for vituperation' and that he had been maligned for the 'persuasion to which I belong'. He pointed out that, of forty wholesale slopsellers and shirt manufacturers in London, 'there are not more than three of the Jewish community', and that his rates were higher than many of the most respectable outfitting warehouses. When he blamed competition from workhouse labour for lowering prices, *The Times* admonished him further for not seeing that 'being innocent, and being less guilty than others, are two different

---

[18]   *Ibid.*

[19]   'Famine and fashion!', *Punch*, 4 November 1843, p. 203. Slop shop garments were sold readymade. On the same page *Punch* also criticised a firm called Moses in the sarcastic poem, 'Moses and Co'. This was followed by 'The cheap clothing' cartoon and a composition warning that Moses' clothes were so shoddy, they quickly disintegrated: *Punch*, March 1845, p. 3.

[20]   *The Times*, 27 October 1843. Elias Moses and Son purchased an advert accompanied by a doggerel verse disassociating themselves (but to no avail) with the company bearing the same surname. In the 1840s, E. Moses and Son owned the most famous show shops. In tailor's slang, show shops belonged to the cheap bespoke (made to measure) end of the trade where goods were displayed with fixed prices behind impressive plate-glass windows. Show shops depended on aggressive advertising, bulk sales, low margins of profit and speed in production. E. Moses' main emporium was modelled on an aristocratic mansion, with mahogany fittings, and ormolu chandeliers for bright lighting. The firm sold to the aristocracy as well as the middle class. See B. Harris, 'All that glitters is not gold: the show-shop and the Victorian seamstress', in Harris, *Famine and Fashion*, pp. 115–37. Many large East End tailoring houses were both show and slop shops. Later, on 4 August 1848, *The Times* falsely alleged that E. Moses' Aldgate branch (on the edge of the City) was guilty of sweating a Lambeth seamstress, Emma Mounser. The firm protested its innocence but secured only an indifferent apology: *The Times*, 8 August 1848.

things'.[21] It added: 'We only used the word "Jew" to which Mr. Moses somewhat indignantly refers, not as a term of reproach to the people, but in the other of its two significations, in which it forms a component part of the language.'[22]

Commenting on Biddell's case, and a similar one heard the same day, *The Times* averred that: '"A fair day's wages for a fair day's work", is one of the Chartists' rallying cries, and one in which, provided we are not excluded from construing it is implying "a fair day's work for a fair day's wages", we can heartily join.'[23] It concluded that a London needlewoman was from 'every moral point of view, as much a slave as any negro who ever toiled under as cruel taskmasters in the West Indies'.[24] On the same page, *The Times* ran a long news item entitled 'The white slaves,' dedicated to the 'hoards of miserable outcasts' who passed as needlewomen.[25] Christians claiming 'the fellowship of a common nature, a common country, and a

---

[21]   In 1848, metropolitan workhouses (but not prisons) discontinued the practice of requiring women inmates to make shirts: 'The distressed needlewoman and cheap prison labour', *Westminster Review*, 50 (1849), p. 376.

[22]   *The Times*, 31 October 1843. The *Oxford English Dictionary* (*OED*) defines to 'Jew' as: 'To cheat or overreach, in the way attributed to Jewish traders or usurers. Also, to drive a hard bargain, and ... to haggle ... to beat down in price ... Hence Jewing. These uses are now considered to be offensive': J.A. Murray, *et al.*, *OED, Volume 8* (Oxford, 1989), p. 229.

[23]   Thomas Attwood utilised the phrase, 'A fair day's wages for a fair day's work' when he presented the Chartists' petition to Parliament: *Hansard* (Commons), 14 June 1839, col. 224. Thomas Carlyle popularised the motto in his *Past and Present* (1872; first published 1843), pp. 16, 171. Engels criticised those who accepted the slogan for not advocating the abolition of the wages system: F. Engels, 'A fair day's wage for a fair day's work', *Labour Standard*, 7 May 1881. See also, J. Saville, 'The ideology of labourism', in R. Benewick, R. Berki, and R. Parekh (eds), *Knowledge and Belief in Politics: The Problem of Ideology* (London, 1973), esp. p. 216.

[24]   *The Times*, 27 October 1843.

[25]   The use of the metaphor, 'white slave', had altered substantially since the beginning of the nineteenth century. Initially employed by pro-slavery propagandists to castigate the wage slavery of the English factory system, by the 1830s (manumission of slaves in British possessions occurred in 1833) it was widely used by reformers such as Richard Oastler to strengthen the case for factory legislation: R. Gray, *The Factory Question and Industrial England, 1830–1860* (Cambridge, 1996), esp. part 1. It was a powerful weapon for building political alliances and for articulating a critique of the market. However, according to Rogers, male radicals were disinclined to use the term since it was 'incompatible with the idea of agency': H. Rogers, '"The good are not always powerful nor the powerful always good": the politics of women's needlework in mid-Victorian London', *Victorian Studies*, 40 (1997), p. 611. Alexander considers that the term became feminised and increasingly associated with pitiable needlewomen between 1840 and 1860: L. Alexander, *Women, Work and Representation: Needlewomen in Victorian Art and Literature* (Athens, Ohio, 2003), pp. 211–21. Beecher Stowe, following a letter in *The Times*, 18 May 1853, accusing her of purchasing a gown from a sweatshop, disagreed with privileging white seamstresses' exploitation over that of chattel, black labour: F.J. Klingberg, 'Harriet Beecher Stowe and social reform in England', *American Historical Review*, 43 (1938), p. 550. See also N. Pullin, '"A heavy bill to settle with humanity": the representation and invisibility of London's principal milliners and dressmakers', in Harris, *Famine and Fashion*, p. 224.

common religion', were urged to relinquish their concern with abolishing slavery abroad. The neglected and wretched at home demanded priority.[26]

Hood, not unaccustomed to poverty himself, concurred.[27] The publication of his poem tripled *Punch's* circulation and gave the seamstresses international fame. Highly praised by professional authors such as Charles Dickens, the work was widely re-printed. It appeared on handkerchiefs, was set to music and even dramatized.[28] It became one of the best known verses in the English language, was translated into German, Italian, French and Russian, and served as a model for a whole school of international social protest literature. To Hood's delight, the seamstresses themselves actually sang it.[29] Paintings inspired by the work were also exhibited in Britain's foremost art galleries.[30] At Hood's request, his epitaph read: 'He Sang the *Song of the Shirt*'.[31]

Hood, a firm believer in social harmony, ended his ode with the hope that the rich would hear the *Song of the Shirt* and intercede on behalf of sweated women. But the poem did not succeed in ending the hardships of overworked seamstresses. Hood himself died in straitened circumstances less than two years after the appearance of his most famous work.[32] Some time later one observer remarked that, powerful though Hood's poem had been, it failed because Hood had been reluctant to advocate a specific reform.[33] More waspishly, Frederich Engels suggested that Hood, like all humorists, was 'full of human feeling, but wanting in mental energy …'.[34]

But other, more powerful forces were at work. The reasons for the extreme reluctance of mid-Victorians to interfere in the wages contract lay deep in political economy and economic individualism. Since the abandonment of the old regulations in the early nineteenth century, classical economists had steadfastly predicted that

---

[26]   *The Times*, 27 October 1843.

[27]   A mildly anti-Catholic, broad Church of England humanitarian, Hood respected Evangelicals and Quakers for their anti-slavery stance. But he objected to the more excessive forms of evangelical piety. See Clubbe, *Victorian Forerunner*, pp. 38, 140–42.

[28]   Mark Lemon dramatised it as *The Sempstress*, first produced at the Theatre Royal, Haymarket, London on 25 May 1844: S. Casteras, '"Weary stitches": illustrations and paintings for Thomas Hood's *Song of the Shirt* and other poems', in Harris, *Famine and Fashion*, p. 19.

[29]   J.C. Reid, *Thomas Hood* (London, 1963), pp. 208–9.

[30]   Artists, beginning with Richard Redgrave's *The Sempstress* (1844), usually portrayed the latter as working in an attic alone. But most worked in groups and often inhabited damp, polluted cellars. Between 1840 and 1890 the seamstress was the focus of nearly fifty illustrations in widely read English periodicals and paintings: Alexander, *Women, Work and Representation*, pp. 2, 8, 18, 65–8.

[31]   Reid, *Thomas Hood*, pp. 208, 262; Clubbe, *Victorian Forerunner*, pp. 153–4. See also T.J. Edelstein, 'They Sang "The Song Of the Shirt"', *Victorian Studies*, 23 (1980), pp. 183–210.

[32]   Hood had been compelled to spend five years in Koblenz and Ostend to escape creditors. The success of the *Song of the Shirt* and a Civil List pension came too late to mend his fortunes or his health: *The Times*, 9 July 1845.

[33]   Rev. H. Davidson, Dundee sweated industries exhibition, *Dundee Advertiser*, 28 August 1914. Hood's father had been born in Errol, close to Dundee and as a child Hood had convalesced in the region.

[34]   Engels, *The Condition of the Working Class*, p. 221.

state interference in the realm of industry would be ruinous for Britain.[35] As Edward Thompson commented:

> True enough, much of this paternalistic legislation had been in origin not only restrictive, but for the working man, punitive. Nevertheless, there was within it the shadowy image of a benevolent corporate state, in which there were legislative as well as moral sanctions against the unscrupulous manufacturer or the unjust employer ....[36]

The triumph of wage fund theorists marked a fundamental breach in economic and social thought. Such thinkers believed that wages could not be advanced unless capital to finance them was increased. Capital, in turn, was influenced by savings. There was a given number of labourers and a given level of savings to cover wages. Long term, labour supply was determined by the minimum subsistence required to maintain the workforce. Even John Stuart Mill, referred to by Ernest Barker as having one of the 'most generous natures of the nineteenth century', examined the viability of a fixed minimum wage to curb low pay, but eventually discarded it on Malthusian principles.[37]

Orthodox political economists also disliked the poem because it directly rebuked them for the hardships imposed by the 1834 reform of the poor law.[38] The Poor Law Amendment Act distinguished sharply between the 'deserving' and the 'undeserving'

---

[35] Until the early part of the nineteenth century, legal regulations had supported guilds in their aims to preserve control over their work. Under the Statute of Artificers (1563) fines were levied on those who employed other than time-served apprentices in specified trades. Masters in these industries were also obliged to limit the number of apprentices. The apprenticeship clauses of the Act were repealed in 1813 following a long period of decay and vigorous agitation by artisans to have them more effectively enforced. In the following year those clauses permitting magistrates to fix a minimum wage were also rescinded, though those making it an offence to leave work unfinished remained. In 1824 the demise of the 1773 Spitalfields Act ended legislative protection for silk weavers. The latter, like many labourers such as framework knitters, saw their customary rights eroded by the expanding market. Perquisites were also diminished. See J. Clapham, 'The Spitalfields Acts, 1773–1824, *Economic Journal*, 20 (1916), pp. 459–71; H. Cassidy, 'The emergence of the free labour contract in England', *American Economic Review*, 18 (1928), pp. 219–26; T. Derry, 'The repeal of the apprenticeship clauses of the Statute of Artificers', *Economic History Review* (*EHR*), 3 (1931), pp. 67–87; George, *London Life*, pp. 200–201, 233–4; E.P. Thompson, *The Making of the English Working Class* (London, 1963), pp. 245, 517, 526, 542–3, 565, 595–6; J. Rule, *The Experience of Labour in Eighteenth-Century Industry* (London, 1981), pp. 95–119; N. Thompson, *The Real Rights of Man: Political Economics For the Working Class, 1775–1850* (London, 1998), pp. 37–44.

[36] Thompson, *The Making*, p. 543.

[37] J.S. Mill, *Principles of Political Economy* (London, 1878; first published 1848), ch. 12. See also E. Barker, *Political Thought in England From Herbert Spencer to the Present Day* (London, 1915), p. 9. For a recent review of classical political economy discourse and Malthusian population theories, see S. Deakin and F. Wilkinson, *The Law of the Labour Market: Industrialization, Employment and Legal Evolution* (Oxford, 2005), pp. 130–34.

[38] Hood censured them further in his, *The Workhouse Clock: An Allegory* (1844). The Poor Law returns for 1844 revealed that one and a half million (9. 3 per cent of the population)

in England and Wales. Technically, anyone applying for relief was required to enter the workhouse, and the principle of less eligibility was sufficiently enforced to make the prospect of the workhouse terrifying. In practice, the severity of this ruling varied according to locality and region. London permitted less outdoor relief than in other areas. The workings of the new poor law were particularly harsh on females – the principal adult claimants. As Pat Thane notes of the policy makers of 1834:

> They took for granted the universality of the stable two-parent family, primarily dependent upon the father's wage ... These were assumptions quite incompatible with the realities ... of industrial low pay and recurrent unemployment, and early or sudden death. Many deserted or abandoned wives were left to support children or other dependents on less than subsistence wages.[39]

Thane adds:

> Women had a longer life expectancy than men at all ages ... poor women were more likely to be widowed with young children ... and were more likely than men to survive ... into old age and dependency ... Marriage break-up was also more likely to cause poverty among women than men, especially when there were young children to care for. Women were less likely than men to marry, less likely to remarry if widowed, and were less able to support themselves if unmarried or widowed ... Women's work opportunities were more limited ... and they could only earn between one-third and one-half of male manual workers' wages ....[40]

Opposition to the new poor law came from various groups including some Tories (in defiance of party support for the New Poor Law), Radicals (excluding philosophical radicals who assisted in designing the new legislation), certain Whigs, *The Times*, the radical underground press and Chartists.[41] A great deal of the resistance hinged on the question of centralisation. Animus on the part of *The Times* was also personal. The proprietor of the paper, John Walter, quarrelled with Edwin Chadwick, secretary of the Poor Law Commissioners, over the former's sanctioning of generous outdoor relief in Berkshire. Traditional magistrates like Walter were inclined to support paternalistic poor law policies in the interests of social harmony. But political economists' arguments that generous poor relief interfered with the working of the 'natural' laws of supply and demand held firm.

Although Victorians in the 1840s were prepared to countenance legislation to regulate the hours and working conditions of children and women in factories, they could not, despite public sympathy for the distressed seamstress, bring themselves

---

were in receipt of indoor or outdoor relief: J.F.C. Harrison, *Early Victorian Britain, 1832–51* (London, 1988; first published 1971), p. 57.

[39]   P. Thane, 'Women and the Poor Law in Victorian and Edwardian England', *History Workshop Journal*, 6 (1978), pp. 29–51.

[40]   Between 1846 and 1848 guardians were legally empowered to grant outdoor relief to widows but this was not necessarily forthcoming: *ibid.*, pp. 33, 36, 42.

[41]   See G. Himmelfarb, *The Idea of Poverty: England in the Early Industrial Age* (London, 1984), pp. 177–8; D. R. Green, *From Artisans to Paupers: Economic Change and Poverty in London, 1790–1870* (London, 1995), ch. 8.

to sanction control or inspection of work carried out by adults in the sanctity of the home. Such surveillance, it was argued, would force women out of their dwelling into the moral danger of the market place. Legal control of homework would also threaten the patriarchal family and the liberty of the individual. Impropriety would occur if male inspectors (no females were appointed until 1893) were allowed access to the bedrooms of sweated females. Home was home – even if it was as stifling as a slave ship.[42] So far as political economists were concerned, the possible cures would be worse than the disease.

It was therefore convenient to dismiss Hood's seamstress as an individual case of suffering, a *London* rather than a national problem – a suitable case for private charity rather than state relief. As Helen Roberts has succinctly pointed out: 'Middle-class Victorians could ruthlessly exploit the working woman, but they did not want to be reminded of their exploitation.'[43] The contradictions in the law, whereby seamstresses were prosecuted for attempting suicide but were allowed slowly to starve to death in an unsanitary hovel, were brushed aside. Sweating quietly continued. Engels was moved to comment that Hood's poem, 'drew sympathetic but unavailing tears from the eyes of the daughters of the bourgeoisie'.[44] *The Times* added: 'Poor Hood's "Song of the Shirt" set people speechifying, and giving concerts or balls – but, after a little singing, a little dancing, and a good deal of talking, the sempstresses were dropped for some newer object of benevolent interest.'[45]

I

Six years after the publication of the *Song of the Shirt*, the bohemian journalist and former editor of *Punch*, Henry Mayhew, produced a series of letters on sweating in the well-respected *Morning Chronicle*. Bought in February 1848 by a liberal-conservative or Peelite group, who included Sidney Herbert, the *Morning Chronicle* was decidedly philanthropic and evangelical.[46] With its large audience, good resources and impressive array of contributors, including Dickens, it was a serious rival to *The Times*. Written just after the Irish Famine (1846–1848) and at the time of the 1848 Chartist demonstration and the cholera epidemics of 1848–1849, Mayhew's graphic reports, accompanied by etchings, were widely reproduced.[47] Initially Mayhew had viewed exposés of exploited seamstresses as exaggerated. He quickly changed his opinion and deeply regretted his former complacency: 'I was unprepared for the

42   Hutchins and Harrison, *History of Factory Legislation*, chs 4–5.

43   H. Roberts, 'Marriage, redundancy or sin', in Martha Vicinus (ed.), *Suffer and Be Still* (London, 1980; first published 1972), p. 63.

44   Engels, *Condition of the Working Class*, p. 221.

45   *The Times*, 27 March 1846.

46   E.P. Thompson, 'Mayhew and the *Morning Chronicle*', in E.P. Thompson and E.Yeo (eds), *The Unknown Mayhew* (London, 1971), p. 20.

47   Inspired by Mayhew's revelations, John Leech chose to satirise the Victorian wealth gap in his 'Pin money' and 'Needle money'. The diptych juxtaposes an affluent woman admiring the trinkets her allowance has bought with that of a famished seamstress diligently sewing in a tumbledown tenement: *Punch*, 22 December 1849, pp. 240–41. See Figure 1.

NEEDLE MONEY.

PIN MONEY.

Figure 1 John Leech, 'Pin money' and 'Needle money', *Punch*, 22 December 1849

amount of suffering that I have lately witnessed. I could not have believed that there were human beings toiling for so long and gaining so little, and starving so silently and heroically....'[48]

At the same time, he insisted that he had not sought extreme cases.[49] In contrast to Hood, Mayhew was willing to delve into the 'darker' side of the Victorian underworld. Hood's shirt maker had been associated in the public mind with a young, single, beautiful, solitary and almost saintly figure. A martyr to her work, she was deserving of assistance.[50] Mayhew, although he established that most of the needlewomen were aged less than twenty, portrayed them as predominately widows, abandoned partners, mothers several times over and the main breadwinner of the family. He found that many routinely supplemented their meagre earnings with prostitution, merely in order to exist. As a result of his sensational surveys, employment as a needlewoman became virtually co-terminus with living on immoral earnings. Mayhew first interviewed needlewomen in their own homes. One poor 'creature', the daughter of a dead minister and the mother of an illegitimate child, since consigned to the workhouse, told how she had been driven onto the streets to feed her child. She had recently been rescued from a suicide attempt. Another needlewoman, aged nearly twenty and seven months pregnant, had been forced 'to go wrong' after being deserted by her 'young man'. To extenuate her circumstances she remarked: 'if I had been born a lady it wouldn't have been very hard to act like one. To be poor and to be honest, especially with young girls is the hardest struggle of all ... Young as I am, my life is a curse to me.'[51]

In order to verify the correct averages of wages and to establish how many women actually supplemented their earnings with prostitution, Mayhew called a public meeting of 'fallen' needlewomen. To ensure 'strict privacy', the room was only dimly lit, cards of admission were issued, and males, with the exception of Mayhew and three assistants, were not allowed admittance. Twenty-five women presented themselves. Some appeared in rags, others wore their only set of clothes because the remainder were pawned – 'the very idea of a change of garments appeared to excite a smile.' Several women suckled infants. They laughed and cried together as each recounted their personal tragedies. Some had lost more than one child from starvation.[52] The women's outpourings, as Rogers notes, 'captured the atmosphere of the confessional ...'.[53] Whilst this gathering was taking place, sixty-two female slop workers who could not get into the crowded meeting room assembled outside. When questioned, they told Mayhew that one-quarter of all needlewomen, and at least fifty per cent of those with no parent, resorted to prostitution to eke out their

---

[48]   *Morning Chronicle* (*MC*), Letter VI, 6 November 1849 in Thompson and Yeo, *Unknown Mayhew*, p. 116.

[49]   *MC*, Letter VII, 9 November 1849, in Thompson and Yeo, *Unknown Mayhew*, p. 127.

[50]   Edelstein comments on the traditional association of the single figure with the images of saints: 'They sang "The Song Of the Shirt"', p. 190.

[51]   *MC*, Letter VIII, 13 November 1849, in Thompson and Yeo, *Unknown Mayhew*, pp. 147–52.

[52]   *MC*, Letter XI, 23 November 1849, in Thompson and Yeo, *Unknown Mayhew*, pp. 167–78.

[53]   Rogers, '"The good are not always powerful"', p. 599.

living. Mayhew concluded that, since upward of 11,000 females under twenty were engaged in garment work, assuming the census was accurate, then 'the numerical amount of prostitution becomes awful to contemplate.'[54] He condemned shirt making and government contract work for uniforms as the worst sweated work of all.

It is commonly assumed that Mayhew's revelations on the needlewomen assisted the transformation of Chartist literature, that Chartist writers such as Ernest Jones employed Mayhew's images of vulnerable young seamstresses to mount a radical political critique of Victorian capitalism.[55] Sally Ledger insists that Jones' *Women's Wrongs*, 'presents a cross-class analysis of female oppression that posits women as an oppressed group in their own right, and not just as adjuncts to working-class men'.[56] On the whole, though, Mayhew was not primarily concerned with helpless, female workers. The major focus of his study was how sweating impinged on small groups of male artisans such as tailors, boot and shoemakers, carpenters and joiners. He revealed how the skilled or 'honourable', West-End section was being undermined by East-London, unskilled, 'dishonourable', non-society men and women. This had occurred because a new class of exploitative masters had abandoned union-agreed time rates for piecework paid at starvation levels. He contrasted the subdued appearance of the 'honourable' tailor's abode with the tawdry exterior of the show shop master:

> The quiet house of the honourable tailor, with the name inscribed on the window blinds, or on the brass-plate on the door, tells you that the proprietor has no wish to compete with or undersell his neighbour. But at the show and slop-shops every art and trick that scheming

---

[54]   *MC*, Letter XI, 23 November 1849, in Thompson and Yeo, *Unknown Mayhew*, p. 180.

[55]   I. Haywood, *The Literature of Struggle: An Anthology of Chartist Fiction* (Aldershot, 1995), p. 18; I. Haywood, 'The retailoring of Dickens: *Christmas Shadows*, radicalism, and the needlewoman myth', in Harris, *Famine and Fashion*, p. 73; E. Dzelzainis, 'Chartism and gender politics in Ernest Jones's *The Young Milliner*' in Harris, *Famine and Fashion*, p. 91. After his release from prison, Jones had serialised *De Bassier: A Democratic Romance* in his periodical, *Notes to the People* (1851). This focussed on the ruin of a starving seamstress. Jones later serialised in the same journal four short stories of women's moral and physical destruction. The second of the tales features a young milliner abandoned by her lover. She dies and her cadaver is dissected as a demonstration corpse. The stories were later published as *Women's Wrongs: A Novel in Four Books* (London, 1855), and are reprinted in I. Haywood (ed.), *Chartist Fiction, Volume Two* (Aldershot, 2001). See also, George W.M. Reynolds', *The Seamstress*, which first appeared in *Reynolds's Miscellany* between March and August 1850 as 'The slaves of England, no. 1'.

[56]   S. Ledger, 'Chartist aesthetics in the mid-nineteenth century: Ernest Jones, a novelist of the people', *Nineteenth-Century Literature*, 57 (2002), p. 60. Ledger argues that competition from the emerging popular press forced Chartist writers to broaden their appeal by emphasising quasi-historical reportage, crime, seduction, social abuse and the melodramatic. Dzelzainis adds that Jones wrote for a female audience following criticisms from radical feminists that the movement neglected women's enfranchisement: 'Chartism and gender politics in Ernest Jones's *The Young Milliner*', pp. 87–97. Cf. M. Taylor, *Ernest Jones, Chartism and the Romance of Politics, 1819-69* (Oxford, 2003), pp. 158–60. Taylor claims that the impact of *Women's Wrongs* was insignificant.

can devise or avarice suggest, is displayed to attract the notice of the passer-by, and filch the customer from another.

He added of the show shops, 'books of crude, bald verse are thrust in your hands, or thrown into your carriage window – the panels of every omnibus are plastered with showy placards ....'[57]

Journeymen, previously only employed in their master's workshop, had also been forced into becoming small capitalists working at home on their own account. In order to survive, the latter utilised various means to increase their productivity, such as skimping on quality, and labouring for long hours, including Sundays. These small masters had often been driven to become middlemen themselves, engaging cheap labour from apprentices, foreigners, females and even their own family. To Mayhew, these middlemen, caught in a jungle of unregulated competition, were simultaneously both the victims and the villains of sweating.

This insight caused Mayhew to reject the conventional political economists' explanation for sweating: that these trades were over-stocked with redundant workers. He dismissed orthodox economists as 'big bottomed spiders', spinning doctrinaire webs in remote isolation and evincing a loathing of objective evidence akin to that of mad dogs to water.[58] He maintained that it was over-productivity and driving which had created an artificial surplus of hands and reduced wages. From this he evolved his thesis that 'overwork leads to low pay' and conversely, 'low pay leads to overwork.'[59]

This bias towards a certain category of skilled worker and their downward mobility was not unproblematic. It deluded him (and his readers) into thinking that there was such a thing as a 'sweated trade', that sweating was an actual industrial system – bound up with small masters, domestic pieceworkers and subcontract. But the worst cases of sweating had nothing to do with subcontracting. In shirt making and matchbox making, the work was often given out directly from the factory without the intervention of a middleman. Subcontracting and piecework also occurred in industries where sweating rarely occurred – such as shipbuilding. Other London crafts, which did not fit his framework, were ignored.[60] The largest occupational group in the working class, the quarter of a million domestic servants, was similarly overlooked, as were railwaymen and gas stokers who worked for large concerns rather than for back street, small employers. Yet, if we adopt Mayhew's own definition of sweating, these activities were good examples of overwork and often low-waged. As Anne Humpherys concludes, 'Mayhew combined brilliant observation with a shallow analysis of only a few trades.'[61]

---

[57]   *MC*, Letter XVII, 14 December 1849, in Thompson and Yeo, *Unknown Mayhew*, pp. 196–8.

[58]   'Answers to correspondents number 34', *MC*, 2 August 1851, in B. Taithe (ed.), *The Essential Mayhew: Representing and Communicating the Poor* (London, 1996), p. 179.

[59]   *MC*, Letter LXVI, August 22 1850, in Thompson and Yeo, *Unknown Mayhew*, pp. 384–99.

[60]   K. Williams, *From Pauperism to Poverty* (London, 1981), p. 247.

[61]   A. Humpherys, *Travels Into the Poor Man's Country: The Work of Henry Mayhew* (Athens, GA, 1977), p. 49.

Mayhew also dealt more sympathetically with the skilled worker. He appreciated the fact that the 'society' men kept written records and could speak authoritatively on the labour process.[62] He respected their independence, sobriety and cultured life-style, whereas the unskilled and sweated, he considered, acquiesced in their exploitation. Those 'dishonourable' tailors who lived on the sweater's premises were portrayed as being defrauded at every turn. They paid for bed and board, but were half-starved and obliged to sleep in over-crowded, consumptive-ridden workrooms. Some had been forced to pawn their clothes. They had become captives of the sweater – reduced to sharing one communal coat, a 'reliever' which each would wear in turn when permitted to go out. Others, especially those from Ireland, had been 'kidnapped' and bound in debt to the middleman. Wily Irish sweaters' wives, he commented, were used to entrap inexperienced fellow countrymen into 'bondage'. Promised good wages, on arrival they would find themselves 'in a den of a place'.[63] Despite such exploitation, they did not rebel. They were as 'unpolitical' as footmen.

Of the 'honourable' and 'dishonourable' tailors, he asserted:

> The very dwellings of the people are sufficient to tell you the wide difference between the two classes. In the one you occasionally find small statues of Shakespeare beneath glass shades; in the other all is dirt and foetor. The working tailor's comfortable first-floor at the West-end is redolent with the perfume of the small bunch of violets that stand in a tumbler over the mantelpiece; the sweater's wretched garret is rank with the stench of filth and herrings. The honourable part of the trade are really intelligent artisans, while the slopworkers are generally almost brutified with their incessant toil, wretched pay, miserable food, and filthy homes.[64]

Prone to drunkenness and disease, the 'dishonourable' tailors were seen by Mayhew as a danger to health. The hovels of the slop-workers were lice-infested; they slept with the garments of customers upon their beds – even when racked with disease. In winter, when blankets had been pawned, it was common for tailors to sleep with the sleeves of a coat they were making drawn over their arms. He assured his readers that ladies' riding habits were especially prized as covers for the poor and their children on account of the cloth in their skirts.[65] *Punch* exclaimed: 'What a thought to check the triumph of a canter in Rotten Row, to imagine that the flowing robe has been used as a counterpane for the filthy slop-worker and his squalid little one.'[66]

---

[62] D. Englander, 'Comparisons and contrasts: Henry Mayhew and Charles Booth as social investigators', in D. Englander and R. O'Day (eds), *Retrieved Riches: Social Investigation in Britain, 1840–1914* (Aldershot, 1995), pp. 112–13.

[63] *MC*, Letter XVIII, 18 December 1849, in Thompson and Yeo, *Unknown Mayhew*, pp. 223–6.

[64] *MC*, Letter XVII, 14 December 1849, in Thompson and Yeo, *Unknown Mayhew*, pp. 196–8.

[65] *MC*, Letter XVI, 11 December 1849, Letter XVII, 14 December 1849, Letter XVIII, 18 December 1849, in Thompson and Yeo, *Unknown Mayhew*, pp.193–4, 214, 220–21.

[66] 'Beware of cheap tailors', *Punch*, 23 December 17, 1849, p. 238. Rotten Row is a corruption of 'Route de Roi' (King's Road). A broad avenue situated to the south side of Hyde Park, it was a popular meeting place for polite society.

Mayhew's bias towards the skilled, male artisan also meant that females other than the needlewomen hardly figure in his account.[67] When women do appear, they are portrayed as helpless victims – poor Magdalenes telling 'stories' of their seduction and 'fall'. He narrates rather than analyses his meetings with them. He never questions them, unlike the men, about their political opinions. He apparently shares skilled workers' sentiments that women have been the ruin of the trades. He empathised, too, with those males who lamented the loss of being the breadwinner, their wives and daughters having to work to maintain a satisfactory standard of life. Yet on Mayhew's own evidence the majority of the needlewomen were under twenty and widows, orphans, or wives of unemployed or ill husbands. They had no wage-earning male to support them.

It has been suggested that Mayhew formulated a new theory of capitalism, that he provoked a discussion on the ethics of sweated employment drawing on ideals of 'fair exchange' and 'just prices'.[68] Yet Mayhew's sensational revelations amounted to little in terms of possible solutions. As David Englander shrewdly observed: 'Viewed in the round his theoretical interventions seemed much more like an attempt to modify or moralize political economy than to replace it.'[69] Mayhew advocated a muddled range of reforms – including protective tariffs, trade union organisation and co-operative workshops – but offered no precise advice on how to attain these. He assisted in the establishment of a Tailor's Guild, a type of friendly society, but this was short-lived.

One reform was a scheme to despatch distressed needlewomen with exemplary references to the colonies. Perturbed by Mayhew's revelations, Sir Sidney Herbert established the Fund for Promoting Female Emigration.[70] Linking philanthropy and political economy, Herbert believed that there were 500,000 excess females in England and Wales and a shortfall of precisely 500,000 women in the colonies. He attributed this imbalance to men's propensity to emigrate, to join the armed services and the result of wars.[71] But the venture quickly ran into financial difficulties, despite the fact that Prince Albert and Queen Victoria headed its subscription list.[72] Moreover,

---

[67] Humpherys, *Travels*, p. 49.

[68] Rogers, '"The good are not always powerful"', p. 603.

[69] Englander, 'Comparisons and contrasts', p. 117.

[70] The scheme was launched via a letter in the *MC*, 5 December 1849, which was subsequently re-printed in *The Times* on 6 December 1849.

[71] J. Chimes, '"Wanted: 1000 spirited young milliners": the fund for promoting female emigration', in Harris, *Famine and Fashion*, pp. 229–32. John Leech's cartoon: 'Needlewoman at home and abroad', *Punch*, 12 January 1850, p. 15, also recommended emigration. A diptych, it contrasted, a needlewoman's prospects: in England she is an isolated and starving city dweller; in Australia she is well fed, prosperous, and surrounded by contented children and a husband. See Figure 2.

[72] The passage for each woman was estimated at £15. Although figures are unreliable, Herbert's scheme was widely considered to be ineffective. See: A.J. Hammerton, *Emigrant Gentlewomen: Genteel Poverty and Female Emigration, 1830–1914* (London, 1979), p. 107. For a more positive account of emigration schemes, see: G. Howells, '" On account of their disreputable characters": parish assisted emigration from rural England, 1834–1860', *History*, 88 (2003), pp. 587–605.

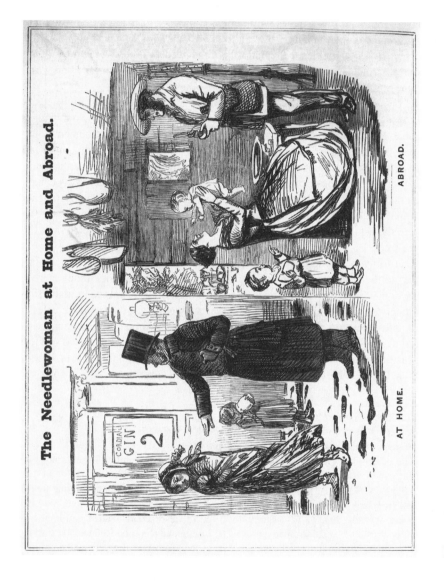

Figure 2   John Leech, 'The needlewoman at home and abroad', *Punch*, 12 January 1850

since Mayhew believed that the problem was not one of excess labour but driving, he quickly argued with the advocates of emigration programmes.[73] He also fell foul of Messrs H.J. and D. Nicholl, one of the *Morning Chronicle*'s wealthiest advertisers when he accused the firm of profiting from sweated tailoring.[74] Assailed by powerful enemies, compelled to resign from his post and forced to seek alternative means of support, Mayhew's interest in sweating was abruptly halted.[75] By the 1860s, if recalled at all, he was chiefly remembered not for his penetrating, investigative journalism but for his colourful vignettes on London's 'low' life.[76]

II

In the short term, though, Mayhew's exposé brought the plight of the sweated to the notice of the Christian Socialists. Founded as Chartism was defeated, this small group of Anglican clergy and laymen headed by Frederick Maurice included Charles Kingsley, Tom Hughes, Edward Vansittart Neale and John Ludlow. Ludlow drew attention to the sweated when he used Mayhew's material on the needlewomen for an article, which appeared in January 1850.[77] According to Edward Thompson, this essay set the theme for Christian Socialist activity.[78] But it was Mayhew's letters on the tailors, less so those on the needlewomen, which inspired the Christian Socialists to take action. In February 1850 they helped to form the Working Tailor's Association (WTA) for co-operative production.[79] Charles Kingsley, under the pseudonym 'Parson Lot', also produced a tract, 'Cheap clothes and nasty', to solicit support for the WTA.[80]

Kingsley had been deeply agitated by Mayhew's letters on the tailors. In his pamphlet he wrote: 'From two articles in the *Morning Chronicle* of Friday, 14th December, and Tuesday, 18th December, on the Condition of the Working Tailors,

---

[73]   Humpherys, *Travels*, pp. 55–6; Thompson, 'Mayhew and the *Morning Chronicle*', pp. 24–32.

[74]   The Nicholls owned a large show-shop in Regent Street: Humpherys, *Travels*, p. 20.

[75]   The editor of the *MC*, John Douglas Cook, published a laudatory article praising Messrs Nicholl and refused to print Mayhew's reply. Mayhew had already quarrelled with Cook over the paper's advocacy of free trade. Mayhew called a meeting of 1,500 tailors to expose the falsehoods. At the same time as denouncing Messrs Nicholl, he used the opportunity to criticise Messrs Moses: Thompson, 'Mayhew and the *Morning Chronicle*', pp. 34–8.

[76]   Beatrice Webb, for example, dismissed Mayhew's work on the grounds that it was 'good material spoilt by bad dressing ...': British Library of Political and Economic Science (BLPES), Passfield Papers, Beatrice Webb's Manuscript Diary, August 1887.

[77]   J. Ludlow, 'Labour and the poor', *Fraser's Magazine*, 41 (1850), pp. 4–7, 11. Founded in 1830, *Fraser's Magazine* supported Tory paternalistic campaigns for factory reform.

[78]   Thompson, 'Mayhew and the *Morning Chronicle*', p. 30.

[79]   Humpherys, *Travels*, p. 168.

[80]   He signed the tract 'Parson Lot' following a meeting at Maurice's house when he found himself alone: L. Cazamian (translated by M. Fido), *The Social Novel in England, 1830–1850* (London, 1973; first published, 1903), p. 342, n. 41.

we learnt too much to leave us altogether masters of ourselves.'[81] The tract was an impassioned attack on the slop system, and urged all of those who wanted to curb it to aid the tailors to form associations. It also portrayed middlemen as often being wealthy Jewish entrepreneurs and grinders of the faces of the poor. The former were, in Kingsley's opinion, infinitely worse than the mythical King Ryence who wore a cloak trimmed with his victims' beards, or French revolutionary monsters who adorned their bodies with freshly flayed flesh.[82]

At the same time, the pamphlet roundly condemned the government for originating and perpetuating sweating through the subcontracting of its uniforms to 'Nebuchadnezzar and Co's' sweatshops.[83] Kingsley wrote:

> Part of the work, if not the whole, is let out to contractors, or middlemen–'*sweaters*'as their victims significantly call them – who, in their turn, let it out again, sometimes to the workmen, sometimes to fresh middle-men; so that out of the price paid for the labour on each article, not only the workmen, but the sweater's sweater, and a third and a fourth, and a fifth, have to draw their profit.[84]

Of the sweated he added: 'We have, thank God, emancipated the black slaves; it would seem a not inconsistent sequel to that act to set about emancipating these white ones.'[85]

At points 'Cheap clothes and nasty' is a series of acknowledged passages from the *Morning Chronicle* loosely joined together. Yet where Mayhew meticulously recorded the genesis of slopwork, Kingsley's tract was superficial. Precision was discarded in order to generate an overwhelming image of oppression. For example, Kingsley transforms Mayhew's restrained account of the ill tailor using a customer's garment as a cover into a grizzly picture of pestilence and death:

> These wretched creatures, when they have pawned their own clothes and bedding, will use as substitutes the very garments they are making. So Lord — 's coat has been seen covering a group of children blotched with small-pox. The Rev. D — finds himself suddenly, unpresentable from a cutaneous disease which it is not polite to mention on the south of the Tweed, little dreaming that the shivering dirty being who made his coat has been sitting with his arms in the sleeves for warmth while he stitched at the tails. The charming Miss C— is swept off by typhus or scarlatina, and her parents talk about 'God's heavy judgement and visitation' – had they tracked the girl's new riding habit back to the stifling undrained hovel where it served as a blanket to the fever-stricken slop worker, they would have seen *why* God had visited them ....[86]

---

[81]   C. Kingsley, 'Cheap clothes and nasty', *Tracts by Christian Socialists II* (1850), in preface to Charles Kingsley, *Alton Locke* (London, 1890; first published 1850), p. vii.

[82]   Ryence, a king of Wales and Ireland, figured in Arthurian legends. Carlyle alleged that, during the French revolution, the skins of the guillotined were tanned at Meudon. Kingsley, 'Cheap', p. vii.

[83]   *Ibid.*, p. xv.

[84]   *Ibid.*, p. vii.

[85]   *Ibid.*, p. xi.

[86]   *Ibid.*, p. xiii.

Despite his careless disregard for the manner in which Kingsley used Mayhew's understated version of sweating, his tract sold well. Written like 'an excited Carlylean sermon', according to Margaret Thorp, it was even popular at Eton and 'lay on the table at the Guard's Club and caused young officers to order coats from the … co-operative workrooms'.[87]

Kingsley followed this success with the publication of his novel, *Alton Locke*, in 1850.[88] The book depicts the life of a sickly Chartist and Cockney tailor who refuses to become a slop worker. Forced to make a living as a writer and seeking to experience the grim realism of sweating, Locke visits starving seamstresses with his guide, Sandy Mackaye.[89] He discovers the wretched Ellen who praises God that her disfigurement has released her from the burden of taking to the streets. Pockmarked, clothed only in rags and racked with consumption, the hollow-eyed girl's sole bedding is a fine new riding habit which two of her distressed companions are busy sewing. Pathetically, one of these repeats Hood's refrain of 'stitch, stitch, stitch', but does not know any more or who wrote it. She concludes that she will learn to sing it – after all, what could be more fitting than the sound of such a ballad in the sweating hovel in which she lives and toils? Another seamstress, Lizzie, an unwilling prostitute, recounts how the poor law has refused them outdoor relief. She can no longer support Ellen, four other seamstresses and a sick old woman, the daughter of an officer, for whom she is responsible. Lizzie's prayers for deliverance are finally answered when a saintly gentlewoman, Lady Ellerton, sacrifices her comfort and wealth, saves the 'fallen' women and finances their passage to Australia.[90]

Locke's help is also enlisted to rescue 'dishonourable' tailors 'kidnapped' by a sweater, Jemmy Downes, a former workmate of his who has taken to government contract work with a Jewish partner, Shemei Solomons. Unfairly imprisoned for Chartist activities, on his release Locke is lured to Downes' sweatshop – an abhorrent slum built over an open sewer. Here Locke is forced to look at the naked corpses of Downes' Irish wife and two children lying under a half-finished coat. They have died from typhus and rats have begun to gnaw them. When completed, Locke's prosperous cousin, a champion of laissez-faire and a pioneer of the 'buy cheap and sell dear commercialism', purchases the infected garment.[91] The customer and his valet handle it; both perish.[92] Locke himself, weakened by the contagion of the sweating den, eventually emigrates but expires in sight of the New World.

According to Una Pope-Hennessy, *Alton Locke* was 'the one novel of the Victorian era that no one interested in social conditions can afford to neglect'.[93]

---

[87]   M. Thorp, *Charles Kingsley* (New York, 1969; first published 1937), p. 67.

[88]   The firm of John Parker had serialised Kingsley's first novel *Yeast* in *Fraser's Magazine* but refused to publish *Alton Locke* on the grounds that Parker's business had suffered adverse publicity. Carlyle interceded and Chapman and Hall produced the book: F. Kingsley, *Charles Kingsley: His Letters and Memories of His Life, Volume 1* (London, 1879), pp. 189–90.

[89]   Mackaye, probably Kingsley's best character, was modelled on Carlyle: Thorp, *Charles Kingsley*, p. 73.

[90]   Kingsley, *Alton Locke*, chs 8 and 41.

[91]   *Ibid.*, ch. 35.

[92]   *Ibid.*, pp. 141–2.

[93]   U. Pope-Hennessy, *Canon Charles Kingsley* (London, 1948), p. 92.

To Schmiechen, *Alton Locke* 'is a graphic picture of the fallen artisan'.[94] Raymond Williams praises it for being 'an informed, angry and sustained account of sweated labour...'.[95] In many ways, the novel was a dramatised and more subtle version of 'Cheap clothes and nasty'. Yet like the latter, it was grossly inaccurate.[96] Once again, Kingsley had drawn on Mayhew's material and embellished it.[97] The narrative was based on the life of Thomas Cooper whom Kingsley knew intimately.[98] But in order to heighten the fear of infection, Kingsley transformed Cooper from a Leicester shoemaker into a Bermondsey tailor. Even Mayhew's respectable tailor's Elysium workroom, with its discrete blinds to distinguish it from a dwelling house, becomes in *Alton Locke* a 'Consumptive Hospital'. It is:

> A low, lean-to room, stifling ... with the combined odours of human breath and perspiration, stale beer, the sweet sickly smell of gin, and the sour and hardly less disgusting one of new cloth. On the floor, thick with dust and dirt, scraps of stuff and ends of thread, sat some dozen, haggard, untidy, shoeless men ... The windows were tight closed to keep out the cold winter air; and the condensed breath ran in streams down the panes, chequering the dreary outlook of chimney-tops and smoke.[99]

Yet Kingsley's hero concedes that it was 'still as good, alas! as those of three tailors out of four'.[100]

The novel largely linked sweating to the downward descent of male, skilled artisans. Schmiechen suggests that Kingsley was concerned about women.[101] However, they only appear briefly – as pathetic 'fallen' seamstresses or as an impossibly pious rescue worker. A further flaw is the undue stress on government subcontracting of military uniforms as the source of sweating – also derived from Mayhew and exaggerated. But sweating was present in cutlery and nail manufacture where no government department could be blamed for initiating anti-social employment methods.

---

[94]   Schmiechen, *Sweated Industries*, p. 1.

[95]   R. Williams, *Culture and Society, 1780–1950* (London, 1967), p. 100.

[96]   Kingsley also gave a very false picture in *Alton Locke* of Chartism: J. Saville, 'The Christian Socialists of 1848', in J. Saville (ed.), *Democracy and the Labour Movement* (London, 1954), pp. 157–8.

[97]   Kingsley was sensitive to the charges of plagiarism concerning *Alton Locke*: Kingsley, *Charles Kingsley: His Letters and Memories*, p. 248.

[98]   Thomas Cooper (1805–1892) was an enterprising, self-educated man who, after relinquishing cobbling, attained national acclaim as a Chartist writer and lecturer. Arrested for his involvement in a riot, he was imprisoned for sedition. While serving his sentence in Stafford jail, he wrote *The Purgatory of Suicides* (1845), an epic poem which attracted the attention of Kingsley. Cooper was converted to religious faith by Kingsley: A.J. Hartley, *The Novels of Charles Kingsley: A Christian Social Interpretation* (Folkestone, 1977), pp. 64–5; Thorp, *Charles Kingsley*, p. 73; E. Norman, *The Victorian Christian Socialists* (Cambridge, 1987), p. 44. See also S. Roberts, 'Thomas Cooper', in J. Bellamy and J. Saville (eds), *Dictionary of Labour Biography, Volume 9* (London, 1993), pp. 51–6.

[99]   Kingsley, *Alton Locke*, p. 8.

[100]   *Ibid.*, p. 37.

[101]   Schmiechen, *Sweated Industries*, p. 2.

The most prominent defect is the bigoted judgements on those who do not share Kingsley's Anglican faith.[102] As Allan Hartley remarks: 'He condemned Calvinism for its materialism in this world and decried Romanism for its emphasis on the next ....'[103] Baptists are depicted as obdurate and bigoted. Alton Locke's Calvinistic, widowed mother 'glorified in her dissent', but her rigid beliefs distort her sense of judgement, and blight her son's happiness. 'She moved by rule and method ... She seldom smiled. Her word was absolute. She never commanded twice without punishing.'[104] The Catholic Irish with 'their slavish and exclusive creed' are characterised as 'feather-headed' and 'scatter-brained' brutish savages, lacking in moral fibre, undercutters to a man of the 'honourable' garment worker.[105] Alton Locke poses the question: 'if the Irish 'are always crying "Ireland for the Irish"; why can't they leave England for the English?'.[106]

Kingsley's support for evolutionary theories led him to divide those who were fit, and those who were unfit for 'self-government'. Not all those who were white belonged in the first category. In his opinion, the Irish were 'white chimpanzees'.[107] Although considerable divisions existed within the Irish community, in Kingsley's view, they were all destitute, uneducated and ultimately infatuated with cleaving to their own separate culture. His dismay at the sudden and vast increase in the Catholic Irish was compounded by his antipathy towards the resuscitation of Catholicism by the Oxford Movement during the mid-Victorian years.[108] The Jews are indicted for more heinous crimes. When Locke's 'honourable' employer dies, the late master's son adopts new management techniques to imitate those Jews, who sacrifice all moral constraints for instant gratification:

> His father had made money very slowly of late; while dozens, who had begun business long after him, had now retired to luxurious ease and suburban villas. Why should he remain in the minority? Why should he not get rich as fast as he could? Why should he stick to the old, slow-going honourable trade? ... Such I suppose, were some of the arguments which led to an official announcement, one Saturday night, that our young

---

[102] Legislation to reduce discrimination against groups outside the Church of England was passed in 1828 (Nonconformists), 1829 (Roman Catholics) and 1858 (Jews).

[103] Hartley, *Novels of Charles Kingsley*, p. 57.

[104] Kingsley, *Alton Locke*, p. 2.

[105] *Ibid.*, pp. 75–8; 116–18. Despite Kingsley's anti-Catholic propaganda, he was draw to Catholic rituals: he wore a hair shirt, slept on thorns and practised flagellation as mortification of the flesh. See S. Chitty, *The Beast and the Monk: A Life of Charles Kingsley* (London, 1974), pp. 75, 80. His anti-Catholicism eventually embroiled him in a disastrous personal clash with John Henry Newman.

[106] Kingsley, *Alton Locke*, p. 117.

[107] Kingsley, *Charles Kingsley: His Letters and Memories, Volume 2*, p. 107.

[108] The latter, sometimes know as Tractarianism, renounced the Protestant components of Anglicanism in favour of its pre-Reformation, Catholic practices. In 1841 the Irish in Britain totalled about 400,000 and had increased to 806,000 by 1861. This was largely the result of the Irish famine. Mainly from rural backgrounds, the migrants settled in the poorer sections of urban areas and were concentrated in London, Western Scotland and parts of Lancashire and Yorkshire: D. Feldman, 'Migrants, immigrants and welfare from the Old Poor Law to the welfare state', *Transactions of the Royal Historical Society*, 13 (2003), p. 93.

employer intended to enlarge his establishment, for the purpose of commencing business in the 'show trade' ... emulous of Messrs. Aaron Levi, and the rest of that class ....[109]

Jewish middlemen are branded as avaricious, inveterate and whining liars, smart at turning a bargain to their advantage.[110] Jemmy Downes becomes more downcast than 'a negro slave' as a punishment for going into business with a Jewish sweater. The latter is described as possessing 'a most un-"Caucasian" cast of features, however "high nosed", as Mr. Disraeli has it'.[111]

Where Mayhew had been prepared to see the middleman as both victim and transgressor, in Kingsley he has no redeeming features. In his eagerness to unmask the prosperous retailers, Messrs Nicholl and Moses, for farming out work to sweating middlemen, Mayhew's rhetoric was sometimes tinged with anti-Semitism. But he did not single-out the Jewish middleman for special disapprobation. Kingsley, on the other hand, insisted Jews were 'clannish' and 'other' – despite the fact that there were probably fewer than 35,000 Jews in England and Wales and around 20,000 in London. Increasingly, they were British born and beginning to emerge from their separate social, cultural and legal existence. Kingsley felt that accommodating the Jews, and the Catholic Irish, might lead to the collapse of the Anglican faith. As a radical Tory, monarchist and patriot, he considered the Anglican aristocracy to be the natural leaders of society, and that only the Church of England could regenerate and bring harmony to Britain.

Kingsley also despised the 'Mammonism' of the industrial bourgeoisie. The fact that London Jews were predominately middle-class and engaged in trade added to his prejudice.[112] The upshot was that the public associated sweating with a single, frequently Jewish, figure who could be despised and scapegoated as an inhuman vampire. Even eminent scholars, such as William Aytoun, by no means sympathetic to Kingsley's Christian Socialism, praised the latter for exposing in 'these days of projected Jewish emancipation', that:

These sweaters are commonly Jews ... Few people who emerge from Euston Square Station are left in ignorance as to the fact, it being the insolent custom of a gang of hook-nosed and blubber-lipped Israelites to shower their fetid tracts, indicating the localities of the principal dealers of their tribe, into every cab as it issues at the gate. These are, in plain terms, advertisements of a more odious cannibalism than exists in the Sandwich Islands. Very often have we wished that the miscreant who so assailed us were within reach of our black-thorn cudgel, that we might have knocked all ideas of fried fish out of his head for at least a fortnight to come! ... Shylock was and is the true type of his class; only that the modern London Jew is six times more personally offensive, mean, sordid, and rapacious than the merchant of the Rialto ... It is notorious to the whole world that

---

[109] Kingsley, *Alton Locke*, pp. 37–8.

[110] *Ibid.*, pp. 76–7.

[111] *Ibid.*, p. 76. Disraeli insisted that, as a superior race, Jews spiritualised those of more lowly ancestry: U.R.Q. Henriques, 'The Jewish emancipation controversy in nineteenth-century Britain', *Past and Present*, 40 (1986), p. 140.

[112] See Feldman, *Englishmen and Jews*, pp. 4, 21; Norman, *Victorian Christian Socialists*, p. 52.

these human leeches acquire their wealth, not by honest labour and industry, but by bill-broking, sweating, discounting, and other nefarious arts ....[113]

Forty years later, the distinguished economist, J.A. Hobson, could observe: '*Alton Locke* gave us a powerful picture of the sub-contracting tailor, who spider-like, lured into his web the unfortunate victim, and sucked his blood for gain.'[114]

Whilst Kingsley, like Mayhew, perpetuated the idea that sweating was a 'system', he contributed little by way of a cure. As *Harper's New Monthly Magazine* was quick to note, Kingsley was 'vague and fragmentary in his statement of remedies, and leads us to doubt whether he has discovered the true "Balm of Gilead" for the healing of nations'.[115] His advocacy of emigration as a solution was not without controversy. Some leading Christian Socialists supported the endeavour, others did not.[116] Ludlow, probably the most significant Christian Socialist leader of the century, especially regretted that Kingsley felt that such a scheme would be a success. He considered that 'whilst emigration may profit the individual, and colonization the country colonized ... it is but a palliative for the radical evil of competition.' Categorising emigration as 'a ruinous and deadly delusion', he exclaimed: 'how can any one trade be adequately thinned, whilst there are two millions of paupers ready to fill every gap?'[117] Later developments provided support for Ludlow's reservations. Australia required not 'redundant' seamstresses but females with farming skills. Emigration gave only temporary respite to a few while leaving the long-term problems of sweated needlewomen still unsolved.[118] Colonial surveys catalogued a succession of inauspicious incidents during the emigrants' passage and their arrival in the New World.[119]

The other alternative Kingsley offered to sweating dens was co-operative workshops. But where these were tried, they failed. Only a small number were engaged in these projects; they were based on light rather than heavy industry; and

---

[113] W.E. Aytoun, 'Alton Locke: an autobiography', *Blackwood's Edinburgh Magazine*, 68 (1850), pp. 598–9. Aytoun, a staunch Jacobite, was Professor of Rhetoric and Belles Lettres at Edinburgh University.

[114] J.A. Hobson, *Problems of Poverty* (London, 1891), p. 76.

[115] *Harper's New Monthly Magazine*, 1 (1850), p. 858. Gilead was a renowned exporter of aromatic, soothing substances.

[116] Maurice commended colonisation not as transportation, but as 'a brave, hearty, Saxon, Christian work': F. Maurice, *Life of F.D. Maurice, Volume 2* (London, 1884), p. 28; T. Christensen, *Origin and History of Christian Socialism, 1848–54* (Aarhus, 1962), pp. 125–6.

[117] Ludlow, 'Labour and the poor', p. 13.

[118] *Economist*, 15 and 23 December 1849. The *Economist* also alleged that Irish immigration would still contribute to over-population and sweating. Popular Radicals and Chartists viewed emigration schemes as a form of transportation: Thompson, 'Mayhew and the *Morning Chronicle*', p. 28.

[119] These involved insobriety and impropriety on the part of the exuberant women supposedly carefully sifted for the experiment and sexual harassment on the part of male passengers and crew. See Chimes, '"Wanted: 1000 spirited young milliners"', pp. 229, 234 and 236.

disillusionment set in when leading officials were discredited.[120] According to Sidney and Beatrice Webb, they were not co-operatives in the true sense. Unlike the earlier Owenites, the Christian Socialists only intended to replace the individual capitalist with self-governing bodies of profit-making workmen.[121] The needlewomen's co-operatives were not even allowed to be self-governing. Here a superintendent organised the work and had the ability to discharge the women subject to the consent of the 'ladies' committee or the ladies' visitor of the day.[122]

In the final analysis, the Christian Socialists emphasised the first word of their title and relied on the power of religion to humanise and harmonise. Even if they rejected the principle of competition and Malthusian population theories, they accepted the main tenets of political economy. This was particularly true of Kingsley, whose conservatism became more evident in the later part of his life. In 1856 he could counsel the sweated worker: 'Emigrate, but never *strike* … I see little before the Englishman but to abide … and endure.'[123] Soon after his appointment as Regius Professor of Modern History at Cambridge University, he added a new preface to the 1862 edition of *Alton Locke* congratulating the upper classes on: 'labouring for and among the working classes, as no aristocracy on earth have ever laboured before'.[124] He rapidly became a pillar of the establishment, eventually becoming Queen Victoria's private chaplain. A close friend of the Prince of Wales from 1861, he was tended by the latter's physician on his deathbed. In a personal letter of condolence to Mrs Kingsley, the Queen eulogised him for being: 'noble, loyal, warm-hearted, talented and chivalrous …'.[125]

More generally, Kingsley's revelations were eclipsed by wider events. Interest in sweating declined as a result of the fragmentation of social inquiry during the following twenty-five years. Groups such as doctors and lawyers, eager to establish their credentials as professionals, only concentrated on one small aspect of sweating, such as its relation to disease and sanitary reform. Inadvertently, they hindered the understanding of how sweating was actually part of a more complex problem – that of poverty.[126] In addition, the ending of the 'Hungry Forties', the termination of the cholera outbreaks and the apparent return of economic prosperity all led to a diminution of interest in sweating. By May 1851 Britain was preoccupied with the

---

[120] Christian Socialists were only directly responsible for founding twelve workingmen's associations: these included three of tailors, two of shoemakers, two of builders, one of piano-makers, one of smiths, and one of bakers. Walter Cooper, who became manager of the Castle Street tailor's co-operative in 1849, appropriated the funds and absconded. Charles Scully, secretary of the Tailors' association had to be removed from the country to avoid a charge of bigamy: Norman, *Victorian Christian Socialists*, pp. 27, 44, 54–5, 78.

[121] S. and B. Webb, *The History of Trade Unionism* (London, 1894), pp. 225–6. See also, C. Vulliamy, 'Charles Kingsley and Christian Socialism', *Fabian Tract*, 174 (1914), p. 3.

[122] Neff, *Victorian Working Women*, p. 142.

[123] Kingsley, *Charles Kingsley: His Letters and Memories, Volume 2*, p. 13.

[124] 'Preface to the undergraduates of Cambridge', in Kingsley, *Alton Locke*, p. xx.

[125] Thorp, *Charles Kingsley*, pp. 144, 151, 188–9.

[126] E. Yeo, *The Contest for Social Science: Relations and Representations of Gender and Class* (London, 1996), ch. 4. Ironically, Kingsley had assisted this compartmentalisation with his sanitary reform work. Norman considers Kingsley's preoccupation with health issues his only lasting legacy: *Victorian Christian Socialists*, p. 57.

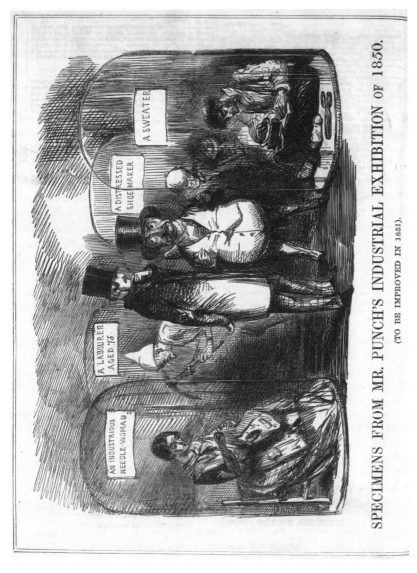

Figure 3 John Leech, 'Specimens from Mr. Punch's industrial exhibition of 1850. (To be improved in 1851)', *Punch*, 13 April 1850

Great Exhibition. Opened by Queen Victoria, the spectacle attracted six million paying customers which, taking into account foreign and repeat visitors, represented approximately one-fifth of Britain's population.[127] During the first three weeks, admission charges were above five shillings. On 26 May the show was opened to shilling visitors – a sum equivalent to four days' labour in a good week for a sweated needlewoman.[128]

For many such as Kingsley, the show ratified both their Christian and Protestant identity.[129] Basking in the optimistic spirit of the 1850s, Kingsley was moved to tears on entering the exhibition's building. To him, it was equivalent to 'going into a sacred place'.[130] Mayhew, equally confident that the class tensions of the previous two decades had abated, argued that the exhibition accorded labour a recognised and respected position in society. Industrialism and technology could solve society's ills.[131] Although famously dubbed by Douglas Jerrold, a founding editor of *Punch*, the 'Crystal Palace', the magazine's own cartoon depicting an alternative spectacle of sweated workers displayed under bell jars for inspection, passed virtually unnoticed.[132]In the end, even the political lampooning of *Punch* waned. Gloomy images of trapped and exploited workers were replaced with Anglo-centric and self-indulgent paeans celebrating England's manufacturing and imperial supremacy. By the eighteen-sixties the journal had mellowed and became less disposed to assailing officialdom or to supplicating on behalf of the sweated underdog. The *Lancet* remarked: 'as the Chartist movement died out, and the depression and distress of the "forties" were forgotten, so the old grievances disappeared, drowned in a sea of prosperity ....'[133]

---

[127] P. Gurney, 'An appropriated space: the Great Exhibition, the Crystal Palace and the working class', in L. Purbrick (ed.), *The Great Exhibition of 1851: New Interdisciplinary Essays* (Manchester, 2001), p. 120. For further details of the exhibition as a monument to consumption, see: T. Richards, *The Commodity Culture of Victorian England: Advertising and Spectacle, 1851–1914* (Stanford, CA, 1990), p. 3.

[128] Testimony of an operative of 'excellent character', *MC*, Letter VI, 5 November 1849, in Thompson and Yeo, *Unknown Mayhew*, pp. 120–21.

[129] J. Auerbach, *The Great Exhibition of 1851: A Nation on Display* (New Haven, CT, 1990), p. 170.

[130] Pope-Hennessy, *Canon Charles Kingsley*, p. 105.

[131] H. Mayhew and G. Cruickshank, *1851: Or, the Adventures of Mr. And Mrs. Sandboys and Family, Who Came Up to London to 'Enjoy Themselves' and to See the Great Exhibition* (London, 1851), pp. 129, 132.

[132] J. Leech, 'Specimens from Mr. Punch's industrial exhibition of 1850. (To be improved in 1851)', *Punch*, 13 April 1850, p. 145. See Figure 3. The cartoon depicts a grim Mr. Punch showing a thoughtful Prince Albert the emaciated victims of industry: R. Pearson, 'Thackeray and Punch at the Great Exhibition: authority and ambivalence in verbal and visual caricatures', in Purbrick, *Great Exhibition*, p. 182. Mayhew had married Jerrold's daughter in 1844. See Thompson, 'Mayhew and the *Morning Chronicle*', pp. 18, 47. *Punch* also referred to the exhibition as a 'glass bazaar' and a 'shop of glass': J.R. Davies, *The Great Exhibition* (Stroud, 1999), p. 186.

[133] *Lancet*, 3 March 1888, pp. 430–31.

Chapter 2

The 'Rediscovery' of Sweating, 1876–1890

Sweating was briefly 're-discovered' in the early years of the 'Great Depression' (1873–1896) when the *Lancet* appointed a commission to report on the spread of infectious diseases through garments made in unsanitary London tenements. But it was Kingsley's highly emotive explanation of the problem not Mayhew's more qualified definition that was remembered. Equating sweating with subcontracting and avaricious middlemen, the commission started from the mistaken premise that: 'The fearful realism of "Alton Locke" first drew attention to the subject, and since then cases have from time to time come to light which afford powerful evidence of its accuracy.'[1] On this occasion, the victim referred to was not one of Kingsley's fictitious characters but the daughter of Sir Robert Peel, whose death on the eve of her wedding was traced to the tailors who had made her riding habit in the same room as a fever patient. The gist of the report was that: 'Similar incidents are no doubt of constant occurrence, and are familiar to many medical practitioners, who do their best to protect the public, but who freely admit the imperfection of their power.'[2] The report described in detail the noxious conditions under which the sweated workers lived and laboured:

> Many of the 'sweaters' cannot, or do not, keep workshops, but crowd their assistants in the small and filthy apartments in which they live and sleep … In one room the family cook, sleep, work, are sick and die. Dirt accumulates unheeded. The bedding of the night time is thrust by day under the tailor's boards, and a swarm of dirty and neglected children often help to vitiate the air and pollute the work.[3]

Nothing happened as a result of this outcry but, by the 1880s, interest in the topic was once more renewed. This time, however, it was overcrowding rather than infection, which became the main source of concern. Andrew Mearns' *The Bitter Cry of Outcast London* highlighted how the sweated were dragged down by their environment.[4] Defrauded by rack-renting landlords, they were forced to live and mingle with the worst criminal elements. Local authorities had intensified this process through large-scale slum clearances. Vile living conditions were exacerbated

---

[1] *Lancet*, 29 January 1876, p. 175.

[2] *Ibid.*

[3] *Ibid.*

[4] A. Mearns, *The Bitter Cry of Outcast London* (London, 1883). Initially, the author's name remained one of speculation: A.S. Wohl, 'The bitter cry of outcast London', *IRSH*, 13 (1968), pp. 189–245.

by the nature of sweated home industries. The air was laden with suffocating dander arising from fur pulled from the skins of rats, rabbits and dogs. The nauseating smell of paste and drying matchboxes mingled with other offensive odours. There was no point in opening windows, even were this possible, since 'the external air is scarcely less heavily charged with poison than the atmosphere within'.[5] This savage environment, Mearns intimated, had also led to 'unspeakable immoral practices'. The brutalised children of the sweated, themselves the products of 'drunken and dissolute parents', were not only being lured into prostitution, they were also becoming prey to incestuous relationships.[6] Amongst these 'miserable outcasts', he warned, 'no cause of vice and sensuality causes surprise or attracts attention.' Hood's respectable seamstress ate her 'crust of bread' and faced her daily grind of seventeen hours surrounded by horrors that could not be 'set forth either by pen or artist's pencil'. Eager to press home the point that the established church had lost contact with the urban poor, Mearns, a Congregationalist, stressed not just the poverty of the sweated but their potential for becoming godless and depraved.[7]

The following year, the *Lancet*, whilst praising Mearns' sensational pamphlet, also published its own exposé.[8] But the *Lancet* was primarily concerned, whereas Mearns was not, with the influx of impoverished foreigners, chiefly Russian and Polish Jews. Whilst Jewish immigration from Eastern Europe was not unprecedented, it was the waves of Jewish immigrants, particularly after 1880, that occasioned antagonism and resulted in a significant anti-sweating movement. Probably some two million Jews migrated out of Russia, Austria and Rumania between 1880 and 1914. Although most proceeded to the United States of America, possibly some 120,000 to 150,000 settled in Britain.[9] The majority of the latter, around sixty per cent, established themselves in East London, making them the second largest ethnic population in the capital after the Irish.[10] Other centres of settlement were the Jewish quarters of Manchester, Leeds, Liverpool, Birmingham and Glasgow. Although some of these immigrants were victims of pogroms and persecution in Russia, Poland and Germany, the majority were economic refugees.[11] In London, the newly-arrived immigrants tended to cluster in the 'special' Jewish trades: tailoring, the

---

[5]   Mearns, *Bitter Cry*, pp. 59–60.

[6]   *Ibid.*, p. 61. Mearns, under cross-examination, later partially retracted this statement. See Royal Commission on the Housing of the Working Classes (RCHWC), *Second Report* (PP XXX, 1884–1885), p. 177.

[7]   Mearns, *Bitter Cry*, pp. 62–5. Mearns' pamphlet led directly to the appointment of the RCHWC. It also encouraged the university settlement movement at Toynbee Hall (Whitechapel): Wohl, 'The bitter cry', p. 190. See also, L. Goldman, 'Ruskin, Oxford, and the British labour movement, 1880–1914', in D. Birch (ed.), *Ruskin and the Dawn of the Modern* (Oxford, 1999), p. 63.

[8]   'Report of the special sanitary commission on the Polish colony of Jew tailors',*Lancet*, 3 May 1884, pp. 817–18.

[9]   Feldman, *Englishmen and Jews*, p. 141. See also, V. Lipman, *A History of the Jews in Britain Since 1858* (Leicester, 1990), p. 45.

[10]   D. Englander, 'Booth's Jews: the presentation of Jews and Judaism in *Life and Labour of the People in London*', *Victorian Studies*, 32 (1989), p. 551.

[11]   Feldman, *Englishmen and Jews*, pp. 147–57.

most significant source of employment, making boots and shoes, cabinets, tobacco products and several minor occupations such as making brushes, caps, slippers, fur work and artificial flowers. The immigrants increased the demand for both housing and workshop premises. Unfortunately for them, they arrived at precisely the time when accommodation in the East End was diminishing.

The *Lancet*, although aware of this mitigating factor, chose to ignore it. Its commission observed: 'we found all the difficulties attached to the question of the housing of the poor are aggravated by the special habits of this peculiar people.'[12] The commission perceived the immigrants as largely destitute, uneducated and un-neighbourly. The 'miserable thoroughfare' of Pelham Street, Spitalfields, it was claimed, reverberated day and night with 'the rattle and whirr' of countless sewing machines. Whitechapel had not recovered 'from the overcrowding that arose when, night after night, waggon loads of poor Jews were brought up from the docks ...'. Conditions in Hanbury Street were considered to be especially offensive:

> we found eighteen workers crowded in a small room measuring eight yards by four yards and a half, and not quite eight feet high. The first two floors of this house were let to lodgers, who were also Jews ... The sink was not trapped ... while the closet was a permanent source of trouble. A flushing apparatus had been provided, but this discharged the water *outside* the pan; the water consequently ... flowed across the yard to the wall opposite ... where the slops accumulate and emit foul odours ....[13]

It was even alleged that the newly arrived possessed their own strange débris. The dustbins belonging to Jewish tailoring tenements were especially singled out as being so foul that steam arose from them. This was the result of 'the large quantity of refuse from the fish, which forms a staple of the Jewish diet, mixing with the cloth dust coming from the workrooms'. The extensive use of disinfectants was recommended.[14]

Newer or modernised dwellings, it was suggested, had not escaped the blight of the Jews since the latter were still, to a great extent: 'Poles in their instincts, customs, and predilections'. In Shepherd's buildings, although modern lavatory facilities were provided, 'the whole system was so foreign to the inhabitants that they had not yet learnt to pull the chain so as to flush and clear the pan.' In Booth Street, rather than descending the stairs to access recently refurbished closets in the yard below, the Jews allegedly ejected their 'soil out of the windows, according to the practice of the Middle Ages'.[15]

I

The *Lancet's* report considerably embarrassed the wealthy, long-settled Anglo-Jewish community whose origins lay in Amsterdam and central, rather than eastern, Europe. The Rev. Dr H. Adler, Delegate Chief Rabbi, commented: 'I am aware

---

[12] *Lancet*, 3 May 1884, p. 817.

[13] *Ibid.*

[14] *Ibid.*, p. 818.

[15] *Ibid.*

that in Booth-Street Buildings ... there is a great lack of cleanliness, and practices occur repugnant to our civilised ideas.' But, he added by way of extenuation, this 'is due to the inadequate number and bad construction of the sanitary conveniences, evils for which surveyors and sanitary inspectors should be made responsible rather than the poor inmates.'[16] Nevertheless, the *Lancet* proceeded to blame the victims and concluded that: 'the presence in our midst of this numerous colony of foreign Jews' with their 'uncleanly habits and ignorance of English ways', caused a sanitary problem in sweated workrooms of a most perilous nature.[17]

The alarm that these reports generated led the Jewish Board of Guardians (JBG) to establish a sanitary committee to persuade 'foreign Jews to conform with our English principle of hygiene'.[18] It also resulted in the Board of Trade despatching its labour correspondent, John Burnett, to investigate sweating in East End tailoring. Burnett heightened the moral panic by lambasting the Jews for not only over-crowding dwellings but also the labour market. He drew heavily on Kingsley's interpretation that the decline of the skilled tailor was related to subcontracting and rapacious Jewish middlemen. He recorded how the introduction of the sewing machine and the manipulation by unscrupulous capitalists of the demand for cheap clothes without regard for quality had greatly accelerated the development of the ready-made clothing trade. Of the minute subdivision of labour, he lamented:

> Instead of there being ... only the customer, the master tailor and his journeymen and apprentices, we have ... the customer, the master tailor, the contractor, and possibly several other middlemen between the consumer and the producer, each making his profit out of the worker at the bottom of the scale. Instead of the complete tailor we have now men who only make coats, or waistcoats or trousers ... We have cutters, basters, machinists, pressers, fellers, button hole workers, and general workers, all brought to bear upon the construction of a coat.[19]

He insisted matters had been made considerably worse since Kingsley's day in other ways: foreign immigrants now flooded the market to such an extent that 'thousands of native workers' had been reduced to 'the verge of destitution'. But for this special cause, he added, 'there would be no demand for inquiry on the subject.'[20] He later recalled that some parts of the East End resembled a foreign country: 'the fact that stuck me especially in reference to a few streets, was that absolutely the whole of the inhabitants were Jews.'[21] The aliens, he declared, lacked self-respect and succumbed to the economic and spiritual slavery of sweating. The Jewish male was deficient in manly virtues. He ate less, accepted a lower standard of comfort than the English artisan and, despite assistance from the native union, the Amalgamated Society of

---

[16] SCSS, *First Report* (PP 1888, XX), Q. 5,740.

[17] *Lancet*, 3 May 1884, pp. 817–18.

[18] *Lancet*, 4 February 1888, p. 236. Founded in 1859, the London JBG dispensed relief to worthy cases of impoverished Jews: Lipman, *A History of the Jews*, pp. 32–3.

[19] *Report to the Board of Trade on the Sweating System at the East End of London* (PP 1887, LXXXIX), p. 256.

[20] *Ibid.*

[21] SCSS, *Second Report* (PP 1888, XXI), Q. 17,285.

Tailors (AST), was totally bereft of class loyalty and trade union consciousness. To Burnett the sweated Jew was a pathetic specimen morally and physically and belonged to a 'patient, submissive race …'. [22]

Conversely, Burnett asserted that the Jews were simultaneously Ricardo's Economic Man incarnate. Unskilled when they arrived, they were prepared to work all hours in the hope of one day becoming small capitalists – 'princes of the sweating system'.[23] Their goal was to extract the maximum of work for the minimum of pay. According to Burnett, the 'cunning' Jewish and 'artful sweater', in the pursuit of gain, was very astute and always on the 'look out' to outwit government officials:

> the inspector is regarded as the common enemy, and as soon as he is seen in any locality where sweaters abound, the signal of his presence is flashed from house to house with almost electric speed, so that one or at most two unexpected visits are all he can make in any one locality.[24]

These middlemen also found it convenient that there were two Sabbaths in the week, Saturday and Sunday, because they observed neither.[25] He concluded that many opponents of sweating believed that 'the influx of these foreigners' nullified 'the sacrifice of thousands of our own emigrants who go or are sent abroad', and hinted that restricting the cheap supply of labour would not lead to the loss of Britain's export trade in clothing. Those who objected to the free trade in alien paupers, he counselled, were adamant that, unless the tide of immigration was stemmed, then 'race hatreds and their natural results' were inevitable. An Aliens Act was passed in 1905.[26]

Burnett claimed that he had drawn on sources describing the problems of sweating 'in moderate language and without exaggeration'.[27] Nothing was further from the truth. He was unable to produce conclusive evidence on how many English tailors had been displaced by Jewish competition, confessed that he had never visited the East End before and had spent only one day there conducting his inquiry.[28] There is also scant evidence of high social mobility among Jewish immigrants during the period 1880–1914, despite Burnett's insistence that many had access to modest amounts of

---

[22] *Report to the Board of Trade on the Sweating System*, p. 261.

[23] *Ibid.*, p. 259.

[24] *Ibid.*, p. 261.

[25] As Saturday was the Jewish Sabbath, Jews were permitted to work on Sundays until 4.00pm.

[26] *Report to the Board of Trade on the Sweating System*, p. 270. Feldman considers that the legislation produced a radical diminution in the rate of Jewish immigration to Britain. See: D. Feldman, 'The importance of being English: Jewish immigration and the decay of liberal England', in Feldman and Stedman Jones, *Metropolis London*, p. 76. But it is likely that the impact of the Act was counteracted by the large numbers of young workers (children of earlier migrants), entering the East End labour market. By this time, though, hostility towards Jews had reverted to one of concern with housing, rather than sweating. See Lipman, *History of the Jews*, p. 69.

[27] *Report to the Board of Trade on the Sweating System*, p. 269.

[28] *Ibid.*, p. 256. See also, SCSS, *Second Report*, Q. 17,285.

capital, such as small loans for a sewing machine from the JBG.[29] Those few who became subcontractors probably did so more out of desperation than through avarice or culturally determined reasons. Self-employment was one means of obviating seasonal worklessness. If there was a Jewish aspiration for upward social mobility, it probably sprang more from their situation as vulnerable workers than from their ethnic identity.[30]

The representation of the Jewish workshop as being populated by unskilled labour and only able to compete by driving the workforce also needs to be questioned. It is probable that approximately forty per cent of immigrants had worked at a craft in Eastern Europe.[31] Moreover, wages in Jewish workshops were often above subsistence levels and, in the busy season, could be substantial. Nor is there any evidence that Jewish workers laboured the excessive hours claimed by Burnett.[32] On the contrary, Tawney considered that Jewish garment shops held their own because of their greater proficiency and superior management.[33]

The lack of permanent organisation among immigrants had little to do, as Burnett insisted, with ethnicity or a deficient sense of morality. Rather, it mirrored the system of workshop production. Trade unionism was most successful in large concerns with impersonal management techniques. Workshop labour, both Jewish and non-Jewish, was severely disadvantaged in this respect.[34] In the complicated world of small-scale production, relations between employers and workers could combine friendship and mutuality as well as hostility and disdain.[35] In the same situation, the native working class responded in much the same manner. Moreover, trade unionism was only one method among many through which immigrants sought to combat sweating. They were also prepared to utilise legal remedies involving the courts and the factory inspectorate but Burnett failed to investigate these alternative strategies.[36]

Burnett's findings did not go unchallenged. Two of Charles Booth's social investigators, Beatrice Potter and David Schloss, denied that sweating was caused by vicious subcontractors or by immigrants replacing native labour.[37] More recently

---

[29]   *Report to the Board of Trade on the Sweating System*, p. 259.

[30]   Feldman, *Englishmen and Jews*, pp. 248–9.

[31]   *Ibid.*, p. 213. Buckman probably overstates when he comments that most of the immigrants were artisans: J. Buckman, *Immigrants and the Class Struggle: The Jewish Immigrant in Leeds, 1880–1914* (Manchester, 1983), pp. 2–3.

[32]   SCSS, *First Report*, QQ. 3,261, 3,281, 3,286, 3,292.

[33]   Tawney, *Minimum Rates in Tailoring*, pp. 18–20.

[34]   Jewish trade unionism had more success in Leeds where workshops were larger. Buckman, Williams and Maitles challenge the view that Jewish workers were essentially individualistic: Buckman, *Immigrants and the Class Struggle*, esp. chs 3–4; B. Williams, 'The beginnings of Jewish trade unionism in Manchester, 1889–91', in K. Lunn (ed.), *Hosts, Immigrants and Minorities: Historical Responses to Newcomers in British Society, 1870–1914* (Folkestone, 1980), pp. 263–307; H. Maitles, 'Jewish trade unionists in Glasgow', *Immigrants and Minorities*, 10 (1991), pp. 46–69.

[35]   Feldman, *Englishmen and Jews*, pp. 239–40.

[36]   *Ibid.*, p. 231.

[37]   D. Schloss, 'The sweating system–I'; B. Potter, 'The sweating system–II', *Charity Organisation Review*, 4 (1888), pp. 11–12, 12–16. Apart from Schloss, none of those connected

Bernard Gainer has remarked that Burnett, as a former trade union leader, should have produced a more circumspect report.[38] Yet Burnett's views were shared by a large section of British society – including the organised working class.[39] Indeed, Burnett had been highly influenced by the AST officials who had acted as his guides around the East End.[40] A crowded conference of tailors in Brick lane, Whitechapel, enthusiastically endorsed the report.[41] Burnett's sentiments were also harboured by a broad spectrum of middle-class opinion, including Home Office officials. James Lakeman, an inspector of workshops for twenty-four years, claimed the credit for much of the evidence in Burnett's report and was irritated that his input had not been acknowledged.[42] *The Times* dignified Burnett's findings with a lead article and dwelt on the 'haunting picture of the sweating system drawn by Mr. Burnett ...'. [43] The *Lancet* observed approvingly how, as a consequence of Burnett's endeavours, the public was now fully cognisant that 'thousands of Polish and German Jews have entered into competition with the English tailor ...'.[44] It complimented Burnett on his 'masterly report' which had 'justly attracted great attention'. The *Lancet* also preened itself for initially bringing the problem of the Polish colony of Jew tailors to public notice.[45]

Even those like Potter who criticised Burnett continued to perpetuate the stereotype of the Jews as being only interested in the pursuit of gain. She professed that Jews were predisposed to profit maximisation due to their perspicacity, their flexibility due to persecution, and Talmudic training.[46] As Feldman has noted, the

---

with Booth's surveys was Jewish: Englander, 'Booth's Jews', p. 554.

[38] B. Gainer, *The Alien Invasion: The Origins of the Aliens Act of 1905* (London, 1972), p. 24. Burnett had been general secretary of the Amalgamated Society of Engineers (ASE) between 1875 and 1886. In 1886, the ASE had a union membership of 51,689 and possessed 432 branches worldwide: *Hansard* (Lords), 28 February 1888, col. 1,618.

[39] Lee suggests that most anti-alienists in the trade union movement took great pains to distance themselves from claims of racism or anti-Semitism: A. Lee, 'Aspects of the working-class response to the Jews in Britain, 1880–1914', in Lunn, *Hosts, Immigrants and Minorities*, p. 119. After 1895, Gainer considers that the Trades Union Congress (TUC), and trade councils curbed their anti-alien activities. Trade recovery, the rise of socialism and the growing belief in asylum for refugees helped to soften anti-alien sentiments: Gainer, *Alien Invasion*, pp. 96–7. Yet, according to Buckman, anti-alienism did not disappear entirely. In Leeds, the destruction of Jewish workshops by new factories, and the subsequent proliferation of Jews working from sweating dens at home provoked anti-alien feeling down to the First World War: Buckman, *Immigrants and the Class Struggle*, esp. pp. 26–30.

[40] *Report to the Board of Trade on the Sweating System*, p. 263.

[41] *The Times*, 6 February 1888.

[42] Webb, *My Apprenticeship*, p. 319.

[43] *The Times*, 21 January 1888.

[44] *Lancet*, 10 December 1887, p. 1176.

[45] *Ibid.*, 3 March 1888, p. 430.

[46] B. Potter, 'East London labour', *Nineteenth Century*, 24 (1888), p. 167. She contrasted the Jewish immigrant (temperate, provident and self-controlled), with the Irish migrant (no care for tomorrow, incapable of sustained thought, and of mutinous disposition). Some recent writers reproduce similar assumptions concerning Jews: See L.P. Gartner, *The Jewish Immigrant in England, 1870–1914* (London, 1973), p. 100.

Jews, whether middlemen or sweated, were viewed as aberrations in Victorian England whose national identity was envisaged as Protestant, Christian, freeborn and imperialist.[47] Alan Lee adds: 'in the perception of race and perhaps of religious differences there seems to have been a greater degree of ideological consensus between classes than on most other issues.'[48]

II

When the Tory democrat and leading fair trader, the Earl of Dunraven, called for a select committee on the sweating system, he rested virtually his entire case on Burnett's report.[49] Dunraven declared that the labour correspondent's survey 'disclosed a state of things in the East End which was disgraceful to a civilised State ...'. Reiterating Burnett's conclusions, he insisted that, although sweating had existed in clothing since the 1840s, the evil 'had been greatly aggravated by' the perfection of machinery, subdivision and, above all, by 'the intense competition ... which was, to a great extent, the result of foreign immigration.'[50] Lord Sandhurst, when seconding the motion, agreed that foreign immigration and sweating were 'inseparably bound up'.[51]

The Secretary to the Board of Trade, the Earl of Onslow, reminded Dunraven that Jewish sweaters 'were really to be commiserated' since, in the lowest class, they were frequently sweated themselves. Nevertheless, he assented to the motion on the grounds that it was too often believed 'that the streets of London were paved with gold, and that foreigners had only to come here to find plenty of work. He had heard it said that advertisements were even inserted in foreign newspapers in the Jewish language announcing that there was plenty of work to be obtained in London.'[52] *Punch* joined in the debate and typified the righteous anger provoked by Dunraven's speech when it represented the sweater as an oafish, splendidly arrayed, cigar-puffing, fur-coated Hebrew who, as he gleefully amassed gold sovereigns, grew corpulent, while his victims were immolated to his avarice. The caption read: 'The sweater's furnace: or the real "curse" of labour'.[53] A similarly disturbing cartoon depicting skeletal workers being preyed upon by a bloated Jewish capitalist, headed 'Sweaters and their victims', appeared in the *Illustrated Police News.*[54]

Composed of Liberals and Conservatives sitting in equal numbers, the SCSS began its sittings in March 1888 and reported two years later. Originally confined

---

[47] Feldman, *Englishmen and Jews*, p. 11.

[48] Lee, 'Aspects of the working-class response', p. 109.

[49] *Hansard* (Lords), 28 February 1888, cols, 1,598–609. Dunraven was President of the Fair Trade League, and advocated the reorganisation of the Conservative Party along Chamberlainite lines. He scorned radicalism as 'communistic': *The Times*, 15 June 1926. Anti-alienism and protection were closely linked: Lipman, *History of the Jews*, p. 68.

[50] *Hansard* (Lords), 28 February 1888, cols, 1,599–600.

[51] *Ibid*, col. 1,609.

[52] *Ibid*, col. 1,617.

[53] *Punch*, 17 March 1888, p. 122. The illustrator was E. Linley Sambourne. See Figure 4.

[54] *Illustrated Police News*, 21 July 1888.

Figure 4 E. Linley Sambourne, 'The sweater's furnace: or the real "curse" of labour', *Punch*, 17 March 1888

to London's East End, the committee's terms of reference were extended after five months when it was reluctantly admitted that sweating pervaded the provinces too.[55]

In its final form, the inquiry covered twenty-seven trades and embraced clothing, boots and shoes, cabinet making and upholstery, shirt making, mantle making, furriery, saddlery and the making of army accoutrements, nails, chains, gun-locks, nuts and bolts, cutlery, hardware and waterproofing.

When calling for the inquiry, Dunraven, the committee's first chair, insisted that sweated workers were more brutalised than slaves:

> At any rate, the slave was the property of his owner, and from mere selfish motives a man would not damage his own property; an owner would not underfeed or overwork a slave so as to lessen his value. But these people, who were nominally free men and women, free citizens of a free country, were just as much bound by their environment as slaves were; and they might die of starvation or rot of disease and their masters would not suffer one farthing of damage. It was not strange to find that women were driven upon the streets, and even the strongest men among the machinists and pressers were killed out in the course of eight to ten years.[56]

Dunraven was dismayed, therefore, when many of the working-class witnesses summoned before the SCSS seemed neither abject nor forlorn. Desperate to sustain the popular anti-alien chorus, he insisted that the self-esteem of the sweated had led them to borrow plumes and clothes so as 'to present a favourable appearance ...'.[57] 'It was the hardest thing in the world', he lamented, 'to get them to admit the way they were fed and clothed and housed.' The final report also commended the sweated on their dignity.[58]

It is doubtful whether their lordships had been brought face to face, as they asserted, with the typical sweated worker or the grim industrial world they inhabited. The sweated were unwilling to come forward because the committee only paid one day's expenses and offered no indemnity against the possible loss of employment.[59] Some who did come forward were dismissed.[60] Others who were approached were unable to understand or to speak English and turned out to be middlemen rather than the sweated. This problem of obtaining *bona fide* victims of sweating resulted in the

---

[55]   The localities investigated included London, Woolwich, Chatham, Sheffield, Newcastle, Leeds, Glasgow, Edinburgh, Liverpool, Manchester, Birmingham, Shrewsbury, Walsall, Dudley, Cradley Heath and district: SCSS, *Fifth Report* (PP 1890, XVII), p. 259.

[56]   *Hansard* (Lords), 28 February 1888, col. 1,603.

[57]   Earl of Dunraven, *Past Times and Pastimes, Volume 2* (London, 1922), p. 106.

[58]   SCSS, *Fifth Report*, p. 299.

[59]   *Ibid.*, p. 259. See also, SCSS, *First Report*, QQ. 2,636–38; *Fourth Report* (PP 1889, XIV), Q. 32,152. Several dockers claimed they would be 'marked men and would probably lose their chance of getting further work in consequence of having given evidence before the Committee': *The Times*, 22 November 1888. The Unitarian minister, Rev. Harold Rylett stated that Black Country witnesses were 'afraid of the consequences to themselves': *The Times*, 7 March 1889.

[60]   Solomon Platt confirmed that he had been discharged for giving evidence: SCSS, *First Report*, QQ. 2,049, 2,114, 2,116.

Earl of Aberdeen, a prominent member of the committee, enlisting the assistance of the popular journalist and eugenicist, Arnold White, to help provide witnesses.[61] According to Beatrice Potter, White was, at that time, the 'great authority on the subject'.[62] The son of a chairman of the Congregational Union, White was a member of the radical right. Convinced of the inherent superiority of the landed aristocracy, he proclaimed that if the 'natural' leaders of society exerted themselves, than all would be well.[63] He extolled the virtues of empire and national efficiency, and zealously opposed home rule and socialism. A prolific writer and ardent 'restrictionist', he was the author of several sensational anti-alien works.[64] In his *Problems of a Great City* (1886), White had insisted that urban degeneration in the East End was due to overcrowding, early marriage and, above all, to uncontrolled immigration. He wrote: 'It is monstrous that the weak should be destroyed by the strong, how much more repugnant is it to instinct and to reason that the strong and capable should be overwhelmed by the feeble, ailing and unfit.'[65] One year later in a letter to *The Times,* headed 'England for the English', he alleged that the pauper foreigner 'was successfully colonising Great Britain under the nose of Her Majesty's Government'.[66] On 15 December 1887 he had led a deputation to the Home Secretary to protest against 'the immigration of foreign paupers'.[67]

Not surprisingly, and at considerable personal expense, White produced witnesses who were only prepared to testify against the iniquities of alien labour and subcontracting. The Jewish employer, as a result of White's intervention, was represented before the Committee as a modern Shylock living off the labour of desperate immigrants driven to the sweater's den to survive.[68] Initially, White produced two extreme case of newly arrived Jewish 'greeners', Mayer Feilweil and Solomon Hirsch, and interpreted for them.[69] Both condemned their long hours, low pay and miserable conditions. White narrated how they arrived from Russia via Hamburg with a batch of equally destitute fellow immigrants. Questioned on how they lived, they testified that they worked for next to nothing and had borrowed money to accomplish 'scabbing' in boot finishing within a few weeks. Neither had any previous connection with the clothing trades: Hirsch had been an agricultural labourer, Feilweil a sugar

---

[61]　A. White, 'A typical alien immigrant', *Contemporary Review*, 73 (1898), p. 248.

[62]　Webb, *My Apprenticeship*, p. 333.

[63]　G.R. Searle, 'Introduction,' in A. White, *Efficiency and Empire* (Sussex, 1973; first published 1901), p. xxiv.

[64]　White penned: 'The common sense of colonization and emigration', *Contemporary Review*, 49 (1886), pp. 375–82; *Problems of a Great City* (London, 1886); 'The invasion of foreign paupers', *Nineteenth Century*, 23 (1888), pp. 414–22. See also, A. White (ed.), *The Destitute Alien in Britain* (London, 1892).

[65]　White, *Problems of a Great City*, p. 30.

[66]　*The Times*, 23 July 1887.

[67]　*Ibid.*, 16 December 1888.

[68]　J.A. Dyke, 'The Jewish workman', *Contemporary Review*, 73 (1898), p. 45.

[69]　SCSS, *First Report*, QQ. 651–703. 'Greener' was a slang term for foreign, unskilled immigrants. Greeners were called 'settlers' after seven years when anglicised: *Ibid.*, QQ. 5,584 and 5,590.

baker.[70] While the former had come to evade military conscription in the Tsar's army, Feilweil, an economic migrant, regretted settling in England. He had heard that his 'countryman was well-off' here but had found the opposite.[71]

White also produced long-established 'settlers' to verify that, instead of improving, their conditions were increasingly immiserated. Samuel Wildman, formerly a Hungarian teacher but now a boot finisher, had been in England for ten years. Yet he could not make a living.[72] Speaking, according to *The Times*, in 'imperfect English' and with the assistance of White, he explained that the newly arrived constantly undercut the rates, that men were so crushed down they were frightened to belong to a trade union.[73] He agreed that there were difficulties in keeping unions going since the variety of languages caused as many difficulties as 'in the building of the Tower of Babel'.[74] The Russo-Polish Jew, Solomon Rosenburg, also a boot finisher, had been in England for eighteen years.[75] Despite being a good workman, his condition had deteriorated so much that he had asked for the urgent assistance of the JBG for his wife and seven children.[76] He pleaded for a halt to further immigration. One reviewer observed: 'The men themselves are helpless. It is either work or starve. The labour itself is practically unskilled. A "greener" can learn … in a month; and it is no longer necessary to shut the men up, as in *Alton Locke*. They know that if they leave, others will be found to take their place.'[77]

White gave evidence and declared that immigrants such as Hirsch and Feilweil, unlike the Huguenots who had brought trade, were destructive to national life. Alien Jews, he averred, refused to become naturalised but took full advantage of citizenship rights.[78] They failed to contribute to the strength of the country and, since they neither imbibed alcohol nor tobacco, did not assist taxation![79] Aided by charity from the JBG, they were directly responsible for undercutting Englishmen and for throwing them on the rates. Impoverished and disease-ridden immigrants, he maintained, were declined entry to America and the Colonies. Yet Britain, with her lax approach, was becoming 'the dust-heap of Europe'.[80] He warned that the tension in the East End aroused by unregulated immigration amounted to a 'judën hetze'.[81]

Leading spokesmen in the Jewish community confronted White and strove to diffuse the scaremongering. The honorary secretary of the JBG, Lionel Alexander, insisted that few were enticed over by charity. Indeed, the JBG was as thorough as

---

[70] *Ibid.*, QQ. 681, 668.

[71] *Ibid.*, Q. 659.

[72] *Ibid.*, QQ. 576–87.

[73] *The Times*, 18 April 1888.

[74] SCSS, *First Report*, Q.707.

[75] *Ibid.*, Q. 907.

[76] *Ibid.*, QQ. 1,005–6.

[77] R.M. Smith, review of 'First Report from the Select Committee of the House of Lords on the Sweating System', in *Political Science Quarterly*, 4 (1889), pp. 186–7.

[78] SCSS, *First Report*, QQ. 2,275, 2,277.

[79] *Ibid.*, Q. 2,164.

[80] *Ibid.*, Q. 2,286.

[81] *Ibid.*, Q. 2,146.

the Charity Organisation Society (COS) in its investigation of claimants.[82] Clients were meticulously vetted and they were refused assistance for the first six months after arrival.[83] No relief was granted to those evading military service. They were sent back.[84] Between 1881 and 1906, the JBG supported the return of over 31,000 impecunious Jews to Eastern Europe.[85] Dr. Hermann Adler, son of the Chief Rabbi, pointed out that he discouraged immigrants by impressing on Russian Rabbis that opportunities in England were far from plentiful.[86] Like Samuel Montagu, MP for the Whitechapel division of Tower Hamlets, he held that Jews and Christians co-existed on friendly terms.[87]

III

While giving evidence before the SCSS, White assisted the investigations of the Select Committee on Emigration and Immigration.[88] On 8 May, he ushered along a crowd of fifty Jewish 'greeners'.[89] Wearing long and dilapidated overcoats and the high boots distinctive of the Russian peasant, their condition, according to *The Times*, was far from 'wholesome'.[90] The Committee's Chair, Sir W.T. Marriott, with the full consent of the members, hastily requested that the 'greeners' be removed from their presence to the corridor outside.[91] Only a few testified but the statements of the others were vouchsafed in affidavits. *The Times* spoke of the evidence that day as being of a 'novel character'.[92]

Subsequently, it emerged that many of the group were probably not 'greeners' at all. One, Jacob Grill, had resided in England for four years and had been assured by White's agent, Isaac Levey, that if he claimed to be newly arrived he would receive an assisted passage to America.[93] Having previously declared Levey to be

---

[82] Founded in 1869, the Charity Organisation Society (COS) advocated careful individual casework to distinguish between the deserving and the undeserving poor. Before becoming disillusioned with the COS, Beatrice Webb had acted (1883–1887) as one of its East London rent collectors: Webb, *My Apprenticeship*, pp. 207–25, 264–84.

[83] SCSS, *First Report*, Q. 5,469.

[84] *Ibid.*, QQ. 5,447–51.

[85] Feldman, 'The importance of being English', p. 63.

[86] SCSS, *First Report*, QQ. 5,740, 5,776.

[87] *Ibid.*, QQ. 5,741, 7,939–40.

[88] The question of foreign immigration was excluded from the remit of the SCSS since a Select Committee of the Commons had been appointed to 'inquire into the laws existing in the United States and elsewhere on the subject of the immigration of destitute aliens and to report ... whether it is desirable to impose any, if so what, restrictions on such foreign immigration.'

[89] House of Commons Select Committee on Emigration and Immigration (Foreigners), *First Report* (PP 1888, XI), Q. 1,324.

[90] *The Times*, 10 May 1888. See also, Select Committee on Emigration, *First Report*, Q. 1,349.

[91] Marriott was an ardent Conservative and prominent member of the Primrose League.

[92] *The Times*, 10 May 1888.

[93] *Ibid*. See also, Select Committee on Emigration, *First Report*, QQ. 1,506–11, 1,541–2. White had paid Levey £10 to find fifty greeners, and had promised the latter 5s per day to

'utterly respectable', White was forced to 'absolutely repudiate the man Levey altogether'.[94] Stung by the accusation that his witnesses 'were not substantially what they appeared to be', White found it prudent to declare that he had 'a lame foot' and a prior engagement re-settling Hampshire labourers in South Africa.[95] On his return a month later, he re-appeared at the immigration committee with a further fifty Jewish 'greeners'. Given the opportunity by the acting chair, W. Lowther, to select some of the men to be examined, White singled out three particularly wretched types.[96] He also complained that there was much surreptitious immigration. He alleged that steamers dropped anchor and placed immigrants in boats to row ashore. Others, he insisted, passed themselves off as cattle tenders when their real motive was to secure a free passage and entry into England.[97]

White's evidence did not stand up to cross-examination. He admitted to Baron de Rothschild that he had paid his private secretary to seek out exceptionally desperate men and that their statements were unreliable.[98] Earlier, he volunteered that as far as he knew some could be millionaires![99] Montagu also chastised White for spreading racial hatred. He reminded White that, as a result of religious observation, Jewish incomers were cleanly in habits, often more so than Catholic ones. White was totally unaware that five Jewish bathing establishments were situated within half a mile of Aldgate. He was also ignorant of the fact that Jews served on juries and had 'equal burdens to those of British subjects'.[100] More significantly, the free-thought advocate, Charles Bradlaugh, forced White to confess that much of the evidence he brought before the committee connecting sweating to the influx of Jews since 1880 was based on hearsay. When pressed, White could not even give the street names of where he had allegedly gathered his material on clothing.[101] It transpired that he had made no special inquiries beyond reading Mayhew's *London Labour and the London Poor* and Kingsley's *Alton Locke*.[102]

Following his ignominious dismissal by Bradlaugh, White resumed his inquiries for the SCSS. While pre-occupied with the immigration committee, he had relinquished the task of getting up evidence to support his contention that sweating was expanding from clothing to encompass the cabinet trade, to his solicitors.[103] His legal team, on White's recommendation, in turn hired the services of Henry Miller,

---

testify: *Ibid.*, Q. 1,553.

[94]   *Ibid.*, QQ. 1,340, 1,519.

[95]   *Ibid.*, QQ. 1,553, 1,594.

[96]   *Ibid.*, QQ. 1,570, 1,587, 1,593, 1,595. See also, *The Times*, 8 June 1888.

[97]   Select Committee on Emigration, *First Report*, Q. 1,356. The collection of basic statistics at ports concerning aliens was a Home Office responsibility. Figures were inadequately compiled. Responsibility later shifted to the Board of Trade's statistical department: J. Pellew, 'The Home Office and the Aliens Act', *Historical Journal*, 32 (1989), pp. 370–71.

[98]   Select Committee on Emigration, *First Report*, QQ. 1,987–92.

[99]   *Ibid.*, Q. 1,579.

[100]   *Ibid.*, QQ. 1,820–22, 1,826, 1,839, 1,843, 1,846.

[101]   *Ibid.*, QQ. 1,969, 1,971.

[102]   *Ibid.*, QQ. 1,947, 1,959.

[103]   SCSS, *First Report*, QQ. 8,557–8.

alias Theodore Müller.[104] William Parnell, secretary of the West End branch of the Alliance Cabinet-maker's Association was also personally approached by White to provide assistance.[105] Miller, Parnell and their associates indulged in outright slander when they unfairly accused the furniture-store magnate and Conservative Member of Parliament, John Blundell Maple, of being a sweater of sweaters and a fraudster.[106] White orchestrated the attack and even contended that Maple had furnished Baron Edmund De Rothschild's French château with the products of sweated labour, an accusation no doubt intended to embarrass Lord Rothschild who was a member of the SCSS.[107]

Maple appeared before the committee and declared that statements made at the SCSS had been circulated in the press and 'had done incalculable damage' to the reputation of his firm.[108] White's statements in attack and Maple's replies occupied numerous pages of the report. Maple's rebuttals were also fully recorded in *The Times*.[109] The latter commented on the 'grave charges' brought against Maple by 'Arnold White and others'.[110] On several occasions the committee's rooms had to be cleared when White insisted that Maple's junior partner, Herbert Regnart, had tampered with one of White's witnesses, Julius Adolphe Deintje, on Maple's behalf.[111] Deintje's solicitors denied that he had been corrupted.[112] Maple seized the opportunity as proof of a conspiracy against him.[113] The Conservative MP, Arthur Baumann, although himself in favour of alien restriction, likened White and his inquisitorial methods to those of Robespierre. He declared that: 'White appeared before the Lords' Committee as a kind of Public Accuser, whom nobody was allowed to answer.'[114]

Maple was exonerated by the committee when it became apparent that there was only the 'germ' of sweating in cabinet making, that there were no grievances to answer. All his opponents established was that Maple sub-let a small quantity of his orders.[115] It also transpired that Parnell had a long-standing dispute with Maple and had selected only vindictive and mendacious witnesses.[116] Threatened with legal action by Maple, he withdrew his accusations as not entirely accurate.[117] Miller, it

---

[104] The latter was paid two pounds a week for five weeks plus an allowance for witnesses. Seven witnesses were paid between 2s 6d and one pound. *Ibid.*, QQ. 8,394, 8,460, 8,505.

[105] *Ibid.*, Q. 8,594. Parnell and a union delegate receive a sovereign each from White for expenses, and compensation for their witnesses' loss of time. *Ibid.*, QQ. 8,604, 8,611.

[106] *The Times*, 9 June 1888.

[107] SCSS, *First Report*, Q. 5,844.

[108] *The Times*, 23 June 1888.

[109] *Ibid.*, 9 June and 23 June 1888.

[110] *Ibid.*, 25 November 1903.

[111] SCSS, *First Report*, QQ. 4,650–61, 4,704. See also, *The Times*, 9 June 1888.

[112] SCSS, *First Report*, QQ. 5,926–8.

[113] *Ibid.*, QQ. 5,934–8.

[114] A.A. Baumann, 'The Lords' Committee and the sweating system', *National Review*, 12 (1888), p. 148.

[115] *The Times*, 25 November 1903.

[116] SCSS, *First Report*, QQ. 8,618–21.

[117] *Ibid.*, QQ. 2,135, 7,901, 8,771.

was revealed, was not a sweated worker at all but a failed business rival with a grudge against Maple. Miller had also attempted to bribe his former trading partner, John Wicks, to suppress evidence of their association and to testify against Maple. Wicks refused to commit perjury.[118] Not only had White's solicitors utilised Miller's tainted evidence, they had suborned, through incompetence, one witness and misleadingly edited the statements of others.[119] Baumann exclaimed, 'it is quite painful to think of the amount of perjury that was committed in the name of philanthropy.'[120] White and his entourage were discredited.

White attempted to extricate himself by insisting that he bore Maple no animosity and that stories he intended to stand as a Liberal Unionist candidate against Maple at the next election were untrue.[121] No doubt smarting after being dismissed by the champion of laissez-faire, Lord Thring, as the 'Corypheus prominent among the witnesses', he insisted:

> I never wrote an article on the Sweating Commission for which I was paid. No acknowledgement or reimbursement was ever made to me by the Government or the Commission. Implacable enmity in wealthy and powerful quarters was my reward. Mistakes in detail may have been made. I regret them.[122]

However, this did not deter White from helping, with the aid of Dunraven, to establish the Association for the Prevention of Destitute Aliens in 1891.[123] Gainer insists that White 'was painfully honest and well-meaning, but hasty-tempered, over-zealous and woefully unsystematic'.[124] More recently, Geoffrey Searle has suggested of White that: 'Many of his contemporaries thought him foolish and hot-tempered, but few questioned his honesty or his patriotism.'[125] But against these views White freely admitted that he opposed immigration so vehemently he was prepared to distort the facts in order to accelerate anti-alien legislation.[126]

IV

After withstanding this storm, the Committee quickly found itself drawn into another debacle when the Rev. William Adamson, Vicar of Old Ford (Bow), accused the Salvation Army of profiting from sweated labour. Although Adamson was broadly inclined to agree with White and his associates that the chief cause of sweating was immigration, Adamson also alleged that matchboxes made in Salvation Army

---

[118] *Ibid.*, QQ. 7,682–4, 8,474.

[119] *Ibid.*, QQ. 7,559–66, 8,548, 8,682–4, 8,693–9, 8,726–31.

[120] Baumann, 'The Lords' committee and the sweating system', p. 147.

[121] SCSS, *Second Report*, Q. 15,843.

[122] White, 'A typical alien immigrant', p. 248. For Thring, see *Hansard* (Lords), 10 June 1890, col. 451.

[123] W.J. Fishman, *East End Jewish Radicals, 1875–1914* (London, 1975), p. 74.

[124] Gainer, *Alien Invasion*, p. 82.

[125] G. Searle, 'Arnold White', in H.C.G. Mathews and B. Harrison (eds), *Dictionary of National Biography, Volume 58* (Oxford, 2004), pp. 544–5.

[126] Select Committee on Emigration, *First Report*, esp. QQ. 1,954–5.

workshops were being sold more cheaply than those manufactured by fairly paid labour. He also insisted that the organisation unjustly competed with laundry workers.[127] His evidence, he claimed, rested on substantial personal experience gleaned from public and private conversations:

> I have heard it on Charity Organisation committees and in connexion with the Mansion-house relief fund two winters ago. I have heard it from curate, scripture reader, and mission woman, and from poor women who worked on the boxes. I have heard it from the lips of clergy and ministers, in committee meetings, and on public platforms. I have heard it even on the Riviera, when English people have asked, 'Is it true what we have read, that the Salvation Army offered to make matchboxes at 2¼d. a gross and to do washing at 4d. per dozen?'. I have read it in newspapers and pamphlets ....[128]

Palpably, Adamson knew very little about sweating, even less about Salvation Army operations, and his information was largely based on rumour. At that time the Salvation Army did not engage in matchbox or laundry work. But to members of the COS, and to traditional churchmen like Adamson who eschewed *'dilettante philanthropy'*, nothing was too scandalous to believe of the Salvation Army. The Salvation Army did not follow the strictest rules of eleemosynary relief. This was anathema to COS members like Adamson, who considered that the principal cause of pauperism was ill-judged, and over-lapping philanthropy. Adamson, in line with COS policy, provided meals for needy children, but at a charge on the grounds that even a partial payment preserved self-respect.[129]

Bramwell Booth, in his father's absence abroad, swiftly denied the charges in a series of heated exchanges with Adamson in the press.[130] *The Times*, normally hostile to the Salvation Army, even allowed Booth to reproduce his dying mother's scathing denouncement of sweating:

> It is never convenient for ministers or responsible churchwardens or deacons ... to ask how Mr Money-maker gets the golden sovereigns or crisp notes which look so well in the collection. He may be the most accursed sweater who ever waxed fat on that murderous cheap needlework system which is slowly destroying the bodies and ruining the souls of thousands ... He may keep scores of *employées* standing wearily 16 hours per day ... on salaries so small that all hope of marriage and home is denied them.[131]

Bramwell Booth also appeared before the SCSS to inveigh against Adamson's evidence as a complete fabrication.[132] Adamson was forced to recant his testimony but not without implicating *The Times*. He suggested that the latter, as a result of

---

[127] SCSS, *First Report*, QQ. 2,568, 2,604–8.

[128] *The Times*, 10 May 1888.

[129] SCSS, *First Report*, QQ. 2,681, 2,696–8, 2,725–8. See also, C.L. Mowat, *The Charity Organisation Society, 1869–1913: Its Ideas and Work* (London, 1961). pp. 74–5.

[130] *The Times*, 7 May 1888, 10 May 1888, 12 May 1888.

[131] C. Booth, *Popular Christianity* (London, 1887), p. 136, cited in *The Times*, 7 May 1888.

[132] SCSS, *First Report*, QQ. 10,782–3, 10,790.

abridging his remarks, had inadvertently spread 'confusion and inaccuracy'.[133] Shamefaced, he reverted to the old cry of alien immigration, early marriage and over-population as the chief cause of sweating. He recommended that: 'Emigration of trained boys and girls should be done on an enormous scale ...'.[134]

V

The evidence concerning women proved to be even more problematic. In the mid-nineteenth century Kingsley had largely associated sweating with the declining 'honourable' male tailor. Yet Morris insists that the SCSS focussed mainly on *women* in the needle trades. If dock and building workers are excluded, she maintains, the committee reviewed trades employing a total of 646,880 women and 440,900 men.[135] Such a conclusion requires qualification. Much of the evidence concerning females was supplied by male trade unionists, middle-class observers or witnesses financially supported by White. Few women were invited or were willing to appear before the committee – only 37 out of 291. Working-class opinion was essentially that of the male, labour aristocrat. Although poverty and fears of victimisation militated against the appearance of both unskilled men and women, it was additionally assumed that poor females had no thoughts on the management of the economy – that they were passive victims. Dunraven reproached even the subcontractor, Mrs Dwelly, for not sending her husband to give evidence concerning *her* shirt-making business.[136]

It is true that the bulk of the witnesses spoke mainly on the garment trades. Yet even here, only twenty-eight women were interviewed and they were not entirely representative of sweated womanhood. One was a middle-woman and two were middle-class social investigators.[137] A tailoring contractor, Mark Moses, supplied two females but their testimony is suspect in view of Burnett's insistence that Moses furnished false evidence concerning the wages he paid, that Moses was really a 'first-class East End sweater, doing second-class work'.[138] White produced three tailoresses

---

[133] *The Times*, 10 May 1888. When Adamson resurfaced in Booth's religious survey, the interviewer recorded: 'As you talk to him you are in doubt as to whether he is a saint or a fraud and you incline to the former. But the latter would appear to be the outside judgement': BLPES, Booth Collection, Series B175, p. 167. Cited in R. O' Day, 'Interviews and investigations: Charles Booth and the making of the Religious Influences survey', in Englander and O' Day, *Retrieved Riches*, p. 155. For a sympathetic account of the sweating scandal surrounding the Salvation Army, see R. Hattersley, *Blood and Fire: William and Catherine Booth and Their Salvation Army* (London, 1999), pp. 348–9. The issue of the Salvation Army and sweating re-appeared between 1907 and 1910 when the carpenters at the Hanbury Street Elevator were accused of under-cutting union labour. The accusations were refuted by Salvation Army officials: V. Bailey, '"In Darkest England and the Way Out": The Salvation Army, social reform and the labour movement, 1885–1910', *IRSH*, 29 (1984), p. 145.

[134] *The Times*, 10 May 1888.

[135] Morris, *Women Workers*, p. 8.

[136] SCSS, *Fourth Report*, Q. 31,554.

[137] SCSS, *First Report*, Q. 3,246; *Second Report*, Q. 15,850; *Third Report* (PP 1889, XIII), Q. 31,548.

[138] SCSS, *First Report*, QQ. 9,190, 9,286; *Second Report*, QQ. 17,244–6, 17,253.

employed on government contract work. Unfortunately for White, when interviewed these women exhibited a curious indifference as to their pay and contradicted each other.[139] White had also paid for the services of a female investigator. But she refused to provide written affidavits from tailoresses she had interviewed on the grounds that they feared recrimination.[140] Of the five shirt makers, White supplied four. Brought forward to verify White's claims that shirt making led to the sweating of vulnerable Christian women, they obligingly declared that the life of a shirt maker was exceedingly hard, that the wages were very low.[141] Yet these women were far from typical – they only worked intermittently and were not wholly dependent on their meagre shirt-making income. Apparently unaware of the part played by White in the selection of the shirt makers, the eminent economist J.A. Hobson considered them to be the most wretched of all the workers presented before the committee.[142]

The dubious accolade of being the most sweated victims in Britain was awarded by the SCSS, not to the miserable metropolitan seamstresses, but to the semi-rural female nail and chainmakers of the Black Country (south Staffordshire and east Worcestershire).[143] They were seen as doing men's work and endangering their reproductive capacities. The five women chainmakers and four nailers were portrayed as worn-out, half-starved, old before their time and 'unsexed' by their occupation. One of the women stated that, working from seven in the morning until seven in the evening, she could make one hundred weight of chain a week, for which she received the paltry sum of between four shillings and six shillings and sixpence. 'We do not live very well', she said 'our most living is bacon; we get a bit of butter sometimes.'[144] Caroline Cox, aged only fifteen, complained that she was always hungry. Even bread and potatoes were a luxury.[145] Another woman told the committee that she carried chain weighing one hundredweight around her neck for considerable distances in order to return it to the sweater's warehouse.[146] Burnett, who had been despatched to investigate the conditions in chainmaking, lamented that the work was too heavy, that the workshop took precedence over mothering, that a tidy home was totally unknown among these 'undomesticated' females. He regretted that the women were 'extremely flat-chested, and the vast majority of them look pale and thin, although their arms are wiry and muscular.'[147]

The *Lancet*, which had also sent its commissioner to give evidence before the SCSS and to the Black Country, agreed. The women, stated the commissioner, were 'so thin, so worn, so pale – mere shadows of what a woman should be … A picture of squalor and despair, of depression and starvation'.[148] At the same time, he emphasised

---

[139] *Ibid., Fifth Report*, p. 294.

[140] *Ibid., Second Report*, Q. 15,908.

[141] *Ibid., Fifth Report*, p. 271.

[142] J.A. Hobson, *Problems of Poverty* (London, 1891), p. 74.

[143] SCSS, *Fifth Report*, p. 281.

[144] *Ibid., Third Report*, QQ. 18,843–4.

[145] *Ibid.*, QQ. 20,491, 20,497–8.

[146] *Ibid.*, QQ. 19,264–5.

[147] *Report as to the Condition of Nailmakers and Small Chainmakers in South Staffordshire and East Worcestershire* (PP 1888, XCI), p. 470.

[148] *Lancet*, 16 March 1888, p. 550.

that the occupation of female blacksmith led to serious uterine problems, resulting in frequent miscarriages, sickly infants and high infant mortality.[149] The work was so continuous it was alleged that the women suckled their babies with one hand without pausing to work.[150] One chainmaking official testified that he had lived in Cradley Heath and district for fifty-two years and that during that time there had been a noticeable decline in the physical condition of the children born to chainmaking mothers. Of the women chainmakers' work, he stated:

> I think it tends very much to injure the race of chainmakers; many of them are little tiny dwarfs; and it cannot be expected that there shall be much muscle and bone in them; seeing that while the wife is pregnant she is hard at work from morning to night; it must tend to prevent development even before the little things come into the world, and when they come they are shamefully neglected and cannot afterwards properly develop.[151]

It was also alleged that in hot weather the men and women worked side by side in a state of semi-nudity, that unmarried mothers 'spoke about their off-spring ... without the slightest hesitation or reserve'.[152] The *Daily Telegraph*, no doubt in search of a titillating story, chose to describe the chainmaking women as they appeared before the committee as brazen Amazons:

> One sturdy maiden offered to take off her gown to show Lord Dunraven and his colleagues how they worked when the weather was hot; but his lordship waved his hand and would not pursue the subject – a timidity that excited astonishment, and perhaps scorn, on the part of the Black Country damsel.[153]

The committee found that the craft did not lead to impropriety. The local factory inspector categorically told the Lords: 'You may certainly see far more indecency in the stalls of a London theatre than you may see in the chain and nail shop in the way of clothing.'[154] But the committee did recommend prohibiting females from making *large* chains; this it considered to be 'unfit' work.[155] There were also complaints that the wretchedness of the nail and chainmakers had been overstated in other respects. Some middle-class witnesses were adamant that the operatives, far from being average, were the worst paid. The committee had been hood-winked, it was

---

[149] Adolphe Smith (*Lancet* commissioner), SCSS, *Third Report*, QQ. 22,652, 22,670.

[150] *The Times*, 7 March 1889.

[151] Evidence of Thomas Homer, SCSS, *Third Report*, Q. 18,256.

[152] *Report as to the Condition of Nailmakers and Small Chainmakers*, p. 12.

[153] Cited in *CE*, 16 March 1889.

[154] SCSS, *Third Report*, QQ. 20,247, 23,010.

[155] *Ibid.*, *Fifth Report*, p. 301. The proposals with regard to female nail and chainmakers never became law. A deputation of the women under the leadership of Mrs Fawcett 'stormed' London in 1891 to protest to the Home Secretary, Henry Matthews. Their meeting with the latter did not impress them. As they were about to leave, one woman turned to Mrs Fawcett and said: 'It's very 'ard upon the pore gentleman to 'ave to make the laws, and not know nothing about it.' Cited in R. Strachey, *The Cause* (London, 1928), pp. 236–7.

insinuated, into interviewing 'the very refuse of the trades' by male trade unionists intent on removing female competitors.[156]

The men's unions had made what was a wages issue into a gender problem when, in despair following the failure of such remedies as conciliation boards and co-operative workshops, they had sought to restrict women's entry into the trade.[157] They appreciated only too well that the problem of sweating was one of low pay, yet, rather than recommending the legal control of such wages, they fell back on remedies which were already well worn. This was not altogether surprising considering the establishment's belief that intervention in the wages contract would be disastrous for Britain. On the one occasion when the chainmakers hesitantly proposed a legal minimum wage, their lordships made it plain that Parliament viewed state control of low pay as ridiculous.[158]

Although the 1870s had largely invalidated the wages fund theory, it was superseded by the equally cautious philosophy of marginal utility economists. The latter held that the worker's remuneration was established by the marginal productivity of the group to which he or she belonged. It was thus assumed that workers would seek trades where their skills would obtain the highest rewards and, as such, differences in wages reflected a person's economic worth with regards to skill, efficiency and motivation. Those who received low pay, therefore, either performed work of little economic value or manufactured products commanding only a poor market price. It was contended that, if wages were artificially raised above their natural economic level, then this finely tuned balance would be plunged into disequilibrium and unemployment would result. The only remedy for poverty wages, these economists maintained, was to boost the efficiency and thereby the wages of the low-paid. This was to be attained by encouraging higher moral standards, an improved environment and increased education.[159] Unable to mount a coherent critique of the existing system, and anxious not to be seen as subversive, the chainmakers and their leaders not unnaturally restricted themselves to more predictable, albeit sexist, solutions.

VI

Social explorers proved to be no more enlightened. H.L. Beales declared that: 'Booth's investigations opened the door to Old Age Pensions, Labour Exchanges and Trade

---

[156] SCSS, *Third Report*, QQ. 2,310–18, 23,107–8, 22,722, 22,836, 22,838–9, 22,888.

[157] For further details, see, S. Blackburn, 'Working-class attitudes to social reform: Black Country chainmakers and anti-sweating legislation, 1880–1930', *IRSH*, 33 (1988), pp. 42–69. Morgan draws substantially on this article in: C. Morgan, *Woman Workers and Gender Identities, 1835-1913* (London, 2001), esp. ch. 6. See also, S. Blackburn, 'Gender, work and labour history: a response to Carol Morgan', *Women's History Review*, 10 (2001), pp. 121–35.

[158] SCSS, *Third Report*, QQ. 18,089–92.

[159] See, for instance, H.V. Emy, *Liberals, Radicals and Social Politics, 1892–1914* (Cambridge, 1973), pp. 112–13. See also, E. Biagini, 'British trade unions and popular political economy, 1860-1880', *Historical Journal*, 30 (1987), pp. 811–40.

Boards.'[160] Yet Booth's evidence before the committee was mediocre. Since his East End inquiry would not be available for six months, he hesitated to give evidence or to draw any general conclusions. No doubt much to Dunraven's satisfaction, he pronounced sweating to be 'the advantage that may be taken of unskilled and unorganised labour under the contract system.'[161] Although he later retracted this statement, he still harboured grave doubts concerning government intervention: 'I may say at the outset that my expectations of rapid and certain remedy are not high ... I see no safe policy but "laissez-faire". The road is long and steep, but it is the only one that we can safely follow ....'[162]

It is generally assumed that the most effective witness before the SCSS was a woman – the young Beatrice Potter. She had not yet declared herself to be a socialist, though she would in 1890, but she had already begun to formulate her thesis that under capitalism all employers should accept direct responsibility for the welfare of their employees. She had become involved with sweating through assisting Charles Booth, her cousin's husband, with his poverty survey. Her work for Booth, as well as several articles that she published separately, attracted wide public attention.[163] This led to her being invited in 1888 to give evidence before the SCSS. Her brief testimony proved to be a turning point for the inquiry.[164]

With expertise and expedition she brushed aside the previous assumptions that sweating was caused by subcontracting, middlemen or immigrants. According to one observer, her main strength lay in her positiveness, her ability to interpret the facts and her lack of sensation.[165] She pointed out that the worst cases of sweating had nothing to do with subcontracting.[166] She also denied that middlemen became excessively rich; on the contrary, the middleman in the most poorly paid tailoring work generally earned less than some of their more skilled hands.[167] Moreover, relationships between middlemen and those who worked under them were governed by 'a good deal of geniality and kindness'.[168] She repudiated as sensationalist

---

[160] H.L. Beales, *The Making of British Social Policy* (Oxford, 1946), p. 20. See also, T.S. and M.B. Simey, *Charles Booth: Social Scientist* (Oxford, 1960), p. 261.

[161] SCSS, *First Report*, QQ. 308–10.

[162] A. Fried and R. Elman (eds), *Charles Booth's London* (Harmondsworth, 1971), p. 175. See also, Booth's letter to *The Times*, 18 August 1888.

[163] Potter's contribution to Booth's *Life and Labour* included chapters on the docks, tailoring and Jews: *My Apprenticeship*, pp. 166–85, 264. See also, B. Potter, 'East London labour', *Nineteenth Century*, 24 (1888), pp. 161–83; B. Potter, 'Pages from a work-girl's diary', *Nineteenth Century*, 24 (1888), pp. 301–14.

[164] In case this wasn't observed, she wrote to the *Times*, 26 Sept 1888, pointing out that: 'I differ from most of the witnesses who appeared before the Committee ....' O'Day argues that Collet was a superior investigator to Potter: 'Women and social investigation: Clara Collet and Beatrice Potter', in Englander and O'Day, *Retrieved Riches*, esp. p. 193.

[165] Baumann, 'The Lords Committee on the sweating system', p. 152. In order to avoid luridness, she had omitted references to incest in her early publications: Webb, *My Apprenticeship*, pp. 317, 324 n. 25.

[166] SCSS, *First Report*, Q. 3,250.

[167] *Ibid.*, QQ. 3,397–9. Feldman disagrees: *Englishmen and Jews*, p. 241.

[168] SCSS, *First Report*, Q. 3,357.

the claim that, when immigrants landed, they only knew three words of English: 'Board of Guardians'.[169] She insisted that pauper immigrants were not at the root of the sweating problem: in practice, Jewish and non-Jewish tailoring coexisted in watertight compartments, and there was no competition between them.[170] Jewish workers were not necessarily low-paid. In busy times machinists and pressers could make their own terms.[171]

But her evidence was not above criticism. She was relatively inexperienced as a social investigator and exaggerated the time she had worked in a Jewish East London sweatshop. Much to her embarrassment, the socialist tailor, Lewis Lyons, exposed this fact in the *Pall Mall Gazette*.[172] In private, she admitted that she could not withstand the foetid atmosphere and bodily exhaustion of sweatshop labour for more than a day. As Royden Harrison notes: 'Had she made this admission in public it would have told against much of her testimony and the complacency which it encouraged'.[173] More importantly, she prided herself on adopting a 'male' model of social analysis. This led her to insist that the taproot of sweating was females working at home – even if immigration was curtailed, the problem of the almost inexhaustible supply of indigenous, married female labour competing for work within the sweated sectors would still exist. She later added that: 'The Jews are counted by their thousands; the women dragging in their rear semi-dependent husbands and a huge force of unprotected children, may be numbered by hundred thousands.' Having absolved the Jews for working too hard, she now denounced English women for working for paltry amounts.[174] Eager to take work at any price, these women, she concluded, were the 'Chinamen' of their class, part of a mongrel population grasping after the leavings of the Jews.[175]

This situation, she argued, had been assisted by factory and workshop legislation which had virtually exempted women outworkers from regulation. The Factory and Workshops Act of 1878 had altered the legal definition of 'a factory' from an establishment with fifty persons to any place with motive power, defining those without power as 'workshops'. Although the 1878 Act strengthened control over factories, it permitted workshops considerable flexibility. In textile factories, for example, the working hours of women and young persons were limited to ten a day, between fixed times. All factories were required to register with the Factory Department and to be open to inspection day or night. By contrast, women's workshops and home-workers were exempt from the legal requirements governing cleanliness, effluvia

---

[169] *Ibid.*, Q. 3,374.

[170] *Ibid.*, QQ. 3,292 and 3,331. Feldman (*Englishmen and Jews*, p. 210), disputes that Jewish and non-Jewish tailoring were entirely separate.

[171] SCSS, *First Report*, Q. 3,292.

[172] Webb, *My Apprenticeship*, pp. 326–7. Lyons, in turn, was accused of embezzling the funds of the London Tailors' and Machinists' Society when serving as its secretary. The charge remained unproven, and Lyons blamed Schloss for constantly bringing up the matter to discredit him: SCSS, *First Report*, QQ. 10,723–8.

[173] R. Harrison, 'Sidney and Beatrice Webb', in Carl Levy (ed.), *Socialism and the Intelligentsia, 1880–1914* (London, 1987), p. 52.

[174] SCSS, *First Report*, Q. 3,415.

[175] Potter, 'East London labour', p. 178.

and overcrowding. In women's workshops and domestic workshops, where only family members were employed, work could be undertaken at any time between 6.00 am and 9.00 pm. Along with the lack of a legal obligation to register, this made the enforcement of a maximum working day almost impossible. In the home there were no restrictions at all on women's working hours and practically none for child labour.[176] Potter considered that sweating could be ended swiftly if these loopholes in the law were closed.[177] Ultimately, she hoped that this step would make home-working unprofitable and would drive industry into larger units of production.[178]

Elsewhere, Potter justified these beliefs on the grounds that large employers were obliged by law to be 'responsible' and to meet minimum civilised standards. In the factory, trade unionism prospered; female outworkers, on the other hand, had no such protection and it was among them that sweating flourished.[179] As she observed:

> The mill-owner, coal-owner, or large iron-master, is forced to assume, to some slight extent, the guardianship of his workers. He is compelled by the state to provide healthy accommodation, to regulate the hours of labour of women and young persons, to see to the education of children, to guard against and to insure all workers against accident. Trade unions, arising from the massing of men under the factory system, insist on a recognised rate of wages. Public opinion, whether social or political, observes the actions of a responsible employer in the open light of day. Willingly or unwillingly, he must interpose his brains and his capital between groups of workers on the one hand, and the great mass of conscienceless consumers on the other ... He is, in fact, the first link between the private individual intent on his own gain, and the ideal official of the socialist state administering property in trust for the people. It is the absence of this typical figure of the nineteenth century which is at once a distinguishing feature and a main cause of those grosser forms of fraud and oppression known as the sweating system.[180]

---

[176] Hutchins and Harrison, *History of Factory Legislation*, pp. 188–91, 208, 240–42.

[177] At the very minimum, she recommended that all home workshops should be registered. This would necessitate inspection of dwellings through the weekly rent collector, and landlords would be required to notify the inspectorate of manufacturing work carried out on their premises: SCSS, *First Report*, QQ. 3,313, 3,339, 3,366. She later advocated an additional form of surveillance: the giver out of work was to be held responsible, too, for registering workers' premises. See B. Potter, 'The Lords and the sweating system', *Nineteenth Century*, 27 (1890), pp. 895, 901.

[178] SCSS, *First Report*, QQ. 3,322, 3,361. Potter ascribed the unrigorous system of regulation in women's workshops to the opposition of the women's rights movement of the 1870s: Potter, 'The Lords and the sweating system', p. 899. In doing so, she laid herself open to the criticism by Millicent Fawcett and other liberal feminists that her proposals could reduce women's employment opportunities. Potter insisted that the exclusion of middle-class women from the professions and legal protection for working-class women were fundamentally different issues: B. Caine, 'Beatrice Webb and the "Woman Question"', *History Workshop Journal*, 14 (1982), pp. 25–43; B. Caine, *Victorian Feminists* (Oxford, 1992), pp. 243–8. Potter compounded this disapproval of her actions in 1889, when she signed a manifesto drafted by, among others, Mrs Humphrey Ward against the political enfranchisement of women. She recanted this 'false step' in 1906 in a letter to *The Times*, 5 November 1906.

[179] SCSS, *First Report*, QQ. 3,248, 3,310, 3,322, 3,339, 3,361.

[180] Potter, 'The Lords and the sweating system', p. 899.

Her analysis conveniently overlooked the terrible conditions at Bryant and May's match factory, which had occasioned the famous 1888 strike, and the sweating in London's jam, pickle and confectionery establishments. Potter demonstrated a touching faith in the efficacy of factory legislation. As Manny Shinwell remarked: 'The Factory Acts, if they existed at all, were "more honoured in the breach than in the observance". Inspectors were few in number and the law was ignored.'[181] She also ignored the over-supply of casual males, such as agricultural labourers, who were flooding into London and taking whatever work they could. She assumed all homeworkers were unskilled, defenceless and sweated when patently this was not always the case.[182] More importantly, she disregarded the crucial point that the Factory Acts did not regulate pay. As the social investigator Clementina Black observed, factory workers shared 'with the home worker the constant dread of being left without employment and without means to pay for lodgings and food'.[183]

---

[181] M. Shinwell, *Lead With the Left: My First Ninety-Six Years* (London, 1981), p. 43. For evasions of factory legislation, see, Black, *Sweated Industry*, ch. 2.

[182] Select Committee on Homework (SCH) (PP 1907, VI), QQ. 3,042–6.

[183] Black, *Sweated Industry*, p. 47.

PART II
The Search for an Effective Solution

Chapter 3

Anti-Sweating Campaigns, 1890–1905

After two years of collecting and consolidating of information, the SCSS brought its labours to a close in 1890, though not without an element of conflict. Whilst the views of the committee had been gradually modified, Dunraven remained adamant that the root causes of sweating were the advance of machinery, subcontracting and, above all, the competition of foreign immigrants with low living standards.[1] As chairman, he submitted a preliminary paper embodying these ideas.[2] The other committee members unanimously rejected his findings. *The Times* regretted that it was,

> unfortunate that Lord Dunraven has not been able to find a single supporter of his reading of the evidence upon a Committee which includes men of the highest ability ... he must have failed seriously in what is the primary duty of a chairman anxious to expedite business – namely, appreciation of the general feeling of the Committee and approximately accurate expression of its conclusions.[3]

Piqued, Dunraven declared that he was 'in a very unsatisfactory and equivocal position' and asked to be relieved of further duty.[4] The new chair, Lord Derby, assisted by Lords Monkswell and Thring, drafted the final document. Forty pages long in contrast to Dunraven's fifty, their report spoke of sweating but not of a sweating system. Potter observed of its authors, 'by this significant omission they tacitly deny that the evils are co-extensive with, or peculiar to, any one form of industrial organisation.'[5] After eschewing any scientific definition of sweating, the final report merely described the factors which contributed to the problem: earnings barely sufficient to sustain existence; hours of labour such as to make the lives of the workers periods of ceaseless toil, hard and unlovely; sanitary conditions injurious to the health of the person employed, and dangerous to the public. It added: 'These evils can hardly be exaggerated.'[6]

The report completely exonerated machinery as a cause, on the grounds that the most highly mechanised sectors contained the most favourable working conditions. Chainmaking was barely touched by new technology; the majority of sewing machines were unpowered. In as much as sweating occurred in trades unaffected by a foreign element, the report largely acquitted immigrants as contributing to the

---

[1] *Hansard* (Lords), 9 June 1890, col. 289.
[2] *Ibid.*, cols 283–307.
[3] *The Times*, 25 March 1890.
[4] *Ibid.*
[5] Potter, 'The Lords and the sweating system', p. 886.
[6] SCSS, *Fifth Report*, pp. 298–9.

origins of the problem. Middlemen were also excused as 'the consequence, not the cause of the evil; the instrument not the hand which gives motion to the instrument, which does the mischief. Moreover, the middleman is found to be absent in many cases in which the evils complained of abound.'[7] Instead, their lordships placed the blame squarely on the shoulders of the workers, especially married women:

> With more truth it may be said that the inefficiency of many of the lower class of workers, early marriages, and the tendency of the residuum of the population in large towns to form a helpless community, together with a low living standard of life and the excessive supply of unskilled labour, are the chief factors in producing sweating. Moreover, a large supply of cheap female labour is available in consequence of the fact that married women working at unskilled labour in their homes, in the intervals of attendance on their domestic duties and not wholly supporting themselves, can afford to work at what would be starvation wages to unmarried women.[8]

To remedy this state of affairs, the report suggested that co-operative production, despite past failures, and trade union organisation might solve the problem of low wages and long hours. Having discounted the docks as a possible site of sweating since 'the conditions of dock labour have been so materially altered' by the strike of 1889, the committee stressed the problem of domestic workshops.[9] Deciding against the prohibition of homework – 'such a measure would be arbitrary and oppressive' – the report recommended instead that the Commons should discuss the registration of homeworkers. Further proposals included the sanitary inspection of all workshops including domestic ones, administrative reforms to make detection and inspection easier, and the extension of technical education to all classes. The Lords also recommended that government and municipal bodies should take every precaution to see that fair wages were being paid for their contracts, such as those for uniforms – something that the London School Board had been practising since the 1870s.[10] Finally, they piously hoped that: 'When legislation has reached the limit up to which it is effective, the real amelioration of conditions must be due to increased sense of responsibility in the employer and improved habits in the employed.'[11] Its work thus formally completed, the committee's principal recommendations were virtually confined to factory and sanitary legislation.

Schmiechen considers that the 'decade of the 1880s was a watershed for British social theory'.[12] Yet the committee, for all its methods and theories, had left wages unregulated and sweating undisturbed. In 1891 Henry Matthews, Secretary of State for the Home Department, could remark:

---

[7]   *Ibid.*, p. 299. However, Feltes appears to believe that subcontracting was a major factor in sweating: N. Feltes, 'Misery or the production of misery: defining sweated labour in 1890', *Social History*, 17 (1992), p. 450.

[8]   SCSS, *Fifth Report*, p. 299.

[9]   *Ibid.*, p. 278.

[10]   *Ibid.*, p. 301.

[11]   *Ibid.*

[12]   Schmiechen, *Sweated Industries*, p. 134.

There are three leading factors in the workman's life – his work, his wages, and his health. Unhappily, legislation can do but little with regard to the first two. It cannot alter or improve the quantity or the quality of work, and it cannot otherwise than mischievously interfere with the question of wages.[13]

I

Punch wrote witheringly of the application of a 'rose-water cure' and the whitewashing of the fiendish, vampire sweater.[14] White considered that the SCSS had been 'carefully calculated to allay public interest, and to drug the public conscience'.[15] He deplored the report's 'sedative style' and concluded that it was 'fragrant with the frankincense of *Laissez faire*'.[16] Rather disingenuously, considering the 'difficulties' with his own witnesses, he maintained that the case for the sweated had been inadequately set forth for:

> Taken from the garret and the cellar and brought to a stately chamber in a palace in the West End, poor men and women could but feebly tell their story. What they told was a fraction of what was left untold. When the very poor are not inarticulate, their language is often repugnant to men of taste. The case of the capitalists was framed with the moderation, and was generally expressed with the culture, to be expected from their class ... much desirable evidence was left untold ...[17]

White lamented that the SCSS had ignored direct evidence on immigration 'for fear of trenching on the rights and privileges of the Commons Committee, which was concurrently occupied in the ostensible examination of the immigration question'. In order to place before the public what he considered to be the correct estimation of the situation, he edited a 'practical' guide 'bringing out the true physical, moral and economic results' of unrestricted immigration.[18]

Dunraven derided the report in the Lords and later in his biography. He complained that the majority of the Committee 'were imbued with the "Manchester School" theory of cheap labour ...', that Derby's report 'was not clearly, fairly, and justly presented ...'. He maintained that, while Potter's testimony was worthy of respect, it ought to have been 'balanced and weighed against the evidence of other people of greater experience'. He also claimed that seventeen of twenty working-class witnesses had blamed sweating on immigration, that of eighty-six witnesses, eighty-three 'were of opinion that the evils ... were due to the unnecessary number

---

[13]   *Hansard* (Commons), 26 February 1891, col. 1,711.

[14]   Cited in C. Graves, *Mr. Punch's History of Modern England, Volume 3* (London, 1921), p. 96.

[15]   *Lancet*, 2 August 1890, p. 246.

[16]   *The Times*, 12 May 1890.

[17]   *Ibid.*

[18]   White, *The Destitute Alien*, pp. 1–4.

of middlemen and to the system of sub-contracting.'[19] The Archbishop of Canterbury, a member of the SCSS, upbraided him:

> To count 83, or half that number, of poor working men and women, with their heads below water ... against the opinions of three people who have considered the whole matter from the outside, who have, after considering the question in many lights, gone among the workers ... is, I think, absurd to the last degree.[20]

Potter praised the SCSS for describing sweating as long hours, low pay and unsanitary working conditions, all of which were linked by the common bond of the irresponsible employer.[21] She found it gratifying that the SCSS urged Parliament to set fair rates of pay for all central and local government contract work. This, she believed, was the first step 'towards the direct creation by the State of employers responsible to the people for the welfare of the workers'.[22] She also maintained that the report was correct to reject as impracticable the socialist solution for creating the responsible employer – state-subsidised workshops.[23] When John Lincoln Mahon, a socialist engineer, presented the SCSS with a detailed plan for the re-organisation of Black Country chainmaking in state-funded factories, several of their lordships recoiled in horror. Potter observed of Mahon's scheme: 'public opinion is not ripe for the Socialist answer to the labour problem.'[24] But she dismissed the suggestion that voluntary co-operative production might solve sweating as little more than 'a very grim joke'. Its fulfilment required 'exactly those qualities which are conspicuously absent among sweated workers – loyalty, integrity, commercial enterprise – besides the possession of that little trifle capital'.[25]

Above all, Potter was disappointed that the Lords' recommendations did not go further. Her public and private attempts to influence the final report were largely ignored, and it failed to sanction total repeal of those sections of the Factory Acts that exempted domestic workshops.[26] But, despite considering the document to be

---

[19]   Dunraven, *Pastimes*, pp. 105–9. See also, *Hansard* (Lords), 9 June 1890, cols 291, 2,301–2.

[20]   *Hansard* (Lords), 9 June 1890, col. 464.

[21]   Potter, 'The Lords and the sweating system', p. 866.

[22]   *Ibid.*, p. 895. When the House of Commons subsequently adopted fair wage resolutions in 1891 and 1909, workers complained about lack of enforcement: *Morning Leader*, 28 March 1908; *Evening Standard* (London), 30 March 1909.

[23]   Potter, 'The Lords and the sweating system', p. 895.

[24]   *Ibid.* For Mahon's evidence, see SCSS, *Third Report*, QQ. 21,636–769. Mahon was a member of the Social Democratic Federation (SDF), the Socialist League, and later of the Independent Labour Party (ILP). E.P.Thompson, *William Morris: Romantic and Revolutionary* (London, 1955), p. 563, considered that Mahon exemplified '[w]hat is finest in the pioneering spirit which first brought the propaganda of socialism to the masses'.

[25]   Potter, 'The Lords and the sweating system', p. 896. These arguments are developed in B. Potter, *The Co-operative Movement in Great Britain* (London, 1890), pp. 225–6. She was admonished in *The Times* for rejecting voluntary co-ops: *The Times*, 9 June 1892.

[26]   See her letter to *The Times*, 26 September 1888; also Webb, *My Apprenticeship*, pp. 327–9. Attempts were made to compile legal registers of outworkers in 1891, 1895 and 1901, but they were of little value. The Act of 1891 laid down that every occupier of a factory or

'utterly ineffective', she held that it was 'sound as far as it goes, and will serve as a foundation for my own proposals'.[27] In her diary she made her motives for supporting the restriction of homework more explicit:

> What we have to do is to detach the *great employer*, whose profits are too large to feel the immediate pressure of regulation and who stands to gain by the increased efficiency of the factors of production, from the ruck of small employers or stupid ones. What seems clear is that we shall get no further instalments of reform unless we gain the consent of an influential minority of the threatened interest.[28]

II

When Sidney Webb met Beatrice Potter in January 1890 he was already a prominent Fabian socialist and a well-known authority on labour matters. Asked to comment upon her sweating material, he was initially inclined to be critical. He thought that some of her proposals for greater regulation of homework vague and impractical and likely to be politically ineffectual. He informed her that she needed his assistance before she drafted specific proposals for reform since, 'you rather shirk the dry ground of "draft clauses".' Yet he conceded: 'Your point as to the "responsible employer" is magnificent.'[29]

---

workshop, including men's workshops, must, if so required by the Secretary of State, keep lists of all the outworkers employed. These lists were open to inspection by local sanitary officers and the factory inspectorate. The Act of 1895 made it compulsory for lists not only to be kept by the occupier, but also to be sent twice yearly to the factory inspectorate. The last Act, that of 1901, made it compulsory for the occupier or contractor to send lists of outworkers to the district council in which the factory or workshop was situated. The district council then forwarded the names and addresses of these outworkers of firms within its districts to the councils of districts where the outworker lived. While these acts possibly caused some improvements to be made in large cities like Liverpool or Manchester, where municipal authorities took their responsibilities seriously, members of small town councils were reluctant to interfere with fellow tradesmen, lest they made themselves unpopular. The same myopic attitude also applied to the sanitary inspection of the workshops. The 1891 Act, in an attempt to discover unnotified workshops, made local authorities responsible for supervising the sanitary conditions of the shops, for it was felt the sanitary officers in their house-to-house calls were the most likely to bring such shops to light. Few small town councils were prepared to accept the odium of increasing the rates to finance the additional officers, and the number of sanitary inspectors was rarely adequate to permit thorough or systematic investigation. Naturally, where inspection was not regular, and where no special inspectors were appointed, registers were not kept, and workshops were only visited, as in the past, upon complaint: Hutchins and Harrison, *History of Factory Legislation*, pp. 214, 219. Nor did the career prospects of a sanitary inspector attract first class recruits. According to Mess, the profession was a cul-de-sac: H.A. Mess, *Factory Legislation and its Administration, 1891–1924* (London, 1926), p. 6.

27   Webb, *My Apprenticeship*, p. 329.

28   B. Drake and M. Cole (eds), *Our Partnership By Beatrice Webb* (London, 1948), p. 205.

29   N. Mackenzie (ed.), *The Letters of Sidney and Beatrice Webb, Volume 1* (Cambridge, 1978), p. 146. As A.M. McBriar, *An Edwardian Mixed Doubles: The Bosanquets versus the Webbs*

Sidney Webb's own interest in sweating had been stimulated through involvement in the legal eight-hour day movement and the campaign for fair wages for central and local government workers.[30] He considered that enlightened employers would not object to these attempts to remove sweating since: 'The cheapness of their product is the price of blood.' He equated sweating with 'blood-stained commodities' and white slavery.[31] In 1892, the year of the Webbs' marriage, he appeared as a witness before the Royal Commission on Labour (RCL). His evidence regarding sweating took much the same line as his earlier writings. He also drew heavily on Beatrice's thesis concerning the good employer. The upshot of stricter regulation of outwork, he hoped, would 'prevent the bad employers obtaining the advantage which they ... now obtain through their badness'.[32] But he also added an important new element to the debate – that a maximum working day of eight hours should be supplemented with a 'moral' minimum wage 'below which no decent employer would pay the persons whom he employs'.[33] He proposed that this minimum should only be *voluntary*, since workers did not desire it to be a legal one.[34] T. G. Spyers, précis writer to the Commission, wrote wearily:

> Mr. Sidney Webb ... with his characteristic habit of clothing Radical proposals in a Conservative dress ... described an Eight Hours' Law as a mere amendment to the Factory Acts – stated that the value of the relief given under the Poor Law practically fixed a minimum legal wage ... But even Mr. Webb did not include a Wages Regulation Act in his programme of immediate reform.[35]

Although Beatrice Webb denounced the deliberations of the RCL as a 'lamentable fiasco' and the Majority Report as 'a waste of taxpayers' money, she pronounced the Minority Report excellent.[36] Signed by James Mawdsley, secretary of the cotton

---

(Oxford, 1987), p. 371, points out, 'Beatrice's style was rather that of the grand entrepreneur, envisaging large-scale innovation, with Sidney as her reliable advisor, adroit manager, and master of technical detail.'

[30]   S. Webb, 'An eight hours bill', *Fabian Tract*, 9 (1889); S. Webb, 'The case for an eight hours bill', *Fabian Tract*, 23 (1891); S. Webb and H. Cox, *The Eight Hours Day* (London, 1891). For Webb and the fair wages movement, see S. Webb, 'A labour policy for public authorities', *Fabian Tract*, 37 (1891); S. Webb, 'The economics of direct employment', *Fabian Tract*, 84 (1897).

[31]   S. Webb, 'The regulation of the hours of labor', *Contemporary Review*, December 1889, reprinted in S. and B. Webb, *Problems of Modern Industry* (London, 1898), p. 133.

[32]   RCL, *Fourth Report* (PP XXXIX, 1893–1894, Pt. 1), Q. 3,744.

[33]   *Ibid.*, QQ. 3,779–83.

[34]   *Ibid.*, Q. 4,481.

[35]   T.G. Spyers, *The Labour Question: An Epitome of the Evidence and the Report of the Royal Commission on Labour* (London, 1894), pp. 52–3. The only proposal of the majority report, which led to legislative action, was that of conciliation and arbitration. The Conciliation Act, 1896 empowered a labour department to investigate disputes provided that both parties agreed: H. Pelling, *A History of British Trade Unionism* (Harmondsworth, 1973; first published 1963), p. 122.

[36]   B. Webb, 'The failure of the Labour Commission', *Nineteenth Century*, 36 (1894), pp. 4, 8, 22. Her article received a caustic reply from the RCL's secretary. He suggested that she was piqued because she had not been selected as a lady commissioner: G. Drage, 'Mrs Webb's

spinners, the Dockers' president Tom Mann, the Welsh miners' leader William Abraham and the Liberal MP Michael Austin, the Minority Report was in fact written by Sidney Webb with her assistance.[37] Not surprisingly, it contained all of the Webbs' points regarding the responsible employer – including the payment of a moral minimum wage to act as an informal benchmark of goodness.[38] Shortly afterwards, in August 1894, in a paper that he read before some of Britain's leading economists, Sidney Webb elaborated on how the London School Board and the London County Council (LCC) already set such a moral minimum wage. This entailed the payment of the union rate for the trade and at least 6d an hour for adult males and 18s per week to females.[39]

In the years following what the Webbs regarded as their victory over the RCL 'dialecticians', their support for the responsible employer was bolstered by Fabian Society literature. In one notable Fabian tract, H. W. Macrosty concluded that the only remedy 'lies in quickening of the industrial evolution – in taking such steps as will hasten the transformation of the Sweated Trades into factory industries'.[40] Beatrice Webb also published her first tract in which she urged the desirability of transferring work by female homeworkers to the factory. She observed:

> The real enemies of the working woman are not the men, who always insist on higher wages, but the 'amateurs' of her own sex. So long as there are women, married or unmarried, eager and able to take work home, and do it in the intervals of another profession, domestic service, we shall never disentangle ourselves from that vicious circle in which low wages lead to bad work, and bad work compels low wages.

Factory legislation, she concluded, favoured the large-scale employer and squeezed out the 'little master'.[41] The Webbs were also influential in the foundation of the LSE, whose principal purposes included to professionally train disinterested experts to form alliances with responsible employers and to encourage others to rise to the standard of the best masters. As Beatrice recorded in her diary: 'We wish to introduce into politics the professional expert – to extend the sphere of government by adding to its enormous advantages of wholesale and compulsory management, the advantages of the most skilled entrepreneur.'[42]

---

attack on the Labour Commission', *Nineteenth Century*, 36 (1894), p. 457. She was actually furious because Sidney's early evidence was fairly lacklustre. In retaliation, she dismissed the four chairmen of the RCL – G. Balfour, F. Pollock, A. Marshall and L. Courtney (her brother-in-law) – as 'a little knot of dialecticians': Webb, *Our Partnership*, p. 40.

[37]   RCL, *Minority Report* (PP XXXV, 1894, Pt. 1), pp. 136–46. For details of how the Webbs persuaded the staunch Conservative, Mawdsley, to sign the report, see Drake and Cole, *Our Partnership*, p. 41.

[38]   RCL, *Minority Report*, p. 146.

[39]   S. Webb, *The economic heresies of the LCC* (Address to the Economic Section of the British Association for the Advancement of Science, 13 August 1894) cited in R. Harrison, *The Life and Times of Sidney and Beatrice Webb, 1858–1905: The Formative Years* (London, 2000), pp. 281–2.

[40]   H.W. Macrosty,' Sweating: its cause and remedy', *Fabian Tract*, 50 (1894), p. 10.

[41]   B. Webb, 'Women and the factory acts', *Fabian Tract*, 67 (1896), p. 14.

[42]   Drake and Cole, *Our Partnership*, p. 120.

At the same time (in 1894), she assisted a group of middle-class, social feminists to form the Women's Industrial Council (WIC), and sought through it to make sweated female homeworkers an issue central to public interest.[43] The Council published books and pamphlets on the subject, arranged conferences, conducted campaigns, and also gathered data on the issue from other countries. The WIC was particularly impressed by the American licensing system for homework. In New York, Massachusetts and several other states, outwork was prohibited unless the dwelling place had been inspected and licensed. The workers had to apply for this permit, and were to produce it when applying for work. Margaret and Ramsay MacDonald, two leading supporters of the WIC, made a visit to the USA on behalf of the organisation and were converted.[44] As a result, from 1899 the WIC sponsored bills to license all those who worked at home. The Home Office opposed the proposal and argued that it was totally impracticable. To successfully implement such a scheme, it claimed, would require an army of inspectors.[45]

A minority of commentators, following the Webbs' earlier lead on a moral minimum, increasingly linked sweating not simply with uncontrolled homework but with unregulated pay. This analysis led them to advocate not merely licensing but a legal minimum wage. An initial challenge came in 1896 with the publication of J.A. Hobson's article, 'A living wage'.[46] In 1891 Hobson had largely rejected the conventional solutions to sweating. Like Potter, he deemed co-operation amongst the sweated would be doomed to failure.[47] Yet he also insisted that women's wages were low because they were willing to take work at any price. He concluded that females had to learn not to undersell each other.[48] Michael Freeden describes Hobson as a visionary prophet of social welfare thought.[49] However, at that stage in his career Hobson was content to observe that, although he heard a great deal about male prejudice, it was 'women who are the real enemies of women'.[50] But, inspired by the 1893 miners' strike for an adequate wage, he now suggested that the enforcement of

---

[43]   The WIC emerged from the Women's Trade Union Association's inability to organise working women following the disclosures of the SCSS in 1890. See, *WIN*, December 1895, p. 3. The WIC emphasised fact gathering and the dissemination of information to improve the employment opportunities of working-class females: WIC, *What the Council Is and Does* (London, 1909). See also, E. Mappen, *Helping Women at Work: The Women's Industrial Council, 1889–1914* (London, 1985), pp. 12–18. Beatrice was a council member and, from 1895, she sat on its investigation committee: WIC, *Second Annual Report, 1895–6* (1896).

[44]   J.R. MacDonald, *Margaret Ethel MacDonald* (London, 1921), pp. 137–46.

[45]   C. Dilke, 'Sweating and a minimum wage', *The International*, 1 (1907), p. 7.

[46]   For the growth of a living wage movement in Britain, see: H.W. Macrosty, 'The recent history of the living wage movement', *Political Science Quarterly*, 13 (1898), pp. 413–41. In his Encyclical of 1891, Pope Leo XIII fuelled Catholic interest in a living wage when he pronounced that employers had a duty 'to support the wage earner in reasonable but frugal comfort': E.M. Burns, *Wages and the State* (London, 1926), p. 11.

[47]   Hobson, *Problems of Poverty*, p. 178.

[48]   *Ibid.*, p 161.

[49]   M. Freeden, 'J.A. Hobson as a New Liberal theorist', *Journal of History of Ideas*, 34 (1973), p. 421.

[50]   Hobson, *Problems of Poverty*, p. 161.

a living wage for all workers was a practical possibility, even for those engaged in the sweated sectors of industry.[51]

In a qualitative, humanist interpretation of wealth, profit and value undoubtedly derived, though not uncritically, from Carlyle and John Ruskin, he argued that if an industry could not afford to pay its workforce a decent wage then such a trade was not a suitable industry to exist in a civilised society.[52] The maintenance of a 'degraded industry', paying starvation wages and carried on without regard to sanitary and other social conditions, was a plague spot and it was better that such an unsound trade should disappear:

> The policy of an enlightened community towards low and degraded types of industry should be similar to that which is adopted in the case of insanitary towns: it is to the public interest to stamp them out, making all necessary provision at the public expense for those who are injured by the disturbance of an existing order of things.[53]

These sentiments were heightened when Arthur Morrison's *Child of the Jago* (1896) depicted slatternly mothers working at least sixteen hours a day at sewing shirts for less than a shilling, or making one hundred sacks in four days for the pittance of one shilling and seven pence. Such pathetic beings looked upon securing matchbox making as a 'prize'– it paid two pence farthing a gross before deductions for paste and string used for tying the finished products into batches. The East-End sweated in the novel are a distinct, debased and semi-criminal race sharply demarcated from the respectable.[54]

A year later, in 1897, the Webbs advocated not simply greater supervision of homeworkers but the implementation of a legal minimum wage. This was to form an important component of a comprehensive labour code establishing a 'National Minimum' – setting not only weekly earnings but also a minimum of sanitation, education, safety, and maximum hours. The Webbs observed:

---

[51] Hobson, 'A living wage', pp. 128–9, 165–7.

[52] Ruskin blended the ideas of earlier moral economists and the Owenites. He criticised classical economists such as Ricardo for pursuing market regulation through supply and demand – rather than by more ethical means. He aspired to establish a standard of work and a level of prices based on 'just' wages and fair competition. This was to be achieved with the aid of a strong state, benevolent and paternalistic masters, chivalrous merchants and through guilds. Yet despite Hobson's claim that Ruskin, 'laid a solid foundation for social economics', Ruskin failed to provide a blueprint outlining how his visionary society would operate: J.A. Hobson, *John Ruskin: Social Reformer* (London, 1898), p. 120. For further details of Ruskin's influence on Hobson, see: J.A. Hobson, *Work and Wealth: A Human Valuation* (London, 1914), esp. pp. 9–11; J.A. Hobson, *Confessions of an Economic Heretic* (London, 1938), esp. pp. 38–43; H.C.G. Matthew, 'Hobson, Ruskin and Cobden', in M. Freeden (ed.), *Reappraising J.A. Hobson: Humanism and Welfare* (London, 1990), pp. 11–30. Harris notes that Ruskin's social policy recommendations were often greeted with 'bored and baffled bewilderment' in the 1860s, but the onset of the 'Great Depression', and his ability to view social betterment in 'the round', gave them a new pertinence. By the 1890s, his works were widely re-issued in popular editions: J. Harris, 'Ruskin and social reform', in Birch, *Ruskin and the Dawn of the Modern*, esp., 12–15, 24.

[53] Hobson, 'A living wage', p. 167.

[54] A. Morrison, *A Child of the Jago* (London, 1969; first published 1896), pp. 164–5.

> The proposition of a National Minimum of wages – the enactment of a definite sum of earnings per week below which no employer should be allowed to hire any worker – has not yet been put forward by any considerable section of Trade Unionists, nor taken into consideration by any Home Secretary. This reluctance ... arises, we think, from a shrinking, both on the part of workmen and employers, from having all wages fixed by law.[55]

Great captains of industry, they insisted, had long adopted a voluntary minimum wage. They had learnt that, if they paid fair wages, they could select the most efficient workers. As a result of fair wages clauses, the largest employer of labour in the country – central and local government – set acceptable minimum rates.

The Webbs attempted to turn orthodox economic thinking on its head by arguing that the legal control of low pay represented a logical development of factory legislation that already governed hours and conditions of work. Such a measure, they maintained, would increase the cost of home production and drive work into better-managed, large units of production. In such a context the Webbs welcomed the development of monopolies. Eventually the responsible, capitalist entrepreneur would be rendered obsolete by specially trained, selfless professionals democratically running industry, not for personal gain but for the public good.[56]

They contrasted the economically progressive cotton factory with its 'good' employer to the degraded, disease-ridden home workshop. Crucially, they linked the latter to national efficiency. They claimed that, since the income of many workers in this sector was supplemented through poor relief or charity, their employers were receiving a subsidy that gave them an unfair economic advantage over factory owners forced by law to observe ethical employment conditions. This caused sweated homework to expand.[57] Consequently, sweated homeworkers were not self-sufficient but parasitic on the community. They were also instrumental in spawning new generations of unfit workers with no alternative but to augment the growing ranks of the sweated. Such workers were thus 'subtly draining away the vital energy of the community'. They continued:

> Unfortunately, the harm that the sweater does lives after him. Men and women who have, for any length of time, been reduced, to quote the House of Lord's Committee, to 'earnings barely sufficient to sustain an existence; hours of labor such as to make the lives of the workers periods of almost ceaseless toil, hard and unlovely to the last degree; sanitary conditions injurious to the health of the persons employed and dangerous to the public,' become incapable of profitable labor. What they can do is to compete fitfully for the places which they cannot permanently fill, and thus not only drag down the wages of all other unregulated labor, but also contribute, by their irregularity of conduct and incapacity for persistent effort, to the dislocation of the machinery of production. But this is not all.

---

[55]   S. and B. Webb, *Industrial Democracy*, p. 774.

[56]   *Ibid.*, p. 843.

[57]   After the 1870s, following the overtures of organised labour, and the growing realisation that unemployment and illness could frustrate the achievement of the male breadwinner norm, poor law regulations became more flexible. By the 1880s, widows were no longer separated from their children, and they were granted outdoor relief to supplement their wages: A. Clark, 'The new poor law and the breadwinner wage: contrasting assumptions', *Journal of Social History*, 34 (2000), p. 269.

No one who has not himself lived among the poor in London or Glasgow, Liverpool or Manchester, can form any adequate idea of the unseen and unmeasured injury to national character wrought by the social contamination to which this misery inevitably leads.[58]

Women homeworkers were now not only linked to dirt, disease and prostitution but also with the progressive impairment of the strong.[59] The Webbs had reduced them to being breeders of a degenerate race, to being members of a Victorian underclass that posed a real threat to Britain's imperial future.

Although the Webbs argued that a minimum wage was a feasible proposition, they nonetheless recommended, unlike Hobson, that it should be set at a subsistence level. For Hobson, the key issue was not purely one of ensuring efficient workers but of encouraging the workers to produce their best. In his proposal of a living wage there was to be some latitude to allow for leisure and material comforts.[60] He observed:

> The calculation of such a living wage is of course no easy task. Determined as it chiefly is by 'needs' it will differ widely in different classes of workers, under different material and social conditions, and in different stages of development. No principle of absolute or mechanical equality can be maintained.[61]

The Webbs, in contrast, believed that a legal minimum wage above a subsistence level would be as damaging to the economy as one left to the 'higgling of the market'. It followed, therefore, that:

> The minimum wage ... would be determined by practical inquiry as to the costs of the food, clothing and shelter physiologically necessary, according to national habit and custom, to prevent bodily deterioration. Such a minimum would therefore be low, and though its establishment would be welcomed as a boon by the unskilled workers in the unregulated trades, it would not at all correspond with the conception of a 'Living Wage' ....[62]

The Webbs accepted that their theory of the national minimum would compel managers to select the more capable, that a residuum would be refused work in competitive industry. They considered that children, the aged and childbearing women should not be forced to maintain themselves. But those 'unfortunate parasites' who were unemployable, 'physical and moral weaklings and degenerates', were to be incarcerated in non-competing labour colonies. They would be set to work so as not to cast 'an undue burden on the present taxpayer'. However, the goods created would not be sold on the open market; the inmates would labour for their own consumption only. When suitably re-trained and re-educated, the occupants' liberty would be restored. The end result, they maintained, would be a steady reduction in

---

[58] S. and B. Webb, *Industrial Democracy*, pp. 765–6.

[59] *Ibid.*, pp. 749–66.

[60] Hobson, 'A living wage', pp.128–9. Hobson also believed that his living wage should be a variable one taking into account regional differences in the cost of living.

[61] *Ibid.*, p. 129.

[62] S. and B. Webb, *Industrial Democracy*, pp. 774–5.

the number of the 'morally deficient' annually produced.[63] In this respect, as Adrian Vinson notes, '*Industrial Democracy* was the prelude to the Minority Report of the *Royal Commission on the Poor Laws ...*'. [64]

The Webbs had added a new dimension to the debate on sweating. Their new insistence on a statutory minimum wage reflected their realisation that neither improved sanitary provision in the home or domestic workshop nor a legal eight-hour day would provide adequate food or clothing. An employer was still deemed, in their eyes, to be irresponsible if he paid starvation wages. But moral pressure was not enough. The payment of minimum rates by all employers – both good and bad – had to be reinforced by the power of the state.

Beatrice indulged in self-congratulation in her diary:

> Our big book has had a brilliant reception. The *Times* gave us two columns on the day of publication; the *Standard* an abusive leader; the *Daily Chronicle*, the *Daily News*, and half-a-dozen big provincial papers were all properly enthusiastic. Other papers followed suit and produced their reviews the next day: the weeklies treated us quite handsomely. Altogether a small triumph in its way. The scientific character of the work is recognised, though of course the critics chaff us for our 'pompous phraseology'. It is a big plant on the public: a new method and a new theory![65]

III

Although the Webbs' and Hobson's arguments aroused a great deal of interest, their ideas made little progress in subsequent years. R.B. Haldane commented that 'the statement of the principles of the National Minimum and Industrial Parasitism makes clear what has been vaguely floating before the minds of many people, and what they have been unable to grasp.'[66] Yet, most social reformers were doubtful that the implementation of a full-blown minimum wage could be translated into practical politics. As Gertrude Williams observed, 'there were many who accepted the national minimum as theoretically justified, but who still believed its enforcement too drastic a step to be contemplated with equanimity.'[67] The Oxford economist L.L. Price, who was by no means entirely hostile, considered that the Webbs omitted evidence that detracted

---

[63]   *Ibid.*, pp. 784–9. Taussig thought that the Webbs invented the phrase 'parasitic' industry: F.W. Taussig, 'Minimum wages for women', *Quarterly Journal of Economics*, 30 (1916), p. 415. Yet as Harris remarks: 'The Webbs' theory of the National Minimum ... resounds with powerful echoes of Ruskin.' All urged public regulation of the market place, and harsh treatment of those who refused work. See, Harris, 'Ruskin and social reform', pp. 12, 27–8. Marx had also alluded to 'plundering parasites' imposing themselves between the capitalist and the wage earner: K. Marx, *Capital, Volume 1* (translated by B. Fowkes) (Harmondsworth, 1976), p. 591.

[64]   A. Vinson, 'The Edwardians and poverty: towards a minimum wage?', in D. Reid (ed.), *Edwardian England* (London, 1982), p. 83.

[65]   Drake and Cole, *Our Partnership*, p. 56.

[66]   R.B. Haldane to B.Webb, 16 January 1898. BLPES, Passfield Papers, II 4a It. 76, cited in Rickard, 'The anti-sweating movement', p. 584.

[67]   G. Williams, *The State and the Standard of Living* (London, 1936), p. 105.

from their case.[68] He maintained that a statutory minimum wage was not the obvious completion of factory legislation but that the two were fundamentally different.[69] It was also argued that the application of a legal minimum wage to workers who were not sufficiently efficient to be worth such a rate would bankrupt the good employer and would lead to widespread unemployment.[70]

The 1890s were not propitious for experiments in wage bargaining. The employers' counter-attacks against new unionism, their savage anti-labour methods, especially in engineering, and their recourse to blacklisting meant that unions exhibited little faith in the existing legal system or the judges who enforced it.[71] Beatrice's defence of wage regulation at the International Congress of Women (1899) also elicited angry reposts from Millicent Fawcett and her followers. The latter alleged that, by supporting policies which would inevitably curtail female employment opportunities, she was acting in men's interests. Although Beatrice dismissed these accusations as the cries of a misguided, leisured minority, she felt impelled to edit a collection of essays for the Labour Law Association on the dangers of unfettered freedom of competition.[72] She argued that:

> It is, on the face of it, cruel mockery to preach Trade Unionism, and Trade Unionism alone, to the seamstress sewing day and night in her garret, for a bare subsistence ... When any British statesman makes up his mind to grapple seriously with the problem of the 'sweated trades' he will have to expand the Factory Acts into a systematic and comprehensive Labour Code, prescribing minimum conditions of wages, leisure, education and health, for each class of operative, below which the community will not allow its industry to be carried on.[73]

---

[68]   L.L. Price, review of S. and B. Webb, *Industrial Democracy*, in *Economic Journal*, 8 (1898), p. 69. Trained by Alfred Marshall, Price had been appointed to Oxford's first university extension lectureship in 1886. From the mid-1890s, he became increasingly critical of Marshall and, in 1903, committed himself to Tariff Reform. Although he broke with moderate liberalism, he remained a broad conservative: *The Times*, 28 February 1950; G.M. Koot, *English Historical Economics, 1870–1926: The Rise of Economic History and Neomercantilism* (Cambridge, 1987), esp. pp. 92–101.

[69]   Price, review of *Industrial Democracy*. Somewhat later, A.C. Pigou, 'The principle of the minimum wage', *Nineteenth Century*, 73 (1913), pp. 647–8, adopted a similar stance.

[70]   These arguments are summarised in H.B. Lees Smith, 'Economic theory and proposals for a legal minimum wage', *Economic Journal*, 17 (1907), esp. pp. 506–7. See also, Pigou, 'The principle of the minimum wage', p. 649.

[71]   Over thirty million working days were lost as a result of stoppages in 1893; more than 10.3 million in 1897 and 15.2 million in 1898. For the labour management policies of manufacturers, see A.J. McIvor, *Organised Capital, Employers' Associations and Industrial Relations in Northern England, 1880–1939* (Cambridge, 1996), esp. chapter 4. For the specific policies of the Engineering Employers' Federation, see A. McKinlay and J. Zeitlin, 'The meanings of managerial prerogative: industrial relations and the organisation of work in British engineering, 1880–1939', in C. Harvey and J. Turner (eds), *Labour and Business in Modern Britain* (London, 1989), pp. 34–8. For a general overview, see H. Pelling, 'Trade unions, workers and the law', in H. Pelling, *Popular Politics in Late-Victorian Britain* (London, 1968), pp. 62–81.

[72]   B. Webb (ed.), *The Case for the Factory Acts* (London, 1901).

[73]   B. Webb, 'The economics of factory legislation', in Webb, *Case for the Factory Acts*, pp. 73–4.

Her chapter, as Chris Nyland and Gaby Ramin note, was essentially a feminised version of the notion of a minimum wage developed in *Industrial Democracy*.[74] She confided in her diary of the book:

> It is to be a counterblast to the persistent opposition to factory legislation on the part of the 'women's rights' movement reinforced by the employers' wives. This opposition has for the last ten years blocked all progress in the effective application of the Factory Acts to other industries. It is led by a few blatant agitators, who would not count for much if they were not backed up by many 'society women' who belong to the governing clique, and by a solid opposition to further reform from vested interests ... I feel sometimes in despair ....[75]

Such difficulties led Sir Charles Dilke, whose paternal grandfather had been a close associate of Hood, to investigate wage regulation in Australia and New Zealand.[76] Despite the recent industrialisation of Australia and New Zealand as well as their abundance of land and relative scarcity of labour, investigations carried out in the 1880s and early 1890s revealed extensive sweating. Unlike Britain, the former had been prepared to countenance state intervention in the wages contract. In New Zealand the evils of sweating were combated through courts of arbitration. Originally established by an act of 1894 to prevent strikes and lockouts, local courts of arbitration were also empowered in 1898 to fix wages for low-paid workers. In Victoria (Australia), wage regulation was, in contrast, embodied in the Factory Act of 1896, following a campaign by the Victoria Anti-Sweating League. The 1896 Act empowered the governor to appoint special boards to fix legal minimum wages for persons employed in or outside a factory in certain specified trades. Representation on the boards was divided equally between employers' and workers' representatives. Initially, five boards were established. They held office for four years and were under the direction of a chairman appointed by the elected members.[77]

Wages boards were not entirely unknown in Britain. On the eve of the decline of handloom weaving and in response to the disastrous fall in wages after 1815, calls had been made for boards of trade to establish a minimum wage. Although he later rejected them on Malthusian grounds, in 1848 John Stuart Mill had seriously considered wages boards as a possible mechanism to end low pay.[78] Half a century later, Mill's disciple Dilke gave the concept of wages boards a new impetus and definite form.[79] An imperialist with radical leanings, Dilke favoured wages boards,

---

[74]   C. Nyland and G. Ramia, 'The Webbs and the rights of women', in P. Beilharz and C. Nyland (eds), The *Webbs, Fabianism and Feminism* (Aldershot, 1998), p. 68.

[75]   Drake and Cole, *Our Partnership*, p. 205.

[76]   Dilke's grandfather, Charles Wentworth Dilke (1789–1864), editor of *The Athenaeum* between 1830–1846, had been the godfather to Thomas Hood's son (also Thomas): J. Clubbe (ed.), 'Introduction', *Selected Poems of Thomas Hood* (Cambridge, Mass), p. 18.

[77]   W. Pember Reeves, 'The minimum wage law in Victoria and South Australia', *Economic Journal*, 11 (1901), pp. 335–8. By 1905 wages boards ceased to be *ad hoc*, and other Australian states followed Victoria's lead.

[78]   Mill, *Principles of Political Economy*, ch. 12.

[79]   Dilke, before the SCH acknowledge his debt to Mill, SCH, *Report* (PP 1908, VIII), Q. 3,920. Nevertheless, it is highly probable that Charles Deakin, Chief Secretary of Victoria,

as opposed to the state arbitration of New Zealand, since they did not interfere with the more powerful trade unions, which possessed adequate collective bargaining machinery.[80] When the Australian legislation was passed in 1896, Dilke determined to introduce a similar measure in Britain. Four years later, with the aid of the WTUL – his wife was the president of the organisation – he introduced a Bill in the Commons though with little success. Between 1900 and 1905 Dilke's bill was printed annually but it never gained a second reading.[81] The British public was still not ready to accept such a measure – even though it fell far short of the Webbs' national minimum or Hobson's living income scheme. Dilke was probably not the most powerful advocate. Barred from ministerial office following a sensational divorce case, 'in personal relations, though he was not ostracized, he would have met some distance and reserve.'[82]

In order to gather further evidence the Webbs visited the Antipodes in 1898. They, like Dilke, were particularly impressed with the wages boards of Victoria. Beatrice noted:

> Our general impression ... is that the machinery has worked smoothly; that the constitution is superior to the New Zealand Arbitration Act because minimum and not maximum conditions are determined by the Wages Boards, and do not interfere with the workman's right to bargain collectively if he is not satisfied with the legal conditions.[83]

---

later Prime Minister of the Australian Commonwealth, convinced Dilke that wages boards were a practical proposition. See Rickard, 'The anti-sweating movement', p. 585. Other possible influences were the 1885 Industrial Remuneration Conference (chaired by Dilke), and Emilia Dilke, his second wife, and a Ruskin protégé.

[80]   On the whole, large trades unions and the TUC rejected compulsory arbitration: Dilke, 'Sweating and minimum wage', p. 10. Roy Jenkins notes that 'Dilke believed firmly that the Anglo-Saxon race was superior to any other, and that white men ... had a capacity for effective social and economic organisation which the other races were unlikely ever to equal': R. Jenkins, *Sir Charles Dilke: A Victorian Tragedy* (London, 1958), p. 395.

[81]   Several historians, including Tawney, wrongly suppose that Dilke's Bill was first introduced in 1898: Tawney, 'Fixing minimum wages', pp. 22–3. It adopted the familiar procedure of a conciliation board with an independent chair, but the employers' and workers' representatives were to be appointed by the Home Secretary. The latter following an inquiry was immediately empowered to establish wages boards in any region or industry. (Individual trades were not listed). The factory inspectorate was authorised to levy fines for infringements. Dilke sought B. Webb's advice on the form of the Bill. See Dilke's letters to Beatrice Webb, 7 February 1900 and 7 March 1900. BLEPS, Passfield Papers, II, 46 and National Archives (NA), LAB 2/1, CL and SL, 128/1902, cited in Rickard, 'The anti-sweating movement,' p. 585.

[82]   Phelps Brown, *Growth of British Industrial Relations*, p. 208. W.T. Stead (proprietor of the *Pall Mall Gazette*), carried out a prolonged witch-hunt against Dilke. Seventeen dignitaries (including Stead) had signed a letter to *The Times*, 6 March 1891, censuring Dilke for returning to public life.

[83]   A.G. Austin (ed.), *The Webbs' Australian Diary, 1898* (Melbourne, 1965), p. 86. The Webbs had documented their considerable reservations to compulsory arbitration earlier: *Industrial Democracy*, chapter 3. However, Sidney while serving on the Royal Commission on Trade Disputes (PP 1906, LVI), p. 22, signed the report recommending arbitration on the model of New Zealand and Australia: Pelling, 'Trade unions workers and the law', p. 79.

Significantly, she added:

> the good employers in certain other trades – Printers for instance – are considering the
> desirability of asking Parliament to apply the Act to them in order to stop the undercutting
> of small firms. Indeed, the employers of Victoria (possibly owing to the acceptance of
> tariff protection) are not pledged to the theory of 'free competition', and there is a distinct
> feeling among the better ones that the 'unfair competition' of some of their rivals should
> be stopped.[84]

She noted with satisfaction that higher piece rates brought about by the boards in
clothing had driven all the operatives into the factories. This had 'contributed to the
employment of better machinery and to a more perfect organisation of labour'. She
continued: 'I had this morning a long interview with the largest employer: he has
been converted to the principle of a legal minimum wage.'[85]

On their return, the Webbs contended that if fair-minded employers in Australia
were prepared to experiment with wage fixing, those in Britain had nothing to fear.
Their arguments became a common theme of Fabian Society literature and lectures.
Among the Society's members who supported action to end sweating, there was
general agreement that it would advance factory production and lead indirectly to
married females becoming full-time housewives by depriving them of access to
homework.[86] There was also a broad consensus among Fabians that the minimum
should be adjusted to take account of local variations and be set at a lower level for
women than for men.[87] The majority considered that those who would not work for
the legal minimum should be placed in re-training camps, that the old and infirm who
were incapable of earning the minimum rate should become a case for lenient poor
relief.[88] Above all, with the enactment of a minimum wage, it was felt, 'the better
employers will heartily welcome the means of ridding themselves of the competition
of those who employ parasitic labour.'[89]

There were also significant disagreements within the Society as to the best
way to proceed. Some Fabians favoured the state arbitration of New Zealand over
the Webbs' preference for the wages boards of Victoria.[90] Others desired a more

---

[84]   Austin, *Webbs' Australian Diary*, p. 86.

[85]   Mackenzie, *Letters of Sidney and Beatrice Webb, Volume 2*, p. 90.

[86]   Macrosty, 'Sweating', pp. 5, 18; G.B. Shaw (ed.), *Fabianism and the Empire: A Manifesto
by the Fabian Society* (London, 1900), pp. 64–7; Hutchins and Harrison, *History of Factory
Legislation*, pp. 216–19; H. Bland, 'Socialism and labor policy', pp. 12–13; S. Sanders, 'The case
for a legal minimum wage act', *Fabian Tract*, 128 (1906), p. 18; B.L. Hutchins, 'Homework and
sweating: the cause and remedies', *Fabian Tract*, 130 (1907), pp. 3–19; B. Webb, B. Hutchins
and the Fabian Society, *Socialism and National Minimum* (London, 1909), pp. 15–38.

[87]   Bland, 'Socialism and labor policy', p. 12; Sanders, 'The case for a national minimum
wage', pp. 9–10, 13.

[88]   Sanders, 'The case for a legal minimum wage', p. 13; Bland, 'Socialism and labor policy',
p. 10; S. and B. Webb, *Industrial Democracy*, p. 787; Hutchins, 'Homework and sweating', p. 18.

[89]   Sanders, 'The case for a national minimum wage', p. 18.

[90]   Sanders and Money, for example, favoured wages boards. See *ibid.*, pp. 15–17; L. G.
C. Money, 'Legislation and the sweater', in R. Mudie-Smith (ed.), *Sweated Industries: Being
a Handbook of the 'Daily News' Exhibition* (London, 1906), pp. 24–5. For supporters of the

generous wages floor than the subsistence level recommended by the Webbs.[91] The most serious disagreements occurred outside the Fabian Society. Advocates of the minimum wage, notably the Webbs and Barbara Hutchins, were bitterly opposed by Helen Bosanquet of the COS and by the two ex-Fabians, Ramsay and Margaret MacDonald.[92] Bosanquet predicted that, in order to recoup the pay increases that the board system entailed, employers would mechanise their enterprises or raise the price of their products. She took the view that, since the poor were the chief consumers of sweated products, they would suffer disproportionately if a minimum wage was enacted. She agreed with the Webbs that married women should be removed from the labour market and conceded that something had to be done about sweated labour. But she eventually decided that 'no new method is necessary, but only a better working of the old.' Instead of wages control, Bosanquet recommended that unskilled, inefficient workers should be transformed by rigorous training into skilled efficient operatives; what was well made would invariably be well paid.[93]

Fabians such as Emily Townshend tartly responded that Bosanquet was merely attempting to eradicate sweating by improving the moral characteristics of its victims without arresting its causes. Townshend concluded:

> wages are determined in a state of free competition not by the intrinsic value of the work, but by the relative needs of the worker to sell and the employer to buy. Unfortunately ... though good work does not always secure good wages, bad wages will usually produce bad work.[94]

The MacDonalds, on the other hand, argued that wages boards were palliatives which detracted from the fight for socialism. They maintained that, if such a scheme were ever introduced in Britain, then more work would be driven into the home – thus encouraging the bad employer and defeating the purpose of the initiative. The

---

New Zealand arbitration scheme, see Hutchins, 'Homework and sweating', pp. 10–15; Sanders also suggested that local authorities should administer minimum wage setting, but Hutchins doubted the advisability of this: Sanders, 'The case for a legal minimum wage', p. 17; Hutchins, 'Homework and sweating', p. 14.

[91] For those who upheld the subsistence principle, see Sanders, 'The case for a legal minimum wage', pp. 9, 14; Bland, 'Socialism and labor policy', p. 12. For those who advocated above subsistence rates, see H.W. Macrosty, 'State arbitration and the living wage', *Fabian Tract*, 83 (1898), p. 12.

[92] The MacDonalds resigned from the Fabian Society in 1900 because it would not follow an anti-Boer war policy. But relations between the Webbs and Ramsay MacDonald had been strained since 1896. The latter had unfairly accused the Webbs of, among other things, misusing the Henry Hutchinson Trust (a fund left to the society in 1894 to advance Fabian socialism) and of financially benefiting from the London School of Economics (LSE): Harrison, *Life and Times of Sidney and Beatrice Webb*, pp. 336–7. See also D. Marquand, *Ramsay MacDonald* (London, 1977), pp. 41–3. Beatrice Webb acidly remarked in her diary that MacDonald was vexed since the Webbs had considered him unworthy of a lectureship at the LSE: Drake and Cole, *Our Partnership*, p. 132.

[93] H. Bosanquet, *The Strength of the People* (London, 1902), esp. pp. 290–97.

[94] E. Townshend, 'The case against the Charity Organisation Society', *Fabian Tract*, 158 (1911), pp. 15–16.

MacDonalds, too, travelled to Australia and New Zealand in the autumn of 1906 to gather material to support their case at first-hand. They returned early in 1907 more convinced than ever that wages boards would be disastrous if applied to Britain.[95] As Margaret MacDonald remarked in the Independent Labour Party's (ILP) *Labour Leader*:

> I do not think that any legal regulation could be efficiently put into force amongst the worst paid workers under our present industrial system. Indeed, I believe that it would really increase the number of sweated homeworkers, for the minimum wage could be enforced more easily in the factories and workshops than in the homes, and the unscrupulous employer would put more work out in order to evade the law.[96]

Later, she predicted that the boards would need an army of inspectors to enforce their decisions while workers, to protect their employment, would be forced to collude with underpaying masters.[97] She maintained that: 'The Chinese furniture workers in Victoria have proved to the officials there that no legal wage can be enforced if employers and employed agree to evade it.'[98] Even if the scheduling of rates was very thorough, the most indomitable wages board could not keep pace with 'every fashion and individual caprice in dressmaking'.[99] As to the Webbs' argument that minimum-wage setting was simply an extension of the legal provisions governing hours and conditions of work, she retorted:

> The inspector can check the fact that a workroom is insanitary by means of his own eyes and nose ... he can prove by reference to the clock that an employer is keeping his employers beyond the legal hours for closing. But he has no such independent knowledge of what money has gone into a worker's pocket for wages.[100]

The MacDonalds, determined to halt the progress of pro-wages-board opinion, campaigned through the WIC for the licensing of homeworkers. They effectively split that body over the issue in 1908.[101] Their fervent espousal of licensing also caused

---

[95]   MacDonald, *Margaret Ethel MacDonald*, pp. 157–8; Marquand, *Ramsay MacDonald*, p. 100.

[96]   *Labour Leader*, 17 May 1907.

[97]   WIC, *The Case for and Against a Legal Minimum Wage for Sweated Workers* (London, 1909), pp. 11–23. Although the authors of the pamphlet were anonymous, it was widely known that MacDonald had written the section arguing against a statutory minimum wage.

[98]   M. MacDonald, 'Sweated industries and wages boards', *Economic Journal*, 18 (1908), p. 144. This point was conceded by Fabians. According to Sanders 'the cunning of the yellow man was too often superior to that of the representative of the law...': Sanders, 'The case for a legal minimum wage', p. 7. The Webbs considered social and political maturity was synonymous with administrative expertise. While they discovered these virtues in the Japanese, they considered that China and the remainder of Asia were cases of 'arrested development': J. Winter, 'The Webbs and the non-white world: a case of socialist racialism', *Journal of Contemporary History*, 9 (1974), esp. p. 185.

[99]   MacDonald, 'Sweated industries and wages boards', p. 143.

[100] *Ibid.*, p. 12.

[101] In 1898, the WIC agreed to promote a bill providing for the licensing of dwelling-places where work was done. The Bill was introduced several times between then and 1907,

considerable tension within the ranks of the other organisations to which they belonged – including the ILP, the Labour Party and the Women's Labour League (WLL).[102] Subsequently, they also attempted to divide the all-party pressure group, the NASL.[103] The friction that they caused became so great that Dilke, who supported both licensing and wages boards, was forced to declare that for many years he had been terrified of voicing an opinion on the MacDonalds' proposals. In 1907 he disclosed to Herbert Gladstone, the Liberal Home Secretary, that he consequently felt like a heretic.[104]

IV

The inability of social reformers to agree on a remedy, together with the decline of public concern with social issues as a consequence of the Boer War (1899-1902), led to a decline of interest in sweated workers.[105] Reflecting on this lack of concern, the social explorer Robert Sherard commented in 1898:

> matters are to-day even worse than they were eight years ago. Such is the opinion I have formed in my investigations. And eight years hence, matters will be still worse unless other remedies are found, than appeals to the stony heart of Capital. It is a pity that this should be so.[106]

The Salvation Army's *Social Gazette* attempted to revive the flagging interest by re-printing on its front-page Hood's *Song of the Shirt*.[107] But even Jack London's sensational accounts of the sweated in *The People of the Abyss* (1903) and Edith

---

when Ramsay MacDonald re-introduced it. While the MacDonalds vehemently continued to support licensing, some members of the WIC did not, and the well-known socialist-feminist Clementina Black resigned in 1909 from the presidency of the WIC because it refused to endorse wages boards: E. Mappen, 'Strategies for change: socialist-feminist approaches to the problems of women's work', in John, *Unequal Opportunities*, pp. 248–53. Beatrice Webb, especially, disapproved of the MacDonalds' licensing system because the onus was placed on the worker to obtain the permit before applying for outwork: Webb, *My Apprenticeship*, p. 340.

[102] Ramsay MacDonald fought Fabians on the issue of minimum wages at the 1904 ILP conference: A. McBriar, *Fabian Socialism and English Politics, 1884–1918* (Cambridge, 1962), p. 328. Henderson also clashed with MacDonald over the issue of wages boards at the 1908 Labour Party conference: M.A. Hamilton, *Arthur Henderson: A Biography* (London, 1938), pp. 55–7. Margaret MacDonald, as president of the Women's Labour League (WLL), also argued with Mary Macarthur, secretary to the Women's Trade Union League (WTUL), and an executive member of the WLL, over the latter's support for wages boards. Their angry exchanges impeded WLL work on sweating and resulted in Macarthur's resignation: M.A. Hamilton, *Mary Macarthur: A Biographical Sketch* (London, 1925), p. 75; C. Collett, *For Labour and for Women: The Women's Labour League, 1906–1918* (Manchester, 1989), pp. 118–19, 182.

[103] For further details on this point, see chapter four.

[104] British Library Additional Manuscripts 46,064, Herbert Gladstone Papers, 23 May 1907.

[105] These problems were compounded by the fact that the war divided reformers: the Fabian Society was dominated by a pro-war majority while Hobson and the MacDonalds took a strong anti-war line: Harrison, *Life and Times of Sidney and Beatrice Webb*, p. 321.

[106] R. Sherard, *The White Slaves of England* (London, 1898), pp. 318–19.

[107] 'The new echo of an old song', *Social Gazette*, 24 September 1898.

Lyttelton's play, *Warp and Woof* (1904), though they caused unease, failed to stimulate renewed attention to sweating reform.[108] In 1904, Beatrice Webb lamented in her diary of a conversation with Winston Churchill: 'I tried the "national minimum" on him but he was evidently unaware of the most elementary objections to unrestricted competition and was still in the stage of "infant-school economics".'[109]

A similar fate befell Rowntree's statistical revelations concerning abject poverty in the midst of plenty.[110] Tawney remarked that Rowntree's research had 'deprived the word "sweating" of much of its sensationalism, while adding to its significance', for 'if wages inadequate to support physical existence are the criterion of sweating, then a very large proportion of all ... workers must be sweated.'[111] More recently, Deakin and Wilkinson have remarked that Rowntree 'demonstrated that even with "exemplary" behaviour, a large part of the working population could not reach even the lowest possible subsistence level. This refutation of Malthusianism opened the way to the development of economic theories supportive of Rowntree's recommended solution to poverty: high wages, full employment and social security'.[112] Yet experts denied that York was typical.[113] Helen Bosanquet complained that Rowntree's findings were not entirely trustworthy and that his poverty line represented 'no statistical evidence at all, but is merely a summary of impressions...'.[114] The five-member family dependent on a male wage earner proved to be a statistical artefact.[115]

---

[108] Staged at the Camden Theatre, London, *Warp and Woof* depicted how callous customers exploited West End seamstresses. It was inspired by a real event – the prosecution of some dressmakers for the overworking of their employees engaged on last minute garments for Ascot. *The Times* (7 June 1904), referred to it as a 'didactic play', but concluded that its staging was more of a social than a dramatic occasion.

[109] Diary entry 10 June 1904 in N. and J. Mackenzie (eds), *The Diary of Beatrice Webb, Volume Two* (London, 1986), p. 127.

[110] Assuming that wages were spent with the maximum of efficiency, Rowntree concluded that for an average family of a man, wife and three children, the minimum necessary expenditure in York to maintain merely physical efficiency would be 21s 8d. On this basis, he considered that 15.4 per cent of the town's wage-earning class (1,465 families and 7,230 persons) lived below his primary poverty line. Of these, over half (51.9 per cent) owed their condition to inadequate wages: Rowntree, *Poverty: A Study of Town Life*, pp. 111–12, 120.

[111] R.H. Tawney, 'Poverty as an industrial problem', in J.M. Winter (ed.), *R.H. Tawney: The American Labour Movement and Other Essays* (Sussex, 1979), p. 120.

[112] Deakin and Wilkinson, *The Law of the Labour Market*, pp. 150–51.

[113] D.H. MacGregor, 'The poverty figures', *Economic Journal*, 20 (1910), pp. 569–72. See also, Hennock's remarks that Rowntree's discoveries on wages failed to have any impact on social reformers: E.P. Hennock, 'Concepts of poverty in the British social surveys from Charles Booth to Arthur Bowley', in M. Bulmer, K. Bales, and K. Sklar (eds), *The Social Survey in Historical Perspective, 1880–1940* (Cambridge, 1991), p. 204.

[114] H. Bosanquet, 'The "poverty line"', in COS, *Occasional Papers* 11, third series (1905), p. 233.

[115] Only approximately ten per cent of families corresponded to Rowntree's ideal family of husband, wife and three dependent children: A.L. Bowley, 'Earners and dependants in English towns in 1911', *Economica*, 1 (1921), p. 107. Gazeley and Newall suggest that Rowntree overestimated children's requirements. Consequently, his primary poverty line for his standard family was about eleven per cent too high, and even greater for families with

Following a hostile review Rowntree was forced to write to *The Times* denying that, by placing undue weight on the flawed physiological evidence, he had reduced poverty 'to a chemical formula'.[116] Others deemed Rowntree's 'lifeless list of low-rated payments' insufficient on its own to encourage anti-sweating legislation.[117]

A major difficult was the paucity of national statistics. As Peter Hennock observes, Rowntree 'tried to use what there was' but his 'problem was that there was so little that he could use'.[118] The Inter-Departmental Committee on Physical Deterioration was so disturbed by the lack of reliable, general figures that it recommended their immediate compilation.[119] In the meantime, the sweated, as the Liberal politician, C.F.G. Masterman remarked, momentarily exposed to the harsh glare of publicity, were once again consigned to the obscurity of their twilight world.[120]

---

more than three dependent children: I. Gazeley and A. Newall, 'Rowntree revisited: poverty in Britain, 1900', *Explorations in Economic History*, 37 (2000), pp. 174–88.

[116] 'Review of books', *The Times*, 21 December 1901, p. 9. For Rowntree's reply, see *The Times*, 1 January 1902.

[117] T. Wright, 'Sweating – defined and explained', in T. Wright (ed.), *Sweated Labour and the Trade Boards Act* (London, 1911), p. 5.

[118] E.P. Hennock, 'The measurement of urban poverty: from the metropolis to the nation, 1880–1920', *EHR*, 40 (1987), p. 215.

[119] The Inter-Departmental Committee on Physical Deterioration, *Report* (PP 1904, I), esp. section 67.

[120] C.F.G. Masterman, *The Condition of England* (London, 1909), p. 172.

Chapter 4

The Turning Point of 1906 and the
Legal Minimum Wage

Both Queen Victoria's Silver (1887) and Diamond (1897) Jubilees had been accompanied by anti-sweating scandals. Yet when Edward succeeded to the throne in 1901 sweating continued to flourish. Two of Britain's leading industrial law experts, B.L. Hutchins and A. Harrison, were moved to remark: 'Opinion is not yet converted to the legal regulation of wages, nor likely to be for a considerable time ....'[1] A major turning point only occurred in 1906. In that year a Board of Trade Committee on earnings and hours was established to gather authoritative data on pay for the first time.[2] 1906 also saw the advent of a Liberal Government and the election to Parliament of several leading anti-sweating campaigners: Percy Alden, Charles Masterman, Leo Chiozza Money, George Barnes, Keir Hardie and Will Crooks. More importantly, the Liberal owner of the *Daily News*, the chocolate philanthropist, George Cadbury was prevailed upon not only to expose sweating in his newspaper but also to finance a sensational sweated industries exhibition.

Richard Mudie-Smith organised the exposition and A.G. Gardiner, editor of the *Daily News*, chaired its committee.[3] Council and executive committee members included leading Fabians, Radical Liberal and Labour MPs and prominent church figures as well as well-known social investigators.[4] Restricted to homework exhibits, the show was based on a similar event held in Berlin in March 1904.[5] However, the *Daily News* exhibition was a more comprehensive and ambitious affair. Opened by royalty, the Princess Henry of Battenburg, accompanied by her daughter, Princess Ena, and staged in the heart of the West End at the Queen's Hall, Regent's Street, the show

---

[1]   Hutchins and Harrison, *History of Factory Legislation*, p. 216.

[2]   *Earnings and Hours of Labour of Workpeople of the United Kingdom* (PP 1909, LXXX), (PP 1910, LXXXIV), (PP 1911, LXXXVIII), (PP 1912–1913, CVIII). A wage census had been conducted in 1886, but it was unreliable. See J.J. Mallon, 'Women's wages in the wage census of 1906', in B.L. Hutchins, *Women in Modern Industry* (London, 1915), pp. 213–38.

[3]   Gardiner is thought to have conceived the idea after Mary Macarthur, whom he had never seen before, 'broke in upon' him, and 'disarmed and alarmed him by bursting into tears' over the lack of progress on anti-sweating reform. See M.A. Hamilton, *Mary Macarthur: A Biographical Sketch* (London, 1925), p. 65.

[4]   Significantly, at least seven out of the fifty-eight council members were connected with the Rainbow Circle, a dining club which provided a forum for synthesising debates between Radical Liberals and prominent socialists concerning collectivist policies. See M. Freeden (ed.), *Minutes of the Rainbow Circle, 1894–1924* (London, 1989), pp. 3–4.

[5]   In May 1904, too, the Rev. J.E. Watts-Ditchfield, Vicar of St. James the Less, Bethnal Green had organised a small, East-End, two-day show of articles produced by sweated labour.

became an event in the London season.[6] Even the Home Secretary, Herbert Gladstone, and his wife attended the display.[7] Originally scheduled to last a month, the exhibition attracted so much attention that it was extended for a further two weeks.

For the price of a shilling, a day's wage for a sweated seamstress, or five shillings for the duration of the show's run, spectators were admitted to a 'bazaar belonging to Dante's inferno'.[8] Afternoon lectures were delivered daily by leading anti-sweating experts.[9] Margaret MacDonald spoke on American anti-sweating ventures and licences for home industries. B.L. Hutchins lectured on women's position in industry. Mary Macarthur concentrated on the benefits of trade unionism for females. On 25 May George Bernard Shaw addressed around 1,600 fashionably arrayed men and women. After haranguing the crowd for allowing sweating to persist, he taunted the audience: 'I notice some of you are standing. It serves you right. You have been suffering for about half an hour from a mild form of fatigue. Many thousands of women are compelled to suffer fatigue of that kind while working fifteen and sixteen hours a day.'[10] Evening oxy-hydrogen lantern illustrations – the exhibition stayed open until 8 pm – were also provided. Some 450 items of sweated merchandise were displayed. More importantly, the general public (30,000 attended) were invited to observe forty-five sweated workers, mainly women, toiling away at twenty-four stalls.

Viewers had the opportunity to scrutinise for the first time all the details of sweated manufacture – from the making of shirts to the carding of hooks and eyes, from shawl-fringing to glove stitching.[11] They witnessed directly the intensity of the labour process and the martyrdom of human flesh: 'Society came, saw and shuddered', reported the *Daily News*.[12] Kristina Huneault suggests that the workers at the exhibition 'were a voiceless residuum' who were 'spoken for by the economically secure'.[13] Yet sweated seamstresses and other degraded workers were now no longer represented, as they had been in the popular poems, paintings and plays of the past, as uncomplaining and inert victims; they were active participants

---

[6]   The Princess Henry of Battenburg (Princess Beatrice, 1857–1944) was the fifth daughter and youngest child of Queen Victoria and Prince Albert. She married Prince Henry Maurice of Battenburg in 1885, and was widowed in 1896.

[7]   Gladstone, it was noted, bought a shawl for one old lady at work in the exhibition who was sitting in a draught: *Daily News*, 18 May 1906.

[8]   *Daily News*, cited in M. Stewart and L. Hunter, *The Needle is Threaded* (Southampton, 1964), p. 136.

[9]   WIC members contributed 9 of the 21 lectures, and 16 of the 41 accounts of the trades published in the catalogue: WIC, *Twelfth Annual Report* (1905–1906), p. 15.

[10]   Stewart and Hunter, *The Needle is Threaded*, p. 137.

[11]   Private sector 'good' employers, and government workshops provided sewing machines and materials. In addition to garment workers and those engaged in clothing accessories, the show also featured boxmakers, a confirmation wreath maker, tennis and racquet-ball coverers and a maker of pipe and cigarette holders.

[12]   *Daily News*, 4 May 1906.

[13]   K. Huneault, *Difficult Subjects: Working Women and Visual Culture, Britain, 1880–1914* (Aldershot, 2002), p. 156.

in a dynamic, living spectacle.[14] According to Chiozza Money, the exhibition's workers attracted 'the admiration of all the beholders'.[15] The family budgets and personal circumstances of the participants were printed, in their own words, on cards by their stalls and they answered questions put to them by the crowds. They spoke on platforms with renowned celebrities of the day. Emboldened by Cadbury's promise to indemnify them if their employers dismissed them, and much to the discomfiture of Conservatives, they implored the ILP to intervene on their behalf.[16] Some of the women managed to inject an element of sardonic humour into the proceedings. When Princess Ena, recently engaged to the King of Spain, enquired of one worker how many children she had, she replied that she was nursing her seventeenth. She added mockingly of the flabbergasted royal: 'They do tell me that the young lady's going to be married.'[17] Others parried ill-informed and patronising queries with sarcasm. When asked by one grandee how she spent her miserable weekly earnings of nine shillings, the sweatee responded laconically: 'I put my money in the building society. I've just bought one house, and I'm going on for another.'[18]

Starkly and without exaggeration, the exhibition's pocket-sized catalogue also set out the case histories of the workers and chronicled their life stories. When averaged, their wages were found not to exceed one penny an hour and even this was uncertain and irregular. The matchbox maker at Stall II was listed as living in one small room and was described as having five children:

> ... the eldest of whom is 11. She also has to work to support her husband, who is consumptive, and who has been unable to work for 6 years. They have been compelled to take parish relief intermittently since 1901 ... The eldest girl (11) after morning school, makes a gross of outside cases before going back to afternoon lessons at 2 p.m., and again works from 4.30 to 5.30 p.m., fitting up the boxes.[19]

At the next stall, a hook and eye carder worked with only a 'few hours' bed'. Her husband had been a Midland Railway employee for thirty years: 'When 54 years of age he fell from a boiler, but not realising he was seriously hurt, made no report. The next day he found he had lost the use of his right arm. He was dismissed and told he had no claim on the Company, "because he had not reported the accident the same day". Hence he has received neither compensation nor pension.'[20]

At stall V a widower with four children to support struggled at slipper making.[21] The operative at Stall VII belonged to a family of sackmakers:

---

[14]   Earlier exhibitions, merely contained a collection of sweated goods, actual workers were not featured.

[15]   SCH, *Report*, 1907, Q. 2,905.

[16]   *Law Times*, 12 May 1906. Workers were placed in the care of a matron at a centrally located temperance hotel: *Daily News*, 25 April 1906. For intimidation and indemnification of the women, see *Daily News*, 8 May 1906. Margaret MacDonald 'adopted' one victimised worker: L. Herbert, *Mrs Ramsay MacDonald* (London, 1924), p. 28.

[17]   *Daily News*, 3 May 1906.

[18]   *Ibid.*

[19]   Mudie-Smith, *Sweated Industries*, p. 93.

[20]   *Ibid.*, p. 94.

[21]   *Ibid.*, p. 97.

Her mother has had 21 children (8 of whom are now dependent), and has worked at sackmaking since the age of 9. Her husband (worker's father) is a labourer, out of work. The worker's husband is also a labourer, out of work. Worker calling for material at 9.30 am., often has to wait till 12.30. If the sack is spoiled in making, 9d. is deducted – if the sack is better quality, this deduction may reach 2/6.[22]

Whilst huge audiences watched the workers performing their various tasks, still larger numbers read about them in the press.[23] Disturbing and sombre monochrome pictures of the women were also widely circulated in the exhibition's handbook, on postcards and in national newspapers.[24] One reporter spoke of 'realistic lying photographs …'.[25] Yet the exhibition's guide, some 20,000 copies of which were sold, insisted that pictures of sweated workers 'had not been in any way altered or, with two exceptions, touched up'.[26] The workers at the exhibition normally laboured two to a counter. In contrast, the catalogue often depicted the women in family settings. Newspapers (including the *Daily News*) often chose to represent the woman worker at the exhibition as solitary and close to a lighted window. These photographs were often reminiscent of the early paintings inspired by Hood's poem.[27] Yet, as the *Daily News* insisted, the exhibition: 'was not a show, or a Royal Academy display of portraits and landscapes; it was rather an unveiling of the hidden things of … misery.'[28]

Visitors to the exhibition were filled with consternation when they discovered that even expensive garments were often completed in disease-ridden slums.[29] It was revealed that King Edward's coronation robes, the finest velvet in the land, were not immune from the sweating system. Wedding cakes and pastries manufactured in a hygienic factory were highly likely to be packed in fancy boxes glued together in squalid tenements. Nor were sweated workers, as was commonly assumed, necessarily unskilled. It was demonstrated that racquet and tennis-ball covering as well as exquisite artificial flowers manufactured for use by milliners demanded considerable skill. As Black later commented: 'Neither my reader nor I, for instance, could cover a racquet ball so that it would pass muster … it is improbable that either of us could cover an umbrella, and pretty certain that neither could make a passable artificial rose of even the poorest description.'[30] Cannon Edward Lyttelton, headmaster of Eton, was so distressed at finding racquet balls intended for his institution displayed at the

---

[22] *Ibid.*, p. 99.

[23] The circulation of the *Daily News* alone was 200,000. It advertised itself as the largest morning halfpenny newspaper in the world.

[24] See Figures 5–8.

[25] R.B. Suthers, 'The cannibal exhibition', *Clarion*, 18 May 1906.

[26] See Mudie-Smith, *Sweated Industries*, p. 4.

[27] *Ibid.* See also, *Daily News*, 2 and 7 May 1906; *Manchester Weekly Times*, 22 September 1906.

[28] *Daily News*, 4–8 May; 18 May 1906.

[29] Black, *Sweated Industry*, p. 143.

[30] *Ibid.*

Figure 5   'The chain-makers "workshops"', Sweated Industries being a Handbook of the 'Daily News' Exhibition (1906)

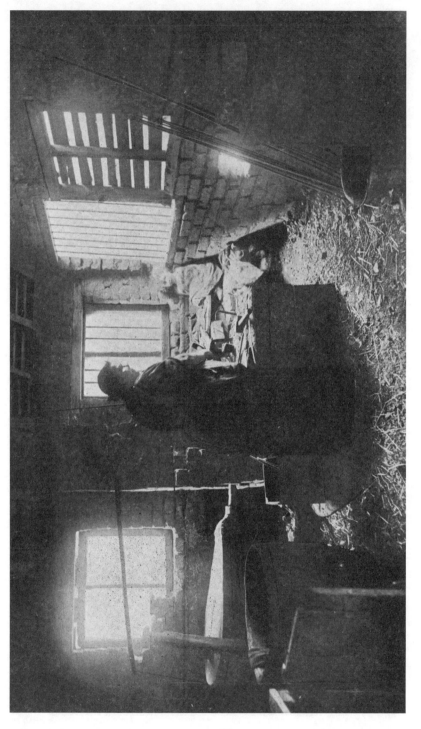

Figure 6   'A Cradley chain-maker', *Sweated Industries being a Handbook of the 'Daily News' Exhibition* (1906)

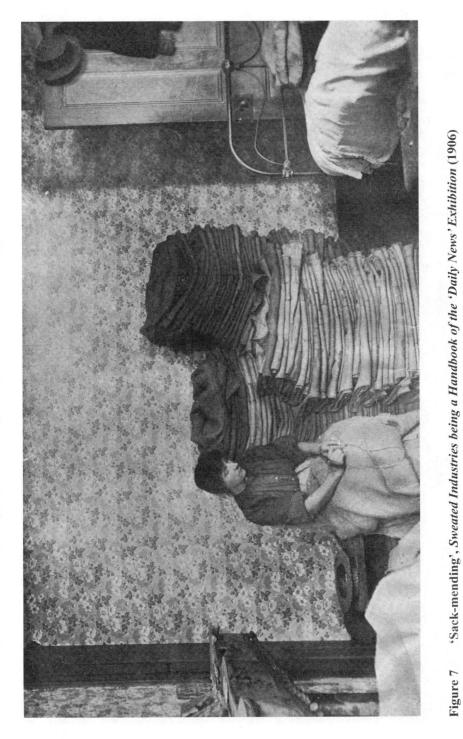

Figure 7   'Sack-mending', Sweated Industries being a Handbook of the 'Daily News' Exhibition (1906)

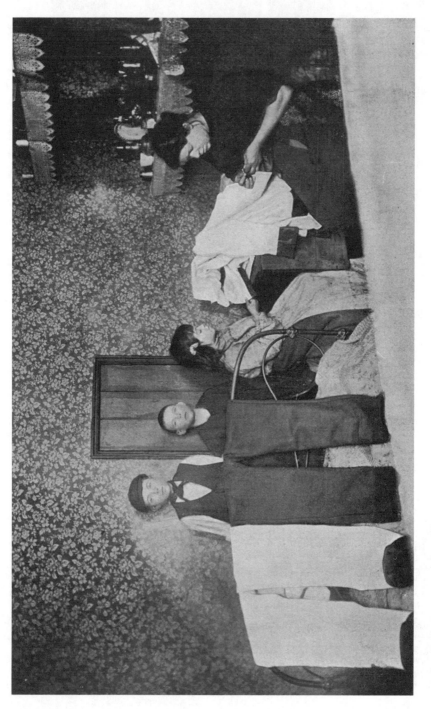

Figure 8 'Trouser finishing', *Sweated Industries being a Handbook of the 'Daily News' Exhibition* (1906)

exhibition that he agreed, with the public schools of Uppingham and Clifton, to pay higher prices to the middleman.[31]

The gravity of the situation was also exposed, for the exhibition revealed that sweating was not confined to a small number of 'sweated trades'. Low rates and bad conditions were to be found at the bottom end of virtually every occupation. Hardly any purchase was free from the taint of sweating. British society could no longer console itself that sweating was purely a phenomenon centred on women's paid work in the home.[32] Those who had advocated consumers' leagues as a possible solution were confounded when they found that clothing made in clean and healthy workshops and by well-paid labour might, nevertheless, be trimmed with braid, buttons or hooks and eyes carded in sweating dens. As one of the exhibition's committee members noted: 'Lists of fair shops are ... thoroughly illusory ....'[33] The exhibition's handbook warned the public:

'The Song of the Shirt' is probably the most effective labour report which has ever been presented to the nation. Unhappily it may still be accepted as a thoroughly up-to-date report of the conditions under which the Home Needlework trades are carried on to-day in any of our cities. The sympathy of the community is easily aroused. What is more difficult is to awaken a sense of the terrible risks to which not only the workers but the purchasing public are exposed through the making of clothing and other articles for general use in insanitary houses ... woollen shirts ... are used as coverings for the sick, or ... as bedclothes for the members of the family generally ... It is difficult to give any adequate idea of the dreary squalor of many of these places which have to do duty both as home and workshop, and which do not possess the most elementary requirements of either.[34]

The most disquieting aspect of the show for contemporaries was the implication of sweating for national efficiency.[35] The exhibition's organisers emphasised not simply the social injustice of sweating, or the ease with which infectious diseases could be transmitted, but the danger of racial degeneration. Dwelling on the doubts and fears raised by the poor performance of Britain's recruits in the Boer War, they stressed how sweating added daily to a new generation of unfit and sickly citizens quite incapable of defending the Imperial race.[36] Even the Tory *Morning Post* was

---

[31]   In 1907, following the exhibition and the Headmaster's Conference, a voluntary wages board was set up to establish fair wages for forty female homeworkers covering racquet balls: E. Lyttelton, 'Wages boards', *Contemporary Review*, 95 (1909), pp. 227–38. Lyttelton was the brother of Alfred Lyttelton and brother-in-law to the latter's second wife, Edith Lyttelton, the author of *Warp and Woof*. See V. Markham, *May Tennant* (London, 1949), pp. 40–42.

[32]   C. Smith, 'The workings of the Trade Boards Act in Great Britain and Ireland', *Journal of Political Economy*, 22 (1914), p. 608.

[33]   G. Tuckwell, 'Preface', in Mudie-Smith, *Sweated Industries*, p. 13.

[34]   M. Irwin, 'Shirt finishing', in *Ibid.*, p. 36.

[35]   The emergence of national efficiency beliefs in Britain should be seen against the backcloth of the country's relative economic decline from about 1870, the rapid industrial advance of Germany (only unified in 1871), and the doubts and fears raised by the poor performance of Britain's recruits in the Boer War: G. Searle, *The Quest for National Efficiency* (Oxford, 1971), *passim*.

[36]   A.G. Gardiner 'Introduction', in Black, *Sweated Industry*, pp. xi–xiv.

now willing to embrace the Webbs' treatise, if not their politics, on the importance of regulating wages.[37]

I

The exhibition aroused similar concern when staged in Britain's major industrial towns and cities. In the provinces the event lasted from three days, in Ilford, to ten weeks, in Birmingham. These shows were often adapted to local labour market conditions. The Manchester exhibition emphasised shirts, umbrellas, handkerchief hemming and rag picking. In the metal working city of Birmingham the appearance of female chainmakers labouring at a working forge attracted a great deal of attention.[38] When a further sweated exhibition was held in London at the Prince's Hall, Earl's Court, in 1909, a lone female chainmaker was the topic of public conversation. A 'pleasant-faced young woman' about eighteen, she was described by a special correspondent for the *County Express* as being in high spirits:

> She is having the time of her life. She receives a weekly wage – a wage which is as high above the heads of her companions in the Black Country as the Himalayas are above the Indian Ocean – she is kept in lodgings and she is taken to see the sights of London .... Her first request was that her name should not be mentioned 'because of the visitors', and she added 'At Cradley Heath they know I'm here, and if you say I'm alright and having a good time, they'll know who you mean'. She started making chains ... when she was 15 she worked with her mother and sister, and her earnings for a week's work did not exceed 4s. 6d. – and that after working from 7 to 7 .... [39]

The operative confirmed that she had recently joined a union with a membership in the region of 800 that: '[we] hope things will be a bit better now.' Julia Varley of the Birmingham Women Workers' Federation added:

> I've been perfectly astonished at the revelations which I have had opened out to me since the young woman who makes chain has been here. I have had her lodging with me, and I find the poor girl hardly knows what a decent meal is ... it is difficult to believe that Westminster Abbey, St. Paul's, Madame Tussaud's, and other places of national interest were absolutely meaningless words to her.

She continued that one visitor:

> was very insistent that the poor girl must be vegetarian, as only people of that cult could possible do such labour. And I had to explain that the women chainmakers were very often vegetarians, but out of necessity, and not from choice.[40]

---

[37]   *Morning Post*, 4 May 1906.

[38]   See, *Birmingham Mail*, 23 May 1908. See also, *Handbook of the Manchester Sweated Industries Exhibition* (Manchester, 1906). For further details of the latter's organisation, see Women's Trade Union Council, Manchester, Salford and District, *Twelfth Annual Report, 1906* (Manchester, 1907), esp. pp. 9–12.

[39]   *CE*, 24 July 1909.

[40]   *Ibid.*

Many exhibitions were inaugurated with recitations of Hood's *Song of the Shirt*. Women's suffrage campaigners, eager to demonstrate that sweated females were exploited because they were denied the franchise, staged a large number. These events, in the tradition of suffragette pageants, were frequently decked-out with colourful banners and were still drawing crowds until the First World War.[41] Margaret MacDonald left no doubt as to the power of their visual impact when she spoke of the 'horror awakened ... as to the wretched wages paid to thousands of home workers in the clothing trades ...', or how one 'cannot forget the pale pinched widow, the girl with the consumptive cough, the wife with a sick husband ...'.[42] The introduction to the Ilford sweated industries catalogue commented in similarly graphic vein:

> The facts of sweating are well known ... Yet still, the facts and figures that are given to us ... do not deeply impress us ... They are not visual, they are easily forgotten ... When we read that a woman shirt worker earns one penny an hour we have to be assisted to understand a thing so monstrous. We have to see before us a veritable woman ... hear from her own lips that thus she works each day and each week of her life, learn that she is sober and industrious, perceive for ourselves the pallor of her face and the weariness of her body.[43]

II

According to Gertrude Tuckwell, the overall impact of the exhibitions was not dissimilar to that surrounding the street processions of the stunted mill children of the North, which had helped the passage of the factory, acts almost sixty years earlier.[44] A minority, however, questioned the integrity of parading the most wretched workers in the country before 'pampered' royalty and the wealthy inhabitants of Belgravia. Writing in the *Labour Leader*, T. Gavin-Duffy reflected how one *Daily News* article had dedicated seventy-seven lines to the silks, satins and other trappings worn by third-rate princesses who deigned to grace the opening of the exhibition and only fourteen to describing the condition of the sweated workers. He mused:

> it is questionable whether a fashionable social function adorned even by royalty will do anything to right the wrongs of these poor people. A reference to the Civil List shows that HRH Princess Henry of Battenburg receives the sum of £6,000 per annum, or rather more

---

[41] By this date, though, they appear to have lost their initial impact. The *Daily Herald*, for example, dryly remarked: 'they do not have much more effect on fashionable people than any other way of passing their spare time': *Daily Herald*, 14 November 1914. For an excellent survey of the imagery of the suffrage campaign, see L. Tickner, *The Spectacle of Women* (London, 1988).

[42] *Labour Leader*, 17 May 1907. Margaret MacDonald provided the majority of the workers for the exhibitions: MacDonald, *Margaret Ethel MacDonald*, p. 157.

[43] J.J. Mallon, 'The need for exhibitions of sweated industries,' in *Handbook to the Sweated Industries Exhibition* (Ilford, 1908), p. 7.

[44] G. Tuckwell, 'The story of the Trade Boards Act', *Contemporary Review*, 120 (1921), p. 601.

than £115 per day, and it savours somewhat of mockery for such a painted butterfly, even when surrounded by moths, to mouth sympathy with a woman 57 years of age who has to work seventeen hours a day making blouses at 2¼d. each – earning in that day of struggle and sorrow the sum of 1s. 11½d. – against the Princess's £115 per day for doing nothing … [I]ndeed, after leaving the Exhibition, Princess Ena was so happy that she went off to a waxwork exhibition, spending an hour there playing pranks on King Alfonso, forgetting altogether the women brushmakers.[45]

Justice, the organ of the Marxist Social Democratic Federation (SDF) was equally caustic. In an editorial headed '"Sweated Industries" and high placed hypocrisy', it acidly remarked that: 'Princesses and sweated-wage slaves go well together.'[46]

One trade unionist felt that, since the workers would not appear in their normally thread bare attire, the exhibitions stripped sweating of some of its most ghastly aspects.[47] Others regretted that it was impossible to reproduce in the splendid, lofty halls where the exhibitions were held the vile odours and the unsanitary living and working conditions.[48] R.B. Suthers of the *Clarion* had anticipated, after studying the front-page illustration of the exhibition's catalogue, a foul sweating den populated with emaciated homeworkers and starving children. Instead, he found that:

> When I entered the hall, and glanced around, my … dream vanished, and I laughed … That lurid picture at the door was a fraud. A lure. A simulacrum … My foot fell silently on a soft carpeted floor. Around the walls were neat, varnished stalls displaying goods … it might have been a fancy fair or a bazaar … It was so sadly funny that I laughed. I thought of what the projectors wanted to achieve by the exhibition, and how feebly futile the means were. They did their best; but the thing is impossible. If they got the right real thing … no one would go.[49]

In response to these criticisms, the *Daily News* readily agreed that it was impossible to replicate exactly the misery and privation experienced by sweated workers. The editor, also frankly admitted that to some the experience was merely 'a painful interlude between a visit to the shops in the morning and … the theatre in the evening'. But he denied that the exhibition had been organised for seasonal amusement. The intention was to shock and to shame. Far from being consumed by idle curiosity or listlessness as at the usual society crush, ticket holders had beheld the workers performing their tasks with 'a rapt attention associated with amazement and dismay'.

---

[45]   *Labour Leader*, 11 May 1906.

[46]   *Justice*, 5 May 1906. The contrast between starving seamstresses and the wealthy woman of leisure is reminiscent of Leech's cartoons on adjacent pages in *Punch*, 22 December 1849, pp. 240–41 depicting, 'Needle money' and 'Pin money'. See Figure 1.

[47]   W.A. Appleton, General Secretary of the Amalgamated Society of Operative Lace makers, Nottingham: *Daily News*, 12 May 1906.

[48]   *Ibid.*, 7 May 1906. See also, *Jewish Chronicle*, 27 September 1907. Similar difficulties confronted the Lower East Side Tenement Museum, New York in 2001, when it reconstructed a turn of the century sweatshop: D. Bender, 'Sweatshop subjectivity and the politics of definition and exhibition', *International Labor and Working Class History*, 61 (2002), pp. 19–20.

[49]   Suthers, 'The cannibal exhibition'.

Sweated women were no longer out of sight out of mind.[50] Moreover, the event had encouraged unofficial strikes among sweated garment and cap makers. Some 10,000 strikers had marched behind two brass bands to form a mile-long procession through the streets of London.[51] The exhibition was such a powerful critique of political economy that it inspired similar exhibitions in America.[52]

Despite the misgivings of a few, the *Daily News* was widely praised for its ingenuity.[53] *The Spectator* observed: 'It was an excellent idea to organise the Exhibition of Sweated Industries ... The impersonal character of modern industry makes such an exhibition for many ... their first opportunity of insight into the work of the people, as it exists in London to-day.'[54] Even the rival *Morning Post* was moved to conclude:

> There is no more effective method of impressing on the public conscience the evils of the sweating system than that of holding in populous centres exhibitions showing the conditions under which some of the poorer and less organised sections of the workers are compelled to earn their daily bread.[55]

Looking back on the year 1906, the Christian Socialist historian, G.P. Gooch, recalled: 'I well remember the interest excited by ... the Anti-Sweating Exhibition ... such challenges to complacency ... remind us that we were only just beginning to build Jerusalem in England's green and pleasant land.'[56] G.D.H. Cole could similarly reminisce:

> I remember, when I was a boy, being taken to an Anti-Sweating Exhibition, at which I heard Gilbert Chesterton speak. I remember hearing Will Crooks talk about conditions in the East End, and encountering social workers from Toynbee Hall. I remember being deeply moved by these experiences, and being able in my mind to relate what I heard to what I saw around me'.[57]

The problem of sweating, previously the concern of a few, interested bodies emerged at the forefront of public debate. Nationally the question was posed: 'What can I do?'[58]

---

[50]   *Daily News*, 3–7 May 1906. See also, Gardiner, 'Introduction', p. xv.

[51]   Stewart and Hunter, *The Needle is Threaded*, p. 137.

[52]   *Daily News*, 13–15 June 1906. The *Daily News* exhibition was replicated in Philadelphia and Chicago. The Chicago event was an advance on previous ventures since it featured women working in simulated tenement slums.

[53]   *WIN*, June 1906, p. 558.

[54]   *Spectator*, 5 May 1906.

[55]   *Morning Post*, 28 November 1908.

[56]   G.P. Gooch, 'The Edwardian decade', in F.J.C. Hearnshaw (ed.), *Edwardian England* (London, 1933), p. 23.

[57]   G.D.H. Cole, *Fabian Socialism* (London, 1971; first published 1943), p. 74.

[58]   See, for example, M. MacDonald's comments in the *Labour Leader*, 11 May 1906, where she remarks: 'We all ask what we can do. The princess asks it, the bishop, the fashionable society women, the trade unionist, the man in the street – each asks, "what can I do?"'.

III

The Committee of the first London exhibition considered the various solutions which had been urged during the event, including proposals for the licensing of homeworkers. It decided that the most helpful remedy lay in adopting wage boards, the groundwork for which had been laid a decade earlier. Accordingly, the NASL was formed to achieve this aim in July 1906.[59] The NASL was a non-political body embracing all religious creeds and social philosophies. Many of its chief campaigners were unmarried, middle-class women associated with the WTUL. In addition, the NASL included prominent Fabians, Liberals, Labour and Conservative MPs, Christian Socialists, Roman Catholics, Methodists and the Chief Rabbi, M. Asher Feldmann among its vice-presidents and executive.[60] Branches were quickly inaugurated in Birmingham, Bristol, Chislehurst, Hampstead, Leicester, Liverpool, Manchester, Oxford, West Hartlepool, and Woolwich.[61] In his survey of the sweated trades, Bythell questions the significance of the NASL for the reform of low pay. He remarks that 'it is unclear just how much credit ought to go to the League, in view of the widespread acceptance of the need for something on these lines.'[62] But, as contemporaries were quick to point out, the NASL was crucial in changing people's attitudes to a minimum wage.[63] Despite its rather slender financial base, the NASL worked untiringly in the anti-sweating cause. The campaign which it waged was handled with consummate skill, as was clearly demonstrated in its first major decision. Realising the importance of gaining the united support of the labour movement for its policy of a minimum wage, the NASL decided to submit the principle to a national conference of trade unionists, to which several experts on industrial questions would deliver lectures.

The conference took place in October 1906 at the Guildhall, London, and was opened by the Lord Mayor. Initially intended to last only two days, the announcement of the meeting attracted so much attention that the NASL extended its deliberations to a third day. Fifteen thousand copies of the report of the conference were sold and some 50,000 leaflets distributed.[64] Leo Chiozza Money, George Askwith, W. Pember Reeves, Sidney Webb and J.A. Hobson were among those who addressed 341 delegates representing two million organised workers.[65] Chiozza Money read a paper revealing how one-thirtieth of the population received one third of the total

[59]   NASL, *First Annual Report Adopted at the Annual Meeting Held 18 July 1907* (London, 1908); NASL, *Report of Conference on a Minimum Wage, Held at the Guildhall, London* (London, 1907), p. 3. George Cadbury became the President of the NASL, and also paid the rent on the NASL's headquarters at Mecklenburgh Square. See S. Koss, *Fleet Street Radical: A.G. Gardiner and the Daily News* (London, 1973), pp. 77–8.

[60]   For details of the NASL's committee members, see Appendix 1. Catholic interest had been stimulated by the appearance of J.A. Ryan's, *The Living Wage* (New York, 1906).

[61]   Winston Churchill and other Lancashire MPs served as vice-presidents of the Manchester branch: NASL, *First Annual Report*, p. 6.

[62]   Bythell, *The Sweated Trades*, p. 236.

[63]   G. Lansbury, *Looking Backwards and Forwards* (London, 1935), pp. 217–20. See also T. Wright, 'Operation and co-operation' in Wright, *Sweated Labour*, p. 57.

[64]   NASL, *First Annual Report*, p. 9.

[65]   NASL, *Report of Conference*, p. 6.

national income. Britain, he urged, could afford a minimum wage as high as thirty shillings a week.[66] Hobson demonstrated how he had refined his earlier thesis on a living wage to encompass his theory of under consumption. He argued that cheap labour did not lead to cheap production and that higher wages and shorter hours improved the quality of products: for 'better nourished, more energetic and cheerful workers give out a larger amount and a better quality of labour power.' An enforced rise of wages, he predicted, would be a spur to progress for a trade dependent for its economy upon an abundance of cheap, low-grade labour was an unprogressive one. He stressed that increased wages would also encourage industry in that those formerly sweated would come to have an enlarged share of the national income and would use their increased purchasing power to buy more and better goods. As a result of this improved standard of consumption, the demand for labour for production would increase. This would also lead to increased regularity and stability of employment because the luxurious expenditure of the wealthy would be replaced by the workers' demand for necessities or conveniences.[67] The WTUL declared that Hobson's paper dealt with 'every possible economic objection' to the proposal of a minimum wage while Sidney Webb's contribution constituted a 'brilliant and exhaustive study' which showed conclusively that many arguments against a minimum wage were based on economic misconceptions.[68]

However, there were so many divergent aims that the conference threatened to disintegrate without a coherent plan of campaign. Not a few of the delegates, as the *Women's Industrial News* (*WIN*) noted, used the conference as a good opportunity for roaming over the whole 'social question'.[69] On the second day Mary Macarthur had to point out that 'the conference was not called to solve the social problem, but to deal with one small phase of it'.[70] She reminded the delegates that it was no doubt true that all industries were sweated but that their object was to deal with the 'super sweated' trades.[71] The high point was reached on the third day when Pete Curran, on behalf of the standing orders committee, moved the resolution. He asked the conference to endorse unanimously the policy of the legal minimum wage for sweated workers and to pledge itself to advance that policy by every means in its power. One SDF delegate, Harry Quelch, denied that a minimum wage on its own would be sufficient to prevent sweating and demanded in addition the total suppression of outwork, without which he would not vote in favour of the motion. Eventually, after a pleading speech by Macarthur in which she stressed the urgent need to pass the resolution unanimously, the resolution was put to the meeting and carried without dissent. A further motion in favour of the abolition of outwork was proposed by the SDF delegates and was also carried unanimously, although Charles Dilke afterwards remarked that: 'he did not see

---

[66]   *Ibid.*, pp. 48–54. See also, Chiozza Money, *Riches and Poverty*, p. 127.

[67]   NASL, *Report of Conference*, pp. 54–8.

[68]   *WTUR*, January 1907, p. 14. Even so, the WIC, pronounced Webb's paper 'somewhat academic in style, and lacking in freshness' and a disappointment to his admirers. See *WIN*, December 1906, p. 586.

[69]   *WIN*, December 1906, p. 586.

[70]   NASL, *Report of Conference*, p. 59.

[71]   *Ibid.*

how it was possible to establish a minimum wage without taking into consideration outworkers ....'[72]

IV

It has been suggested that trade unions played little part in the anti-sweating movement.[73] But the effect of the conference, as the first annual report of the NASL noted, was to give its minimum wage proposal the support necessary to transform it into practical politics.[74] Taking the Guildhall resolution as an instruction from the organised workers of the country to press immediately for legislation, the NASL approached the Liberal Prime Minister, Campbell-Bannerman, and requested that wages boards be adopted by the government. Campbell-Bannerman refused to commit himself to this reform but he assured the NASL that he sympathised with their cause.[75] Encouraged by this statement, the NASL circulated members of the various parties in the House of Commons seeking support. No MP was overtly antagonistic to wages boards whilst thirty members placed their result of the ballot for legislation at the service of the NASL.[76] Even more important was the adoption of wages boards by the Labour Party, which placed it fourth in the list of reforms, which it wished to secure.[77] It was a member of the Labour Party, Arthur Henderson, who was most successful in the ballot and Dilke's Wages Boards Bill, renamed the Sweated Industries Bill, was committed to his charge. The Bill was not favoured by good fortune and, on the occasion of its second reading, had taken up less than five minutes of debating time when the rising of the House terminated the discussion.[78] At the same time, a Wages Board Bill introduced by the Liberal, Ernest Lamb, failed to secure a second reading.[79] As the *Women's Trade Union Review (WTUR)* pointed out, the bills shared 'the fate that, in the present state of public business, awaits all Bills not formally adopted by the Government'.[80]

The Liberal Government, though, was not unresponsive to the efforts of the NASL. Permission was granted to exhibit specimens of sweated manufactures in the anteroom of the House of Commons.[81] To satisfy the obvious desire of the public for legislation, in January 1907 a commissioner, Ernest Aves, was sent to investigate the wages boards of Australia. Aves' report was uncertain and inconclusive. He

---

[72]　*Ibid.*

[73]　See, for example, Roberts, *The Trades Union Congress*, pp. 215–17; Rickard, 'The anti-sweating movement', pp. 587–8; Morris, *Women Workers*, p. 131.

[74]　NASL, *First Annual Report*, p. 4.

[75]　*Ibid.*, p. 5.

[76]　*Ibid.*

[77]　*Ibid.*

[78]　*Hansard* (Commons), 15 February 1907, col. 149. Henderson was also instrumental in gaining trade union support for wages boards: M. Cole, *Makers of the Labour Movement* (London, 1938), pp. 55–7.

[79]　*Hansard* (Commons), 15 April 1907, cols 559–60.

[80]　*Women's Trade Union Review (WTUR)*, July 1907, p. 3. The *WTUR* was the organ of the WTUL.

[81]　*Ibid.*

doubted whether the experience of Victoria could be considered applicable to Britain. Margaret MacDonald, fresh from investigating wages boards in Australia, read Aves' report with fascination and specifically seized on the fact that he doubted whether the experiment in protectionist Victoria could be replicated elsewhere.[82] Nevertheless, the NASL found a good deal of evidence in the report to support its case. Aves himself admitted that: 'the boards, especially those formed in the women's trades are greatly valued and are widely believed in ... The boards have helped both in the home and in the factory, and probably not simply in the trades under them to set a more certain standard ....'[83] As the *WTUR* was quick to remark, Aves had been forced against his will to concede that wages boards worked.[84]

The Government also appointed a Select Committee on Homework in June 1907. The SCH began its investigations five months after Aves had departed for Australia. Its terms of reference were to enquire into both wages boards and the licensing of workplaces. However, the committee, much to the chagrin of some members of the WIC, contained no one favourably disposed to licensing but instead several who endorsed wages boards, including the Chairman, Sir Thomas Whittaker.[85] Nevertheless, Margaret Macdonald and Constance Lewis gave evidence on behalf of the WIC to the committee, opposing wages boards and arguing in favour of the licensing of workplaces.[86] Under cross-examination by Arthur Henderson, MacDonald was forced to admit that, from the economic point of view, inadequate homeworkers' wages were a greater evil than lapses in sanitation.[87] Some employers who gave evidence before the committee shared the MacDonalds' antipathy towards wages boards and fell back on the well-worn arguments that, if they were put into operation, Britain would either need to be protectionist or see her foreign and imperial trade ruined and unemployment

---

[82]   M. MacDonald to C. Black, 27 November 1908: BLPES, J.R. MacDonald Papers, volume 1.

[83]   *Report to the Home Secretary on the Wages Boards and Industrial Conciliation and Arbitration Acts of Australia and New Zealand* (PP 1908, LXXI), p. 24.

[84]   *WTUR*, July 1908, p. 6. The *Spectator* was not impressed with this line of arguing. It suggested that Aves did not approve of wages boards, that his report had been misrepresented: 1 August 1908 pp. 155–6.

[85]   The SCH's members included Chiozza Money, Arthur Henderson, Ernest Lamb, Charles Masterman, Charles Trevelyan and G.P. Gooch – all wages boards proponents. The WIC complained to Gladstone, the Home Secretary, that the licensing of homework lobby was inadequately represented. See *WIN*, September 1907, p. 651. The chairman of the SCH, subsequently published an article supporting a legal minimum wage: T. Whittaker, 'A minimum wage for home workers', *Nineteenth Century*, 379 (1908), esp. p. 514.

[86]   SCH *Report* (PP 1907, VI), QQ. 3,165, 4,296–606. Clementina Black gave evidence in support of wages boards and against licensing. Shortly afterwards she resigned from the presidency of the WIC over the issue: *Ibid.*, QQ. 2,854–971. By 1912, the WIC had become reconciled to a minimum wage and elected such trade board enthusiasts as Tawney to its committee: WIC, *Nineteenth Annual Report* (1912–1913), pp. 21, 38. The *Lancet* also regretted that 'medicine had no direct representative. On the whole ... the sanitary side of the problem was unduly subordinated to the industrial': 19 December 1908, p. 1827.

[87]   SCH, *Report*, 1907, QQ. 4,493–7.

increase.[88] One employer went so far as to object to wages boards on the ground that they would ruin patents. Another, Charles Watts, a large box manufacturer, told the SCH: 'A feature of our business is the constant production of novelties, and we should think it a great impediment to our business if we had, having produced a novelty, to ask other members of the trade to fix the wages that we should pay.'[89]

Representatives of the National Home Workers' League (NHWL), a rival organisation to the NASL, condemned both the licensing of workplaces and wages boards. This association had been founded in the early 1900s and, by 1908, consisted of some 3,000 members. Its leadership had strong feminist connections and it was pledged to protect homeworkers from legislation since it considered that further state interference would reduce the amount of work given out to women.[90] Miss Vynne, a NHWL representative, insisted that homeworkers were not in favour of legislation since they did not consider themselves to be sweated. To try to prove the point, she claimed that a homeworker earning over 20 shillings a week was not uncommon. She also informed the Committee that wages boards would squeeze out the old and disabled, since those who could not earn the minimum would receive no work. Finally, she alleged that sweated industries exhibitions were based on untypical cases of incompetent and disabled workers, a comment, which was subsequently repeated in the London *Evening Standard*.[91] It received a sharp denial from J.J. Mallon, secretary of the NASL. In the *Evening Standard*, Mallon replied:

> I desire emphatically to deny Miss Vynne's insinuations. In every case the workers at our exhibitions have been chosen by expert persons who have desired to give a true representation of the facts. The workers have been chosen as average workers, and their plight has been always much less than that of other workers who might have been chosen had the purpose of the League been a sensational one. This charge of misrepresentation comes with particularly bad grace from Miss Vynne, who has the hardihood to produce a worker receiving 22s a week for homework, and suggests that such a worker is typical of the great community of workers whose unhappy circumstances any of your readers who are curious can easily, by a visit to the East End, ascertain for themselves.[92]

Mary Macarthur and George Askwith, both supporters of the NASL, gave the most telling evidence to the committee. The committee had been established to enquire into the conditions of homeworkers only. Yet, Macarthur noted, the factory and the home did not exist in hermetically sealed compartments: 'in the shirt and collar trade, it is the custom for the worker to take the collars home to do a certain process at home known as creasing ... this is very largely done at the home with the help of the children.'[93] Moreover, low rates of pay, were not confined to domestic workshops. Sweating was

---

[88]   See, for example, the evidence of J.G. Newey, the hook and eye manufacturer, and the evidence of Sholto Douglas, a cardboard box manufacturer; SCH, *Report*, 1908, QQ. 217, 3,186.

[89]   *Ibid.*, Q. 2,320.

[90]   *Ibid.*, QQ. 2,708–75.

[91]   *Ibid.*, QQ. 2,704–81.

[92]   *Evening Standard* (London), 22 June 1908.

[93]   SCH, *Report*, 1907, Q. 2,731. Macarthur was secretary of the general union, the National Federation of Women Workers (NFWW).

as rife in the poorly managed factory as in the home and the solution was simple – to raise the bad employer up to the standard of the good.[94] She explained to the committee how the phenomenon appeared wherever meagre wages did not allow the workers to contribute to a trade society. Even when sweated female labour formed a union, as in the case of the women chainmakers of Cradley Heath, they were still handicapped by low pay. The women of Cradley Heath, she explained, were unable to afford sufficiently high trade union subscriptions to build up a strike fund to support them if a dispute should occur. The end result was that the masters did not take the women seriously.[95] Invariably 'good' employers told her that, if they could obtain the support of other masters, that they were prepared to pay better rates. She quoted from her experience with the chain manufacturers:

> Recently I accompanied their official in visits to a number of employers in the district, and in every case the employer admitted to me that the rates were scandalously low, and said that if only we could get a meeting of all the employers he was sure that a 15 or 20 per cent rise could be given. The difficulty is to get a meeting of all the employers.[96]

The Committee also requested to see some sweated workers at first hand and their private meeting with Mary Macarthur's seven anonymous homeworkers settled their last doubts.[97] The testimony of Miss C. was especially compelling. A baby linen maker, she disclosed how she could not maintain herself and her dependent father on eight shillings a week, even though she worked for eleven hours a day. Her rent was six shillings and six pence for two rooms. Virtually every thing in her home had been pawned and she expected the bailiffs. The chairman pronounced himself totally mystified as to how she existed at all.[98] The personal experience of Macarthur was both memorable and terrifying. When collecting evidence from the makers of babies' clothes, she had caught diphtheria and almost died. Macarthur's information so moved one previously sceptical member of the committee, Stuart Samuel, that he told her she had brought wages boards within the realm of practical politics.[99]

George Askwith, a Board of Trade arbitrator, also deeply impressed the committee with his evidence. He insisted that the practical difficulties of regulating wages had been exaggerated; that what arbitration and conciliation boards did continually in a multitude of organised trades, could similarly be done by the state. He dismissed the arguments that wages boards would lead to greater foreign competition on the grounds that both France and Germany were also considering wages boards as a

---

[94] SCH, *Report*, 1907, QQ. 2,693–712.

[95] *Ibid.*, QQ. 2,756–90.

[96] *Ibid.*, Q. 2,721.

[97] The women chose to remain anonymous for fear of victimisation. See SCH, *Report*, 1908, QQ. 1,788–2,221.

[98] *Ibid.*, QQ. 1,906–59.

[99] SCH, *Report*, 1907, Q. 2,834. Stuart Samuel's, younger brother, Herbert was a member of the Rainbow Circle, and under secretary at the Home Office: See H. Samuel, *Memoirs* (London, 1945), pp. 6–7.

solution to sweating.[100] The committee was so convinced by Askwith's argument that they remarked in their report:

> Your Committee attach importance to the experience and opinion of Mr Askwith, of the Board of Trade, who for many years has, from time to time, rendered most valuable service by acting as Arbitrator and Conciliator in trade disputes of various kinds. He has settled piecework rates in industries where the complication and diversity of patterns, etc., is great, and the results have been arrived at without excessive difficulty, and afterwards have worked satisfactorily. He is of opinion that 'Wages Boards are workable and practicable, and would be beneficial, and ought to be tried.'[101]

The evidence of Macarthur and Askwith was reinforced when, on 5 December 1907, the Tariff Reformer, Viscount Milner, opened the Oxford sweated industries exhibition. In his opening speech, which was reported at length and sympathetically by the Conservative *Morning Post* and *The Times*, Milner spoke in favour of wages boards and against licensing.[102] On 28 January 1908, the NASL organised a national demonstration at the Queen's Hall in support of wages boards. Chaired by the Bishop of Birmingham, speeches were delivered by Dilke, Shaw, Gardiner, Henderson, Crooks and Macarthur.[103] A few weeks later, on 21 February 1908, a Sweated Industries Bill was reintroduced and passed its Second Reading unopposed.[104] Herbert Gladstone, the Liberal Home Secretary informed the Cabinet that they would have to decide whether to recognise the principle of Wages Boards for:

> The Labour Party has placed this question next in importance to the grant of Old Age Pensions and the question of the unemployed. A large section of Conservatives, represented by the 'Morning Post', has declared whole-heartedly for it. No doubt it will also be supported by the general body of Tariff Reformers, who openly declare that social reforms depend upon their fiscal methods, and who will argue with plausibility that their tariff will protect minimum wage workers from foreign competition. Under these circumstances the Government will have to consider the course it will take … Undoubtedly the establishment of Wages Boards and the enforcement of a minimum wage will involve a public charge. Mr Askwith, however, does not think that this charge will be considerable.[105]

---

[100] SCH, *Report*, 1907, QQ. 3,932–4,295. See also, G.R. Askwith, *Industrial Problems and Disputes* (London, 1920), pp. 284–9.

[101] SCH, *Report*, 1908, p. xiv.

[102] *Morning Post*, 10 December 1907. The social-imperialist editor of the *Post*, Fabian Ware, was a member of the NASL's executive committee. Despite holding different political convictions, Ware encouraged Tawney and William Beveridge to write lead articles for the paper. See also Dilke's remarks to Deakin that the *Morning Post* championed the anti-sweating cause more than any of the liberal papers (British Library, Dilke Papers, 4, Add. Manuscripts, 43,877, fol.190). See also, *The Times*, 6 December 1907.

[103] Koss, *Fleet Street Radical*, p. 78.

[104] This was Toulmin's Bill. See NASL, *Second Annual Report Adopted at the Annual Meeting Held 21 July 1908* (London, 1909), p. 5.

[105] The Sweated Industries Bill. (Cabinet memo dated 18 February 1908, p. 5, *Board of Trade Papers and Memoranda,* 1902–1909).

Nevertheless, Gladstone considered the Sweated Industries Bill 'extremely crude' and 'unworkable'. He explained how the bill provided for the establishment of wages boards throughout the country and, 'whenever a difficulty occurs to the framers the solution appears to have been left to the Home Secretary.' Under the circumstances, he preferred to refer the bill to the SCH.[106]

V

Conscious of the growing support for wages boards in Parliament and in the country generally, the SCH issued its final report in July 1908. It concluded that sweating prevailed extensively not only amongst homeworkers but also amongst factory workers, especially in those trades where factory work competed with an outwork sector. It was convinced that only legislation could remedy this state of affairs.[107] After dismissing licensing for homeworkers as impractical, the committee recommended instead that the establishment of wages boards went 'to the root of the matter, in so far as the object aimed at is an increase in the wages of Home Workers'.[108] A note of warning was, however, sounded. Such legislation ought to be 'carefully considered' and only entered upon with 'great caution'. The chief safeguard against the unwise use of wages boards was seen to be their constitution. Composed equally of employers and employed, 'no one could be more deeply concerned than they ... that every precaution should be taken that nothing be done that would really curtail the trade ....'[109]

The acceptance of the principle of the minimum wage, together with the arguments used by the committee to justify it, afforded the NASL complete satisfaction. An interval followed, however, in which the Liberal Government would give no promise to legislate for sweated workers. The NASL found it necessary to hold further meetings and to press those organisations in sympathy with their work to urge the government to take immediate action.[110] When the outlook for anti-sweating legislation remained uncertain, the NASL decided in December 1908 to organise a representative deputation to the Prime Minister, Asquith, to urge the need for legislation.[111] The choice of Sidney Webb as one of the intermediaries at the meeting was inopportune. As Stewart and Hunter remark: 'The urbane and scholarly Asquith had little enough in common with this dry statistically-minded expert. Webb soon forgot that his business was to state a case, and started arguing. Asquith's temper was ruffled and something like a quarrel

---

[106] *Ibid.*, pp. 1–2. Gladstone was a vice-president of the NASL, and his wife sat on its executive committee. They each subscribed £2 10s to its funding: NASL, *Second Annual Report*, pp. 3, 18.

[107] SCH, *Report*, 1908, pp. vii, xi.

[108] *Ibid.*, p. xii.

[109] *Ibid.*

[110] This was assisted by the fact that the NASL, the NFWW and the WTUL shared the same premises in Mecklenburgh Square: D.M. Copelman, 'The gendered metropolis: fin-de-siècle London', *Radical History Review*, 60 (1994), p. 46.

[111] The deputation was led by the Archbishop of Canterbury and included Dilke, Mrs Tennant, George Barnes, Sidney and Beatrice Webb and the Earls of Dunraven and Lytton: NASL, *Third Annual Report* (London, 1910), p. 4. See also, *The Times* 15 December 1908.

developed before the deputation was abruptly dismissed ....'[112] Despite what Beatrice called Dilke's 'dog-like devotion' to Sidney, Dilke felt that an important opportunity had been missed.[113] He was mollified when, following the meeting, Churchill, as President of the Board of Trade, persuaded Asquith to relieve the overworked Home Office of the responsibility for wages boards.[114] Instead, Churchill recommended that the Board of Trade be made responsible for the measure, a concession to which Asquith reluctantly agreed.[115] Churchill later wrote in a Cabinet memo that:

> I understand from the Home Secretary that the Home Office would prefer that any measure on this subject should be in the charge of the Board of Trade, feeling that the establishment of Trade Boards is more akin to a development of the province of Boards of Arbitration than an extension of the Factory Acts, and that their existing machinery and inspecting staff are not adapted for the supervision of the working of such a measure.[116]

A further development was the appointment of H.J. Tennant, Asquith's brother-in-law, and an NASL supporter, as Churchill's Under-Secretary at the Board of Trade in December 1908.[117]

Up to this point, civil servants, with the exception of George Askwith, had approached the topic of wages boards with a marked lack of zeal. Ernest Aves had

---

[112]   Stewart and Hunter, *The Needle is Threaded*, p. 139.

[113]   Drake and Cole, *Our Partnership*, p. 48.

[114]   Churchill was probably converted to the Webbs' 'national minimum' in late 1907. From February 1908, he had cultivated the Webbs: Searle, *Quest for National Efficiency*, p. 248.

[115]   J.J. Mallon, whilst serving on the Chain Trade Board (CTB), described the meeting to Mr Albert Head, a member of the board. (Information from interview with A.E. Head, 13 October 1976).

[116]   Sweated Industries, Cabinet memo. Dated 27 January 1909, p. 1, *Board of Trade Papers and Memoranda*, 1902–1909. It is sometimes alleged that, because Herbert Gladstone lacked courage, Churchill took over the Wages Boards Bill. See J.M. Caldwell, 'The genesis of the Ministry of Labour', *Public Administration*, 37 (1959), pp. 371–82; and E. Halévy, *History of the English People in the Nineteenth Century, Volume 6* (London, 1961; first published 1932), pp. 252–3. It is more probable that the Board of Trade was better equipped than the Home Office to handle labour problems. See R. Davidson, 'Llewellyn Smith, the labour department and government growth, 1886–1909', in G. Sutherland (ed.), *Studies in the Growth of Nineteenth Century Government* (London, 1972), pp. 227–62. There is also some suggestion that Churchill drew his inspiration for wages boards not from Australia but Germany. See Churchill to Asquith 12 January 1909, Asquith Papers, 22 (cited in J. Brown, 'Ideas concerning social policy and their influence on legislation in Britain, 1902–11', unpublished Ph.D. thesis, University of London, 1964, p. 246).

[117]   Tennant's support for trade boards sprang from two main influences. As a social-imperialist, he believed that sweating was a threat to the British race and the empire. Additionally, in 1896 he married May Abraham, a leading figure in the WTUL and, before her marriage, the first woman factory inspector. On the eve of the introduction of the government's Trade Boards Bill, Churchill dined at the Tennants' house. Gertrude Tuckwell later remembered how Churchill talked of the 'great revolutionary measure' he was going to introduce the next day: Markham, *May Tennant: A Portrait*, p. 42.

shown little enthusiasm for the board system.[118] Clara Collet, as Senior Investigator for Women's Industries at the Board of Trade, had given evidence against both licensing and wages boards before the SCH.[119] Llewellyn Smith, Permanent Secretary of the Board of Trade, had opposed Dilke's wages boards scheme.[120] But with the arrival of Churchill and Tennant at the Board of Trade, together with the highly favourable SCH report, Llewellyn Smith reluctantly accepted the inevitable.[121] He no doubt took solace from the fact that representatives of the NASL, especially Mallon, persuaded Churchill to abandon Dilke's scheme for a more modest measure limited to only a few industries, and that they dissuaded him from implementing a full-blown minimum wage of £1 per week which would have encompassed some thirty per cent of the working population.[122]

VI

Events progressed quickly. Churchill circulated his confidential draft of the Trade Boards Bill to the Cabinet on 12 March 1909. He stressed that trade boards were 'only defensible as exceptional measures to deal with diseased and parasitic trades', that 'further extensions of the Act to trades not in the schedule must obtain Parliamentary sanction. Thus there is no danger of such principles being unwittingly accepted as the normal basis of industry.'[123] On 24 March 1909, he moved the First Reading of the Trade Boards Bill.[124] Churchill argued that the boards would be very cost-effective, that the total expenditure would be between twelve to fifteen thousand pounds. Economies would be made on rent and staff by arranging for the boards to meet in the new labour exchanges. Fines were to be levied for breaches of the act and the board system was to be upheld by a special class of low-grade inspectors. Employers paying less than the minimum would be liable, on summary conviction, to a fine not exceeding £20 for each offence and a further £5 pounds for each day on which the offence was continued after conviction. In addition, employers found guilty of paying below the minimum were liable to the payment of arrears of wages.[125]

---

[118] However, between 1912 and his death in 1917, he was appointed chair of all the British and Irish boards.

[119] SCH, *Report*, 1907, QQ. 698–700, 822. See also her hostile review of the Victorian system: C. Collett, 'Wages boards in Victoria', *Economic Journal*, 11 (1901), pp. 557–65. Earlier, she had insisted that married women were far better off working in the home than the factory: 'Prospects of marriage for women', *Nineteenth Century*, 31 (1892), p. 544.

[120] It is likely that Llewellyn Smith was instrumental in having Aves appointed as the commissioner to enquire into the Victorian wages boards: R. Davidson, 'Sir Hubert Llewellyn Smith and labour policy, 1886–1916', unpublished Ph.D. thesis, University of Cambridge, 1971, p. 206.

[121] See comments by Llewellyn Smith, NA Lab 2/1, CL and SL, 128/1902.

[122] Stewart and Hunter, *The Needle is Threaded*, pp. 140–42.

[123] Additional trades could only be scheduled as board industries by a provisional order: Cabinet Memo. Dated 12 March 1909, p. 1. *Board of Trade Papers and Memoranda*, 1902–1909.

[124] At the same time, Hills, a Unionist, moved the Second Reading of Dilke's Wages Boards Bill. See *Hansard* (Commons), 26 March 1909, cols 2,061–129.

[125] *Hansard* (Commons), 24 March 1909, col. 961.

Churchill demonstrated how much he had imbibed the rhetoric of the Webbs when he characterised sweating masters as simultaneously being both 'bad' employers and poor businessmen. As he remarked of the Bill, 'the idea was to protect the good employer – and there are always good employers in the worst trades – who are anxious to pay a proper rate of wages from being undercut, and to protect them by compulsory powers.'[126] He later affirmed:

> It is a serious national evil that any class of His Majesty's subjects should receive less than a living wage. ... It was formerly supposed that the workings of the laws of supply and demand would naturally regulate or eliminate the evil ... But where you have no organisation, no parity of bargaining, the good employer is undercut by the bad and the bad employer is undercut by the worst; where these conditions prevail you have not a condition of progress, but a condition of progressive degeneration.[127]

According to the *Nation*, the organ of New Liberalism, the Bill marked 'the most advanced scheme of social reconstruction which the Government has as yet brought forward.'[128] Much to the dismay of the chainmakers, however, the Bill only scheduled four industries: ready-made and wholesale bespoke tailoring; cardboard box making; the machine-made lace and finishing trade; and the ready-made blouse trade. The chain industry, despite its national notoriety, had been omitted. The chainmakers mobilised quickly. Mass demonstrations were held requesting Churchill to include their craft in his Bill. At the same time, Mary Macarthur and the NASL urged the necessity of making domestic chainmaking a minimum wage industry. The aid of the local MP for Dudley, A.G. Hooper was also enlisted, while Arthur Henderson moved an amendment in the Commons to replace blouse making with chainmaking in the schedule. The chain industry, it was argued, was ideal for the new experiment: it was localised and comparatively free from foreign competition; the administration of the board would be easy; the workers were the most abject and pathetic in the country; and the 'good' employers in the industry welcomed the chance to pay fair wages.[129] Churchill acknowledged the strength of these arguments, and dropped the blouse trade from the schedule in favour of domestic chainmaking.[130]

Tennant moved the Second Reading of the Trade Boards Bill on 28 April 1909. It passed its Second Reading without a division. Churchill wrote to his wife: 'The Trade Boards Bill has been beautifully received ... All opposition has faded away.'[131]

---

[126]   *Ibid.*, cols 1,791–2,224.

[127]   *Hansard* (Commons), 28 April 1909, col. 344.

[128]   The *Nation*, 27 March 1909. The *Nation* (3 April 1909), also declared that Churchill's Trade Boards Bill was 'in embryo, the boldest and most far-reaching of all the social reforms which separate Modern Constructive Liberalism from the older policy that bore that name'. Founded in 1907, the *Nation* received substantial financial assistance from the Joseph Rowntree Social Service Trust: A. Briggs, *Social Thought and Social Action: A Study of the Work of Seebohm Rowntree, 1871–1954* (London, 1961), p. 48.

[129]   *County Advertiser for Staffordshire and Worcestershire (CA)*, 10 April 1909; 22 May 1909; 19 June 1909.

[130]   *Hansard* (Commons), 24 May 1909, col. 962.

[131]   Churchill to Clementina Churchill, 28 April 1909 in R.S. Churchill, *Winston S. Churchill, Volume 2: Companion, Part 2, 1907–11* (London, 1969), p. 880.

In support of the Bill, A.G. Hooper told the House how trade boards would end one of the gravest scandals which had existed in British industrial life for decades; the over working and scandalous rates of the women chainmakers of Cradley Heath.[132] Alfred Lyttelton, a Conservative and Tariff Reformer, also spoke warmly in favour of the Bill and the speech, as his biographer noted, 'coming from the opposition produced a considerable effect.' Lyttelton wrote to his wife:

> To-day I had one of my few successes in the House of Commons, on sweating. Here is a note from Masterman, and Dilke told Arthur [Balfour] that it was a splendid speech. It was not this – being unprepared in words – but it had the feeling in it which alone makes a speech for me – and of course a pretty complete knowledge of the subject. It was a blow that you were not there – but still I am happy to have made it … Bless you … let us do a big thing yet.[133]

At the Committee stage, the Labour Party attempted to extend the Bill to more than the four named industries and advocated a speedier and cheaper method of extension other than by a provisional order. Such a move, however, was overruled by Tennant on the grounds that the new legislation had to move cautiously lest it cause apprehension in various quarters of the House and outside it.[134] In the Lords, the Trade Boards Bill, according to Lord Hamilton of Dalzell, received a flattering and favourable reception.[135] Even Conservative peers acknowledged the need for anti-sweating reform. As the Marquess of Salisbury pointed out: 'As far as I myself am concerned, I assent to the establishment of these Trade Boards … I do so because the ordinary trade remedy for these evils appears to be impracticable … I mean the union of the workers.'[136]

The only discordant note in Parliament was registered by a few irreconcilable extremists, notably Sir Frederick Banbury, Unionist, who believed that the bill would lead to state intervention in the fixing of wages in all industries.[137] Ramsay Macdonald, although still opposed to trade boards, took care not to speak against the measure in the Commons.[138] The only serious opposition outside of Parliament came from the *Saturday Review*, the *Spectator* and certain members of the WIC.[139]

The Webbs regretted that the board rates were based on what employers in each trade could bear rather than on their subsistence minimum.[140] Different rates were thus established for the various board industries. The state, they felt, had shirked the

---

[132] *Hansard* (Commons), 28 April 1909, cols 366–9.

[133] E.S. Lyttelton, *Alfred Lyttelton: An Account of His Life* (London, 1923), p. 253. Lyttelton was Herbert Gladstone's first cousin.

[134] *Hansard* (Commons), 16 July 1909, cols 2,430–33.

[135] *Hansard* (Lords), 30 August 1909, col. 1,014.

[136] *Ibid.*, col. 982.

[137] According to Banbury, trade boards were 'a complete surrender to the socialist party': *Hansard* (Commons), 24 March 1909, cols 1,792–3.

[138] See speech by G.P. Gooch, *Hansard* (Commons) 28 April 1909, col. 400.

[139] P. Boyaval, 'La lutte contre le sweating system. Le minimum légal de salaire l'example de l'Australasie et de l'Angleterre', unpublished Ph.D. thesis, University of Paris, 1911, p. 422. See also, the *Spectator*, 1 May 1909, pp. 691–2.

[140] McBriar, *Fabian Socialism*, p. 216.

responsibility of establishing a standard rate. At the very least, they urged, a central trade board should be established to co-ordinate the decisions of the various boards regarding pay. This would, to some extent, make national policy-making more possible.[141] Beatrice Webb also endorsed the campaign to expand the power of trade boards beyond wage setting to embrace hours, overtime, and other conditions – as occurred in Victoria.[142] When addressing a meeting chaired by Winston Churchill in 1910 she pressed home her point that the legislation was seriously inadequate. She argued that sweating was a preventable cause of destitution and insisted: 'There are still sweated workers, but if we choose to apply the principle of making the employer responsible we can prevent all sweating. If sweating still remains it is because we do not choose to prevent it.'[143] Despite their dissatisfaction the Webbs praised Churchill for his 'courage and persistency' and campaigned for the Act's extension.[144] As Royden Harrison remarks, the Webbs did not always get their own way but 'wisely reconciled themselves to such disappointments so long as they could feel something important was happening'.[145]

The Trade Boards Bill finally became law on 20 October 1909. In the four industries in which wages were deemed unduly low the Act established boards consisting of equal numbers of employers' and workers' representatives, plus independent representatives nominated by the state. The independent or appointed members were to be no more than half the number of the elected members. The boards were empowered to fix a minimum time rate on which piece rates could be based. Although the anti-sweating campaigns had chiefly revolved around women homeworkers, the provisions of the act also applied to *factory* labour. As Churchill recognised: 'to screw up by ... special and artificial means the position of the homeworker, while leaving the factory untouched, would be to improve the homeworker out of existence altogether by a process which in practice would be very harsh.'[146] The legislation also encompassed *males*. Parliament could not safeguard sweated females, as Elie Halévy observed, without at the same time extending its protection to incorporate adult male labour.[147]

The *Labour Yearbook* for 1916 claimed that the measure was virtually 'blessed by everyone'.[148] The London *Evening Star* considered that: 'Since Tom Hood wrote his famous "Song of the Shirt" ... no remedy ... has proved so potent for good as the Trade Boards Act of 1909.'[149] To the *Anglian Daily Times*, Mallon, the NASL

---

[141]   S. and B. Webb, *English Local Government,* pp. 563–4.

[142]   The National Committee for the Prevention of Destitution (NCPD), *The Case for the National Minimum* (London, 1913), pp. 8, 11.

[143]   B. Webb, 'Unemployment and sweating prevention', *Journal of the Amalgamated Society of Tailors and Tailoresses*, December 1910, p. 271. For more information on sweating and destitution, see S. and B. Webb, *The Prevention of Destitution* (London, 1911), pp. 86–109.

[144]   S. Webb, 'Preface', in Hutchins and Harrison, *History of Factory Legislation*, p. xiv. The Webbs also considered that trade boards 'may well lessen the number and even mitigate the bitterness' of strikes. See S. and B. Webb, *English Local Government*, p. 564.

[145]   Harrison, 'Sidney and Beatrice Webb', p. 80.

[146]   *Hansard* (Commons), 24 March 1909, cols 1,789–90.

[147]   Halévy, *History of the English People*, p. 490.

[148]   *Labour Yearbook* (London, 1916), p. 214.

[149]   *Evening Star*, 8 March 1913.

secretary, was 'the lineal descendant of Tom Hood' – it was 'chiefly due to his actions and that of his Society ... that the Government was induced to ... fix a minimum wage for four scheduled employments.'[150] On 15 April 1910, a dinner was held at the Westminster Palace Hotel to mark Sir Charles Dilke's 'statesmanship, courage and devotion ... to sweated workers and the consummation of those services in the passage of the Trade Boards Act'. Responding to the toast in his honour, Dilke replied:

> There had been some who had looked forward to adopting a wider plan, one meant to apply to a vast number of workers from the first, one possible of ultimate and universal adoption for the whole labour world. He and the promoters of his Bill had thought that this would delay a start and be less useful as a fruitful experiment. The Government Bill had finally passed in a form such as they could welcome without reserve.[151]

Having won the battle for trade boards, Dilke and his associates now turned their attention to the practical implementation of the new policy to domestic chainmaking, Britain's first minimum wage industry in virtually one hundred years.[152]

---

[150] *Anglian Times*, 11 October 1913.

[151] *The Times*, 15 April 1910.

[152] The NASL, seeking to ensure the effective operation of the system, continued to exist for several years after the establishment of the boards.

PART III
The Minimum Wage in Practice

Chapter 5

The Test Case of the 1910
Cradley Heath Dispute

Until recently, it was commonly assumed that Victorian and Edwardian businessmen were uninterested in welfare reforms. Unlike in America or Germany where it had been demonstrated since the 1960s that corporate leaders played a dynamic role in constructing a new social order, in Britain it was usually believed that business and welfare were mutually incompatible.[1] Moreover, when British employers were the subject of study, research was usually restricted to the paternalism of the industrial revolution's early entrepreneurs or to those late-nineteenth century manufacturers such as George Cadbury or Seebohm Rowntree who ploughed back profits into social schemes.[2] Faced, it was said, with favourable market conditions, the latter were dismissed as Quaker enthusiasts, celebrated exceptions and objects of ridicule for more 'typical' hardheaded businessmen.[3] Eminent economic historians such as Peter Mathias concluded that Cadbury and similar employers, in contrast to those in basic heavy industries, catered for internal consumer demand and, being free from foreign competition, could afford paternalism.[4]

Since the late 1970s new scholarship has begun to indicate that social policy changes did owe much to the direct initiatives of businessmen – including those in the traditional staples geared to export. As Joseph Melling has pointed out, company paternalism was strong amongst large employers in Scottish shipbuilding, in the engineering industry and in armaments manufacture. A key factor in the provision of such benefits as company housing and profit-sharing schemes was not benevolence but, especially after 1880, employers' struggle for workplace control and the creation of an

---

[1] J.R. Hay, 'Employers and social policy in Britain: the evolution of welfare legislation, 1905–1914', *Social History*, 4 (1977), pp. 436–8. For details of American businessmen's attitudes, see, G. Kolko, *The Triumph of Conservativism* (Chicago, 1967); J. Weinstein, *The Corporate Ideal in the Liberal State: 1900–1918* (Boston, 1968); M. Dubofsky, *Industrialism and the American Worker, 1865–1920* (Illinois, 1975), pp. 72–84. For the activities of German industrialists, see E.C. McCreary, 'Social welfare and business–the Krupp welfare program, 1860–1914', *Business History Review*, 42 (1968), pp. 24–49; H.U. Wehler, 'Bismarck's imperialism, 1862–1890', *Past and Present*, 48 (1970), pp. 119–55.

[2] S. Pollard, 'Factory discipline in the industrial revolution', *EHR*, 15 (1963), pp. 254–71; N. McKendrick, 'Josiah Wedgwood and factory discipline', *Historical Journal*, 4 (1961), pp. 30–55. For Quakers, see Briggs, *Seebohm Rowntree, passim*; J.Child, *British Management Thought* (London, 1969), esp. p. 40. See also, J. Child, 'Quaker employers and industrial relations', *Sociological Review*, 12 (1964), pp. 293–315.

[3] Hay, 'Employers and social policy', p. 438.

[4] P. Mathias, *The First Industrial Nation* (London, 1969), pp. 374–5.

efficient labour force.[5] Patrick Joyce and Diane Drummond have similarly investigated the paternalistic policies of Victorian employers in North-West textiles and the Crewe Railway Works respectively.[6] More recently, William and Clifford Staples have revised labour process theory to illustrate the development of a dynamic paternalistic culture in the Midland hollowware firm of Kenricks.[7] Other specialist studies include those on the enlightened paternalist, William Lever, at Port Sunlight.[8] Robert Fitzgerald has added to these regional surveys by utilising company records on a national scale to reveal a range of employers' actions concerning industrial welfare in such industries as railways, gas, chemicals, iron and steel and brewing.[9] In this and his later survey, he lays to rest the idea that the policies of Quaker businessmen such as Rowntree were significantly at odds with those adopted by other employers.[10] Discussing welfare legislation, as opposed to the private provision investigated by Melling, Joyce, Drummond and others, Roy Hay has utilised Birmingham Chamber of Commerce's attitudes to labour exchanges and unemployment and sickness insurance. He demonstrates that many employers, not only Quakers, realised that state welfare was not merely an optional extra but an adjunct to business success.[11] Valuable as these studies are, they need to be extended to encompass the other New Liberal reforms, especially trade boards.

The views of employers in relation to the Trade Boards Act are significant because this piece of legislation drastically curtailed the industrial freedom of the employers that it encompassed. It compelled trade board employers to pay above a certain rate and obliged them to meet the increased wages bill, either by making production more efficient or by passing the rising costs on to the consumer. Such manufacturers, as tariff reformers were quick to point out, were thus fully exposed to the dangers of foreign competition.[12] In this respect, the Trade Boards Act was essentially different

---

[5]   J. Melling, 'Employers, industrial housing and the evolution of company welfare policies in Britain's heavy industry: West Scotland, 1870–1920', *IRSH*, 26 (1981), pp. 255–301. See also, J. Melling, 'Employers, industrial welfare and the struggle for workplace control in British industry, 1880–1921', in H.F. Gospel, and C.R. Littler (eds), *Managerial Strategies and Industrial Relations: An Historical and Comparative Study* (London, 1981), pp. 55–81.

[6]   However, they differ considerably on whether workers actually internalised deferential behaviour. See, P. Joyce, *Work, Politics and Society: The Culture of the Factory in Later Victorian England* (Brighton, 1980); D. Drummond, *Crewe: Railway Town, Company and People, 1840–1914* (Aldershot, 1995).

[7]   W.G. Staples and C.L. Staples, *Power, Profits and Patriarchy, passim*.

[8]   D. Jeremy, 'The enlightened paternalist in action: William Hesketh Lever at Port Sunlight before 1914', *Business History*, 33 (1990), pp. 58–81; J. Griffiths, '"Give my regards to Uncle Billy…": the rites and rituals of company life at Lever Brothers, c.1900–c.1990', *Business History*, 37 (1995), pp. 25–45.

[9]   R. Fitzgerald, *British Labour Management and Industrial Welfare, 1846–1939* (Beckenham, 1988).

[10]   *Ibid.*, esp. pp. 17–19, 184. R. Fitzgerald, *Rowntree and the Marketing Revolution, 1862–1969* (Cambridge, 1995), esp. ch. 8. See also, C. Dellheim, 'The creation of company culture: Cadburys, 1861–1931', *American Historical Review*, 93 (1987), pp. 13–44.

[11]   Hay, 'Employers and social welfare'.

[12]   See, for example, the remarks by Noah Bloomer, chain master, at a Unionist party meeting, *CE*, 19 November 1910. See also the speeches by Wedgwood and Golding, *Hansard* (Commons), 21 February 1908, cols 1,225 and 1,228.

from the other social legislation of the 1906–1914 era, which was financed partly from employers' and workers' contribution or by the state. In contrast, the weight of minimum wage legislation was borne directly by the manufacturer concerned. The state provided the civil servants to maintain the negotiating machinery and paid the expenses of appointed members and representatives; but the employer ultimately met the higher wages bill which resulted from higher pay.

Despite the economic hardships which the Act placed upon them, some manufacturers nevertheless welcomed the legislation. The large chain masters of the Black Country were one such group of industrialists. They had actively campaigned to have their industry scheduled as the first trade board experiment. The large chain employers, at least initially, supported the new trade board legislation because they looked to it to bring about greater product and industrial efficiency. However, as soon as they perceived that the higher wages resulting from the legal rates might run counter to their objectives, they sought to wreck the newly constituted board. In the only serious examination of employers' attitudes towards statutory wage regulating machinery, Morris dismisses owners' concerns as merely connected with considerations of social control.[13] Taking the example of the first trade board industry, domestic chainmaking, this chapter argues that employers' motives were a good deal more sophisticated (and ambivalent) than Morris would have us believe; it places the Webbs' theory of the 'good' employer in a local context; and it corrects the inaccurate assumption of writers such as Morris and Roberts that pressure from the organised labour movement was unimportant. Instead, the chapter demonstrates that the chain employers' calculative and conditional support for a minimum wage meant that the pressure of public opinion and of the chain workers themselves were vital elements if the legislation was to succeed.

I

To fully comprehend the role played by the chain manufacturers in the passage of the Trade Boards Act, it is essential first to outline the nature of the chain trade and to delineate the types of employers in the industry at the turn of the twentieth century. The chain trade was largely concentrated in the southern portion of the Black Country, in an area of two to three square miles radiating out from the small community of Cradley Heath. Although other chain manufacturing centres existed, notably Newcastle-Upon-Tyne and Pontypridd, South Wales, their output and workforce were relatively small compared with the Black Country. In 1909 the latter accounted for almost 90 per cent of Britain's chain production and Cradley Heath, as

---

[13]   Morris, *Women Workers*, pp. 155–66. Fitzgerald and the Staples touch on trade boards, but only briefly. The Staples consider that hollowware employers viewed trade boards as 'unfair, unnecessary, unworkable, or perverse, and usually all of these things': *Power, Profits and Patriarchy*, pp. 97–8. Fitzgerald notes how Rowntree was a firm supporter of boards. Yet, Rowntree was considerably embarrassed in 1914 to discover that the wages of his least skilled hands were barely above the minimum set by the sugar confectionery board: Fitzgerald, *Rowntree*, p. 242.

the centre of the world's chain trade, could boast that she held the world monopoly in a vital commodity.[14]

Despite its significance to the British economy, Cradley Heath remained a by-word for sweated labour. A decade after the chainmakers had made their dramatic appearance at the SCSS, Mary Macarthur could still observe:

> The fame of the district has spread far and wide, and no social investigator from distant lands considers his tour of our country complete without a visit to Cradley Heath. There are hundreds of such visitors, and on all of them is left an impression hardly favourable to our fame as the greatest industrial nation of modern times.[15]

The problem of sweating mainly affected the smaller, lighter chains such as cow ties, horse traces, and gate chains fashioned in home or domestic workshops. The outwork sector was again subdivided into two distinct groups: the hand-hammered and the 'tommied' or 'dollied' branches. Hand-hammered chain was mainly produced in outhouses attached to the dwelling place by women and girls, a few infirm males and by boys who had not graduated to more skilled work. The 'tommied' or 'dollied' work was male dominated and was generally carried out in the larger workshops. The 'tommy' or 'dolly' was an iron instrument lowered down on the link after the welding process and was operated in the case of the 'dolly' by hand or in the case of the 'tommy', by a treadle. The manufacture of larger chains and cables as well as the best quality of small chain was entirely factory-based and free from the problem of sweating. The concentration of skilled chainmakers in large work units from the 1890s had facilitated the growth of collective bargaining, strong union organisation and high wages.[16]

---

[14]   *Daily News*, 24 August 1910; *CA*, 20 September 1909. Absolute numbers engaged in chainmaking are not entirely clear. Statistics extracted from the census indicate that in 1911 there were 6,550 Black Country chainmakers, 4,447 males and 2,103 females: P. Jump, 'Historical notes on chains and chainmaking', *Proceedings of the Staffordshire Iron and Steel Institute*, 4 (1928–1929), p. 4. But Tawney's estimate, based on information supplied by trade union officials, is lower at only 4,170 chainmakers, 1,500 male factory workers, 670 male domestic workers, and about 2,000 female domestic workers. See R.H. Tawney, *The Establishment of Minimum Rates in the Chainmaking Industry, Under the Trade Boards Act of 1909* (London, 1914), p. 4. The likelihood is that both census statistics and Tawney's figures somewhat under estimated numbers involved in chainmaking. This is, first, because in the census many described themselves by non-chainmaking occupations, e.g. blacksmith, or as 'chainmakers' wives' when, in fact, they were involved in chainmaking on at least a part-time basis. Second, because the chainmaking industry was by no means fully unionised. Tawney's union-based statistics, as indeed cross-reference to 1911 census statistics themselves suggest probably contained a substantial under counting. But the dominance of the Black Country in the trade is not in dispute.

[15]   M. Macarthur in *Christian Commonwealth*, 7 September 1910.

[16]   Following the SCSS, the factory chainmakers, ashamed of the stigma of being labelled sweated workers, had formed the Chainmakers' and Strikers' Association in 1889: E. Taylor, 'A craft society in the age of general unions', *West Midland Studies,* 5 (1972), pp. 29–30; *Souvenir of the Semi-Jubilee of the Chainmakers' and Strikers' Association* (Stourbridge, 1914), pp. 8–9, 23.

This fragmentation of chain production had led to the growth of three groups of employers in the trade. First, there were the so-called 'good employers', some thirty factory owners who together employed an aggregate of about 1,400 hands on their premises and who paid their factory workers trade union rates based on an agreed list price.[17] These employers were 'good', not necessarily because they were aware of their social obligations or were concerned with considerations other than maximizing profits, but because the factory acts, government regulations, and the strong trade union organisation of the factory chainmakers ensured that they maintained satisfactory standards in their businesses.[18] The owners of such establishments, as the young Beatrice Webb remarked in 1890, were forced to assume, to some extent, the guardianship of their workers.[19]

Second, there were the small factory owners, twelve in all, who together employed in their works about 200 poorly paid hands. Finally, there were around 140 middlemen in the trade. Between them, these three categories of employers engaged the two thousand or more domestic workers in the industry.[20] Middlemen were important in the domestic branch of the trade, supplying the domestic chainmakers with orders to make iron into chain, fuel, cartage of the finished product to the warehouse and, in the larger domestic workshops, frequently tools and accommodation. According to Tawney, the middlemen were 'if not the principals at any rate, the agents in beating down the workers' remuneration'.[21] More graphically, Beatrice Webb described

---

[17] *Hansard* (Commons), 28 April 1909, cols 367–8 (speech by A.G. Hooper). See also, Hamilton, *Mary Macarthur*, p. 86.

[18] After a series of scandals in the 1880s, reputable firms had been obliged to have chain cables and anchors tested, and provided with a certificate guaranteeing a certain level of quality and tensile strength. Customers in the private sector also began to insist that chains utilised for rigging or cranes should be accompanied by a certificate, although this was not a legal requirement. Additionally, Admiralty and local authorities orders could, as a result of the Fair Wages Clause, only be contracted by factory occupiers. See *Souvenir of Semi-Jubilee*, p. 27; Tawney, *Chainmaking Industry*, pp. 4–5.

[19] Potter, 'The Lords and the sweating system', pp. 889–90. It should be noted, however, that even in the factories, work was organised around an internal subcontract system. Large chainmaking necessitated teamwork, consisting of the actual chainsmith plus his 'first hammer' and his 'second hammer'. Up to 1944 and the introduction of Pay as You Earn taxation, a chain firm only engaged the chainsmith himself, and the later was responsible for employing and paying his helpers, whom he could dismiss without prior consultation with the management. These helpers were frequently the chainsmith's sons or kin who served their apprenticeship under his guidance. In the factories, the chainmakers rarely dealt with standardised products, and practically dictated their own routine. They began work when they chose, usually in the early morning at three or four o'clock; they ceased production when it suited them, generally by midday, and they worked on average, no more than a three and a half day week. It was physically impossible to work more hours in view of he heavy nature of the work. Large chainmaking was heavy and exhausting and could only be carried out by the strongest of men. See W.K.V. Gale, 'Hand wrought chains', *Transactions of the Newcomen Society*, 29 (1953–1955), p. 197.

[20] *Hansard* (Commons), 28 April 1909, cols 367–8. See also, Hamilton, *Mary Macarthur*, p. 86.

[21] Tawney, *Chainmaking Industry*, p. 8.

such subcontractors as the maggots that appeared in meat after decay had set in.[22] Essentially, these middlemen provided a means whereby the factory owners, both 'good' and 'bad', could delegate their responsibilities as managers. The middlemen mediated between the factory owner and the outworker, saving the large chain masters the inconvenience of giving out and receiving small quantities of iron and finished chain. Remote from the actual business transaction, the manufacturer was shielded from the public disapprobation which sweating aroused whilst at the same time gaining the advantage of not being directly responsible for this work force. Whilst the 'good' employers belonged to the Chain Manufacturers Association (CMA), the remaining twelve masters and the middlemen were not organised in any trade association. The demand that domestic chainmaking should be scheduled as a trade board industry came largely from the CMA.

Prior to the formation of the CMA in 1907, the large chain masters had shown little interest in social issues. The initial campaign to gain a minimum wage in chainmaking came from the trade unions and the newly formed NASL. Although the 'good' employers collaborated with the Chainmakers' and Strikers' Association over trade matters such as the legal control of chain test certificates, they made little effort to solve the social problems of the workers.[23] In earlier years, when sweated workers had requested the 'good' employers to help them establish voluntary conciliation boards to end low pay, they had boycotted the meeting.[24] Nor were the members of the CMA men of vision in other respects. Narrow minded, and preoccupied with their own parochial trade interests, they viewed belonging to the local chamber of commerce as a waste of money and of no concern to them.[25]

---

[22]   Webb, *My Apprenticeship*, p. 336.

[23]   See, Chainmakers' and Strikers' Association, *Annual Report for the Year Ending June 1897*, University of Birmingham Library; *Souvenir of the Semi-Jubilee*, pp. 9, 25–9.

[24]   *Royal Commission on Labour* (PP 1892, XXXVI, Pt. 1), QQ. 17,049–52.

[25]   See Dudley and District Chamber of Commerce Minute books, esp. entry dated 31 January 1927. Trainor considers that the Black Country's industrial-based elite performed a significant role in promoting social facilities: R. Trainor, *Black Country Élites: The Exercise of Authority in an Industrialized Area, 1830–1914* (Oxford, 1993), esp. p. 375. Whilst this might have applied to large manufacturers like the Kenricks and larger centres of population such as West Bromich, small hamlets such as Cradley Heath lacked such benefactors. On the whole, the well-off residents of Cradley were relatively few and of fairly modest means. The majority of large chain manufacturers had only been established in business for some three decades. Many originated from upwardly mobile craftsmen's families, still retained personal management of their firms, and only employed, on average, about fifty workers on their premises. See *CE, The Black Country and Its Industries, Part 1* (Stourbridge, 1903), pp. 22–5. An exception was the coal, iron, steel, chain and anchor firm of the Hingley family in nearby Netherton. Built up from small beginnings by Noah Hingley (1795–1877), this establishment employed in the region of 3,000 hands by the late nineteenth century. See W.D. Curzon, *The Manufacturing Industries of Worcestershire* (Birmingham, 1883), p. 54. Hingley's son, Benjamin (1830–1905), was considerably active at the local and national level in iron masters' associations. His workers praised the latter for his company paternalism: R. Trainor, 'Sir Benjamin Hingley', in D. Jeremy and C. Shaw (eds), *Dictionary of Business Biography, Volume 3* (London, 1985), pp. 261–7. But it would seem that, as the MP for North Worcestershire (1885–1895) and Mayor of Dudley, he encouraged civic pride in Dudley rather than in his native Cradley

But once the NASL's campaign gained momentum, the CMA, of its own initiative and without union pressure, sought to have a legal minimum wage applied to the trade. The CMA had little difficulty in supporting a movement, which so strongly propounded the case of the 'good' employer. Indeed, the CMA's secretary, George Williams, told visiting Board of Trade officials in 1909 of his association's goodwill towards the Trade Boards Act and its resolve to do everything possible to eradicate sweating in the industry.[26] A.G. Hooper, the local Liberal MP, was also persuaded by the CMA to speak in favour of the Second Reading of the Trade Boards Bill and in support of having domestic chainmaking added to the schedule of the Act.[27] Trade unionists among chainmakers praised the active support which the CMA gave to the anti-sweating movement, while in 1910 Mallon commented that the CMA had 'acted in a thoroughly public spirited way over the matter of the inclusion of their trade ...'.[28]

The CMA was delighted when the chain industry was scheduled as a sweated trade. Indeed, to the amazement of the NASL, which had so actively pressed the matter on the Liberal Government, they claimed that the scheduling of the chain industry was largely due to their efforts.[29] As N.E. Bloomer, a member of the CMA and an employers' representative on the Chain Trade Board (CTB), remarked at a local Conservative Party meeting:

> The influence which Miss Macarthur exerted did not result in the chain trade being included in the Bill when it was framed, on the contrary the chain trade was ignored, so that it would appear Miss Macarthur had no weight on the Government of the day who drew up the Bill. Mr Hooper and Mr Sitch had done their share ... but the finishing stroke which resulted in the chain trade being included [in the Trade Boards Act] ... was due to the Chain Manufacturers' Association, which had acted as a commercial association quite outside politics.[30]

Heath. Additionally, although he was a proponent of company paternalism, he firmly believed in the owner's right to manage. He opposed a statutory eight hours day for miners and viewed the 1897 Workmen's Compensation Bill as communistic. His successor and nephew, George (1850–1918), an alderman for Worcestershire and High Sheriff of the county, chose to move away from the environs of Cradley to a landed estate near to the spa town of Droitwich. He appears to have been completely detached from the Chain Manufacturers' Association (CMA). See *Birmingham Gazette and Express*, 15 January 1908. By 1913, the local press could declare that employers like Noah Hingley had died out: *CA*, 20 September 1913. See also K. Mallin, 'N. Hingley and Sons Limited: Black Country anchor smith and chain cable maker', unpublished Ph.D. thesis, University of Warwick, 1996, chs, 3, 5, 7, 8.

[26]   *Dudley Herald*, 19 June 1909.

[27]   *Hansard* (Commons), 28 April 1909, cols 368–9. See also *CE*, 3 July 1909. Hooper had pleaded the case of 'those poor beings of Cradley Heath, those heathens', so frequently that he had become something of a curiosity in the Commons: *CA*, 23 March 1907.

[28]   *Dudley Herald*, 17 September 1909. See also *CA*, 16 April 1910.

[29]   *Dudley Herald*, 17 September 1910.

[30]   *Ibid.*, 3 July 1909. Noah Bloomer, a Tariff Reformer, subsequently became a staunch anti-trade board supporter. See Dudley and District Chamber of Commerce Minute Books, 21 January 1921.

The reasons for this warm support on the part of the CMA were neither ethical nor humanitarian. Whilst an occasional reference was made to the plight of the sweated, the motives of the CMA were almost entirely economic. There were few Cadburys or Rowntrees amongst them, as the social facilities of Cradley Heath fully testified. For years the large chain masters had dismissed the squalid environment of the chainmakers as a moral problem and had attributed it to lack of work discipline and intemperance.[31] Whilst they lived in the comfortable villadom of Stourbridge or inhabited country houses in Pedmore and Hagley, their workers in Cradley Heath, as the *Daily News* pointed out, had 'no public baths, no free library, no recreation ground ...'.[32] In 1906, the journalist, Bart Kennedy, had found few social amenities: 'The masters of the workers evidently felt that the beginning and the end of their duty was to exact heavy toll from the labour of the men and the labour of the women ... A mortuary and a workhouse are hardly the fullest contribution towards the social welfare of an English town.'[33]

There were two interrelated economic reasons for the CMA's support for a chain trade board. First, they saw the establishment of a minimum wage as a way of imposing greater control over the industry. Second, they believed that sweating led to the production of poor quality chain and ultimately to the loss of customers abroad. Let us deal with these issues in turn.

By the late nineteenth century, the growth of sweating and the increasing number of middlemen in the domestic chain trade sector had reduced the production of small chain to near chaos. The freedom of access into domestic chainmaking caused an oversupply of labour, a 'reserve army' competing for work, which led to barely sufficient piece rates for the workers. Trade unionism amongst the domestic chainmakers was not unknown but was always weak. Despite short bursts of trade union activity, the settlement of wage rates normally operated through individual bargaining with middlemen.[34] Owing to the small amount of capital needed to establish a workshop or warehouse, the numbers of middlemen in the trade expanded out of all proportion to the needs of the industry.[35] Competition between these contractors was so keen that they were often tempted to take orders for chain that could not be profitable unless wages were beaten down.[36]

These middlemen occupied a unique position, standing between the worker and the market price. The wage earner was ignorant of the amount the middlemen received from the manufacturer and was thus obliged to bargain individually and in the dark. Each worker could be separately persuaded to accept low rates by the

---

[31]   Even the paternalistic Benjamin Hingley blamed the victims. Habituated to working irregular hours, he alleged, the domestic chainmakers preferred the 'liberty' of the chain shop since it allowed them to 'play' when they liked. See *Pall Mall Gazette*, 5 September 1888; *CA*, 26 January 1907.

[32]   Cited in *CA*, 15 December 1906. See also, *CA*, 20 September 1913. The steel magnate and philanthropist, Andrew Carnegie provided £5,000 to build a public library in nearby Old Hill. See *CA*, 2 January 1906.

[33]   B. Kennedy, *Wander Pictures* (London, 1906), pp. 123–4.

[34]   SCSS, *Third Report*, QQ. 17,946–59 (evidence of Richard Juggins).

[35]   Tawney, *Chainmaking Industry*, p. 8.

[36]   *Ibid.*

middlemen. Of necessity, the chainmakers, in order to gain work, were obliged to take whatever they were offered and were thus pitted one against the other.[37] This lack of a standard rate for domestic chainmakers caused piece rates to fluctuate wildly from firm to firm and from one period of time to another. Sweated production prevented the manufacturer from reckoning up his costs or from knowing the lowest price that he could pay for labour.[38] From the manufacturer's point of view, there was a constant and real danger of being undercut.

These problems were intensified from the beginning of 1908 when the chain trade was plunged into its worst economic depression for over thirty years. The downswing particularly affected world demand for large chains and cables. This was directly related to the fact that, as ships were increasing in size, fewer cables were required. Moreover, the Admiralty had recently shortened the cables of their ships.[39] In consequence, factory owners were forced to fall back on to the small chain trade. But large factory owners, with their greater overhead costs, found themselves being undersold by the unassociated masters who paid low wages in sweated conditions.[40] The CMA hoped that a trade board would put an end to this situation by legally enforcing a minimum wage below which no worker could be employed.

There was also the second factor of poor quality chain and foreign competition. Low pay resulted in inferior work. The production of sub-standard chain was not only bringing the industry into disrepute but threatened to cause the loss of foreign customers. The sweating process obliged the domestic chainmakers to make such large amounts of chain to earn a bare subsistence that it negated any pride in craftsmanship.[41] Inevitably, the markets were glutted with very defective chains.[42] The results of this imperfect production were pinpointed exactly by A.G. Hooper. On the occasion of the Second Reading of the Trade Boards Bill, he told the House of Commons how the CMA believed that sweating:

… is fatal to the reputation of the trade itself. Only last Saturday I was speaking to the ex-Mayor of Dudley, who gave me a concrete case illustrating this phase of the question. He told me that a few months ago he was in Canada, going about with his eyes open to gain all the information he could industrially, and when in one of the shipping yards he saw a quantity of chain. He referred to the fact that he was then Mayor of Dudley, near Cradley, the home of the chain trade. 'Oh', said the gentleman to whom he was speaking, 'you know Cradley, do you? All I can say is that we shall have no more chain from Cradley, as this last lot we had was such shoddy stuff that it broke like single wire'. The hope and expectations which the good employers have as to the ultimate effect of the Bill is that it will prevent this shoddy manufacture of chain which is being sent abroad to the detriment of the good name of the trade.[43]

---

37 SCSS, *Third Report*, Q. 17,946 (evidence of Richard Juggins).
38 Tawney, *Chainmaking Industry*, pp. 66–71.
39 *CA*, 17 October 1908.
40 *CE*, 27 March 1909, 1 May 1909.
41 *Labour Leader*, 23 September 1910. See also, Tawney, *Chainmaking Industry*, pp. 111–13.
42 *Ibid.*
43 *Hansard* (Commons), 28 April 1909, col. 369.

Allied to this was the fear that overseas competitors had almost perfected the production of small chain by machine. Machine-produced chain had one major disadvantage in that consumers objected to the unsightly weld on each link.[44] Yet as the CMA were fully aware, if the hand-produced version continued to be unreliable then consumer resistance to the machine variety would soon be broken.[45]

The CMA thus thought that the establishment of the CTB would protect them from rapacious undercutting while simultaneously enhancing the quality of chain and redeeming its reputation in the eyes of overseas customers. From their point of view, the scheduling of the chain trade was not an injury or a menace but a relief. Once the industry was scheduled, however, the CMA's attitude towards the CTB underwent a significant transformation. Although the CMA wanted the state to protect its members from the intense competition of the middlemen and the inferior production of chain, they did not welcome the increased wages bill consequent upon the implementation of the minimum wage. Despite the CMA's initially favourable overtures towards the scheduling of their trade, relations between the CMA and the workers' representatives on the Board were strained almost from the outset.

II

The first meeting of the CTB took place on 7 January 1910.[46] The Board comprised fifteen members – three appointed members, six workers' representatives and six employers' representatives. Of the six employers' representatives, the Board of Trade stipulated that five should be factory owners and one a middle person, since they believed that chain manufacturers were present in that strength in the trade.[47] The five factory owners all belonged to the CMA, giving the association a dominant position among the employers on the Board. Once the CTB was established, the CMA turned its attention to the costs to its members of the implementation of the minimum wage. The association was determined that the new rates should not be set so high that profits would be unduly decreased or business lost. The trade unionists commented ruefully on this *volte-face* on the part of the employers. Thomas Sitch, secretary to the factory chainmakers' trade union and a life-long believer in conciliation and arbitration with the chain masters, told his union in July 1910 that he was bitterly disappointed with the progress of the Board. He added: 'after six months' experience on this Board, I have come to the conclusion, very reluctantly, that we were living in a fool's paradise when we entertained a thought that our employers were anxious to see the trade free from the evils of sweating.'[48]

---

[44] NA, LAB 2/1/TB119/8/1925.

[45] Noah Hingley and Sons had already broken ranks with other chain manufacturers and installed expensive cable and chainmaking machinery. See *CE*, 26 June 1909; *CA*, 3 July 1909.

[46] CTB Minutes, 1910–1916, NA, LAB 35/74.

[47] *Ibid.*

[48] Chainmakers' and Strikers' Association, *Annual Report for the Year Ending June 1910*, p. 8. Sitch was also disappointed when the CMA supported the repeal of the Trade Disputes Act: *Tipton Herald*, 4 November 1911.

Mary Macarthur, who had also been elected as a workers' representative to the CTB, similarly testified to the unyielding manner adopted by the CMA once the Board became operational. Her patience was sorely tried when meeting after meeting broke up with no agreement on a minimum wage, the employers consistently rejecting the workers' demands as excessive. After one such difficult conference, when it seemed likely that no rate would be fixed at all, she collapsed from physical and mental exhaustion. As her biographer pointed out: 'Something like hatred moved in her for the people who, comfortable themselves, had no imagination to see the sufferings they were perpetuating.'[49] The employers managed to delay the settlement of a minimum rate for the women until the fifth meeting of the Board in March 1910, three months after its formation.[50] Even then, it was only pressure from the appointed members that induced the employers to accept a settlement of 11s 3d a week for women workers or 2½d an hour for a fifty-four hour week.[51] Although this sum increased existing rates by almost 100 per cent, it was far from generous and the workers' representatives on the Board clearly found the amount inadequate. They agreed to accept it simply because the employers flatly refused to grant more and threatened to mechanise the trade. As the NFWW remarked:

> The workers' representatives had to consider whether, if they held out for too large an amount they would be thereby ensuring revolutionary changes in the trade to the displacement of many of the women whom machines would supplant… It weighed with them also that whereas they could get a rate of 2½d per hour fixed by general consent, any increase beyond that would be bitterly contested by the employers.[52]

The clearest indication of the attitude of the CMA members was the way in which they attempted to abuse Section 5 of the Trade Boards Act. Angered by what they considered to be a punitively high minimum wage forced upon them by the appointed members, the CMA resorted to more desperate counter-measures by utilising this loophole in the Act. It is necessary to examine this point in some detail because it clearly indicates that the employers, had they been given the chance, would have been willing effectively to destroy the Board.

III

Although the new rates for women chainmakers had been published on 17 May 1910, the Trade Boards Act laid down that an interval of three months had to elapse before the new rates came into force. The first three months came to an end on 17 August

---

[49]   When, at the end of one long and difficulty meeting, a chain employer offered to drive Macarthur to the station, she refused. Instead, she ran all the way, caught the train 'by the skin of her teeth' and collapsed sobbing in the compartment: Hamilton, *Mary Macarthur*, p. 84.

[50]   CTB Minutes, 1910–1916.

[51]   *Ibid*. The employers wanted a minimum rate of 10s a week or 2¼d an hour. They withdrew in protest when the workers' representatives and the appointed members agreed 2½d per hour.

[52]   Untitled typed sheets, pp. 3–4. Tuckwell Papers (TP), folder 405a, TUC Library Collections, London Metropolitan University.

1910 and final notice was given. However, section 5 of the Act permitted workers to contract out of the new rates for a further six months. As Arthur Henderson told a meeting of the women chainmakers, there was little justification for fixing such a period. In his opinion it merely reflected the fight which the working class still had to wage against vested interests.[53] The CMA seized the opportunity. Apparently acting in concert with the unassociated masters and middlemen, the CMA prepared forms of agreement for contracting out and endeavoured to make the women sign them.[54] Few of the women could read or write: they all found legal forms confusing and the majority of them signed.[55] Their employers informed those who refused to comply either that there was no work or that they could not afford to pay the new rates.[56] At the same time, the employers began to stockpile chains at the old price. Their intention was to utilise these stocks, when the new rates became legally operative, to make the majority of the women unemployed and the Act unworkable.[57]

The employers were confident that their plan would be a huge success, for, unlike many trades, the stock did not deteriorate, was easily warehoused and did not, like millinery, for example, become unfashionable.[58] And as the masters were well aware, no more than half of the women belonged to a trade society.[59] They thus calculated on receiving little opposition from the women. On 23 August, when the women's union, the NFWW, drafted another agreement stipulating the women's desire to be paid the minimum rates immediately, the employers locked them out. The union retaliated by calling out on strike those women who were working for less than the new rate.[60] By the evening of 1 September, the number of women on strike amounted to nearly 800, barely half of whom belonged to the union.[61] On 2 September, only ten days after

---

[53]   *CE*, 8 October 1910.

[54]   *CA*, 27 August 1910. Hamilton insisted that only the 'bad' employers produced contracting out forms and that the 'good' employers were not involved: *Mary Macarthur*, pp. 85–6. This story was a smoke screen put up by the CMA to defend itself. One member of the CMA, with a seat on the CTB was the 'victim' of 120 striking women. (See *Daily News*, 1 September 1910). As one 'Disgusted Cradley Heathen' wrote, 'the Chain Manufacturers' Association refuses to pay them [the chainmakers] the proper prices in accordance with the new Trade Boards Wages Bill ....' (Letter to *CA*, 27 August 1910). Of the probationary period, Churchill had stated: 'It is upon the probationary period that we rely to rally to the trade board the best employers in the trade. In most instances the best employers ... are paying wages equal to the probable minimum which the trade board will establish.' *Hansard* (Commons), 28 April 1909, cols 391–2.

[55]   Of the women's illiteracy, the *Belfast Evening Telegraph* (25 August 1906), declared: 'This after forty years of elementary education'.

[56]   *CE*, 27 August 1910.

[57]   *CA*, 27 August 1910. See also, *Northampton Echo*, 23 August 1910.

[58]   *Ibid.*

[59]   TUC, Parliamentary Committee, *Cradley Heath Women Workers: Appeal for Financial Support* (19 September 1910), TP, folder 301.

[60]   Although, as Macarthur pointed out, since the women worked largely at home, the dispute was not a lockout or strike in the technical sense: *CA*, 27 August 1910.

[61]   *Leicester Mercury*, 1 September 1910. The first strike payment was disbursed on Saturday, 27 August. For the convenience of mothers, those with babies were paid first, until it was realised that babies were being borrowed for the occasion. The Conservative *CE, 3*

the start of the dispute, the attitude of the CMA underwent a serious change. Under the auspices of the CTB, the CMA agreed to meet with the women's representatives to negotiate a possible solution.[62] The new tactics of the CMA were motivated by four considerations. First, they had not foreseen the enormous support which the women received from all classes of the public. Second, they had not reckoned with the resolve of the women themselves to fight for the new rates. Third, the CMA was disturbed by the boycott being imposed on their chains. Finally, they had begun to see the strike as an opportunity of removing the middlemen from the trade.

The huge popular support for the chainmakers was stimulated to a great extent by Mary Macarthur, who waged a national publicity campaign to expose the chain masters as perpetuators of sweated labour. She arranged interviews with the women, wrote letters to trade unions and leading newspapers throughout the country, addressed meetings, and even used the power of the music hall and cinema to illustrate to London audiences the plight of the domestic chainmaker.[63] Her campaign caught the imagination of all social classes. As her biographer noted: 'She compelled the world to look at Cradley Heath as she saw it: she brought in countesses and ecclesiastics, charwomen and engine cleaners to share the struggle and suffering of the helpless chainmakers ....'[64]

As well as drawing the whole of the West Midland's Conservative press to the side of the women, Macarthur attracted the interest of major national newspapers.[65] *The Times*, while quick to point out that it did not often positively countenance a strike, made an exception in the case of the women chainmakers for their 'ill clad, destitute appearance evoked universal sympathy'.[66] One leading, local Conservative newspaper observed:

> From the commencement of the dispute, the women had the advantage of whole-hearted support from every class ... The knowledge that many of them worked under the most depressing conditions for a mere pittance of 5s. and 6s. a week touched deeply the human interest of the country. There is no doubt that the women's campaign was handled with consummate skill, and the appeal on behalf of 'women chainmakers fighting for 2½d. per hour' was irresistible ...[67]

Reynolds's News immortalised the women as England's white slaves while other newspapers declared that the conditions of the women were worse than those of the Chinese compounds in South Africa, the exposé of which had contributed to Britain's involvement in the Boer War.[68] Arthur Henderson, at a meeting held in the

---

September 1910, observed: 'It is significant and pitiable that many of the women are actually better off than when they were working, for those who are members of the [union] ... receive 5s. a week during the lockout ....'

[62]   *CA*, 3 September 1910.

[63]   *Birmingham Mail*, 2 September 1910.

[64]   Hamilton, *Mary Macarthur*, p. 95.

[65]   See, for example, comments in the *Lancashire Post*, 30 August 1910; *Primitive Methodist Leader*, 1 September 1910; *Daily News*, 30 August 1910.

[66]   *The Times*, 1 September 1910.

[67]   *CE*, 1 October 1910.

[68]   *Reynolds's Newspaper*, 4 September 1910.

Temperance Hall, Sheffield, voiced a desire to see all of the pulpits of the country hung with chains made by sweated labour. Short of this, he expressed a wish that all chain masters might be made to see their own wives put to chainmaking.[69] The greatest propaganda was reserved for the older women chainmakers, twelve of whom were over seventy and who went soliciting funds carrying placards headed: 'England's disgrace. Help the women chainmakers who are fighting for 2½d per hour.'[70] The *Birmingham Despatch* commented of one of the women, Mrs Patience Round, aged seventy-nine:

> It is now sixty-nine years since Mrs Round ... started on her long career of chainmaking. Since that day her world has been the forge in her backyard. The great happenings in the world outside have never pierced the smoke-begrimed walls of her home, where day after day and year after year she has ceaselessly beaten the glowing iron into shape and worked the bellows until her figure has become bent and her hands indented with the marks of the chains she has forged.[71]

The grievances of the women chainmakers received such notoriety that foreign social investigators flocked to this industrial plague spot. The German researcher, Herr Kummer, remarked of Cradley Heath: 'It is hell.'[72] An Australian conservative, Mr. Bricknell, was amazed to find that the chainmakers were living in accommodation which, in his own country, people 'dare not house our cattle in'.[73] The Black American philanthropist, Booker T. Washington, was depicted in a cartoon headed, 'The bond and the free', as sympathising with the women because: 'I was once a slave my self.'[74] The International Association for Labour Legislation even despatched two American investigators to Cradley Heath to examine the conditions under which the women worked.[75] When Will Anderson, Chairman of the ILP, attended an international conference in Copenhagen, he found the women chainmakers the centre of conversation.[76]

Fellow businessmen criticised the actions of the chain masters. Edward Cadbury commented that, in the Birmingham area, a minimum living income for a woman was 14s a week. In his business, he managed three thousand women and considered it unjust to employ females under twenty years of age at less than 16s a week. Yet the women chainmakers were asking only for a modest 11s in return for an exhausting week's labour. He epitomised the paternalistic businessmen's attitude to the dispute when he pointed out that it was not an ordinary strike. The women were merely attempting by their stand to implement an Act of Parliament. There was nothing revolutionary or syndicalist in this. Whilst he believed strikes were an 'antiquated way of settling a dispute', he saw the strike of the women as 'an important one, as

---

[69] *Sheffield Independent*, 14 September 1910.

[70] *Express and Star* (Wolverhampton), 3 September 1910.

[71] *Birmingham Evening Despatch*, 1 September 1910.

[72] *CE*, 1 October 1910.

[73] *Ibid.*

[74] *Reynolds's Newspaper*, 4 September 1910.

[75] *CA*, 3 September 1910.

[76] *CE*, 1 October 1910.

they were in the forefront for the movement of carrying out a minimum wage fixed by the State.'[77] Messrs Opell and Owen of Liverpool, one of the largest buyers of chain in the England, held that the dispute was largely unnecessary. As experienced shippers to the cheapest buying markets, they testified that Cradley Heath, as yet, suffered very little from foreign competition and that the chain employers could afford to pay the new rates: 'If all the manufacturers in Staffordshire pay fair wages to their workers the trade will continue without diminution. We have a conviction that higher prices to cover advanced wages are establishable without creating foreign competition in the markets now supplied ....'[78]

The CMA, which comprised many church and chapelgoers as well as local dignitaries, did not relish the title of 'sweater' and sought to defend itself by stating that the reports of the women's plight were grossly exaggerated.[79] When impartial investigators concluded that this was not so, the CMA then declared that its hands were tied by the unassociated masters and middlemen.[80] The *County Advertiser* observed:

> The plea of the Employers' Association that they are unable to pledge themselves to the advance because they would be victimised by unassociated rivals is scorned by the operatives. Though there are about 150 master men, big and little, they are subject to the forty or so members of the association, the man of capital being in the relation of employers to many of the smaller men ... It is contended by the operatives that it is a hollow sham to pretend that the Employers' Association could not carry the whole district with them if they officially decided that the minimum rate should be conceded.[81]

Members of the CMA, as the women's leaders pointed out, had not refrained from raising the price of their chains to the consumer.[82]

As well as being surprised by the intensity of public support for the women, the CMA was also astounded by the defiance of the women themselves. Once roused, the women claimed that they would rather drop dead than sign contracting-out forms, that starvation was preferable to a living death.[83] The *County Advertiser* remarked:

> The women's blood is up, and they mean to have their emancipation day now ... they made a fresh vow to have the eleven shillings and three pence which the Trade Board has laid down as the minimum for a week's work, or to throw down their hammers. It is

---

[77]   *CA*, 10 September 1910. Cadbury had previously researched the 'sallow-faced, flat-chested and round-shouldered women' chainmakers in Cadbury and Shann, *Sweating*, pp. 38–40.

[78]   *CA*, 3 September 1910.

[79]   *Ibid*. George Williams, secretary to the CMA, stated that: 'It has been reported that the people had stewed tea and goat's milk, whilst in many cases they had none at all.' Macarthur replied that: 'There might be people in the district who were perfectly prepared to believe that the women chainmakers were working for pleasure ... All that she could reply was, if those people really believed that, they must be blind and deaf and many other things as well.' (*CE*, 1 October 1910).

[80]   *Birmingham Mail*, 1 September 1910; *CA*, 27 August 1910.

[81]   *CA*, 27 August 1910.

[82]   *Ibid*.

[83]   *Ibid*.

inconceivable that the employers can hold out against the demand ... The chain workers are at last learning the secret of united action.[84]

The women organised marches headed by the Cradley Heath brass band, attended torch-lit meetings which crowded the narrow streets of the town and shouted out their determination not to give in.[85] Strike songs satirising their masters and sung to the tunes of popular favourites such as *Every nice girl loves a sailor* and *Men of Harlech*, became a regular feature of the meetings.[86] On such demonstrations, the older women travelled in a wagonette at the back and booing invariably ensued when the work yards of offending masters were passed.[87] On several of the marches the women wore chains around their necks and danced to the band music to illustrate their contempt for their employers.[88]

Some of the women went hop picking to supplement the strike funds whilst others collected donations outside football grounds and places of recreation in the Midlands.[89] One deputation of the women chainmakers attended the annual Trades Union Congress (TUC) at Sheffield. The *Daily News* graphically described the arrival of the women:

> On the flower-decked platform appear three worn and pale-faced women clad in black, and holding forth a chain ... One of them spoke ... but though she scarcely uttered twenty words, the rememberance of her terrible misery gave an eloquent ring to her pleading voice. For making this yard of chain, said she, we get a penny.[90]

As a result, the Congress pledged to the women chainmakers the moral and financial support of the organised labour movement. Similarly, Thomas Sitch warned the employers that they could rest assured that the united strength of the women and the TUC was against them:

> The employers thought they would be able to deal with their employees the same as a few years ago, when there was no organisation amongst the females in the chain trade ... But they had not counted the cost properly this time, because they had an organised body of women to tackle. Further, the women had the undivided support of one of the strongest organizations in the world ... They were determined to win the struggle, let it cost what it might.[91]

Pressure on the CMA was also heightened by the threat to boycott their product. The government, in accordance with Section 7, Subsection 1 (c) of the Trade Boards

---

[84]   *Ibid.*

[85]   *Ibid.* See also *Daily News*, 25 August 1910, and *Birmingham Weekly Post*, 27 August 1910.

[86]   *CA*, 27 August 1910.

[87]   *Ibid.*

[88]   The wearing of chains inevitably led some newspapers to comment that the women were breaking free of their fetters: *The Times*, 1 September 1910.

[89]   *Daily News*, 7 September 1910; *CE*, 17 September 1910.

[90]   Cited in *CE*, 17 September 1910.

[91]   *CA*, 27 August 1910.

Act, refused to tender contracts with those firms not paying the minimum rates. This was a strong bargaining weapon, for chains entered into a large group of articles used only by central and local authorities. Since government contract work was the province of the larger factory owners, they stood to lose most through such a boycott.[92] In addition, one of the largest chain-buying firms in the private sector adopted a similar policy.[93]

Finally, the CMA was well aware of the fact that, with the impending implementation of the minimum rates, it would be cheaper to dispense with the middlemen and to deal directly with the chainmakers themselves. Some employers were now considering erecting additional factories on land near to their present works and having all the workpeople under their immediate control.[94] As George Williams remarked of the middlemen to the *Birmingham Despatch*, 'the possibility was that they [the middlemen] would be cut out', enabling the CMA to gain almost complete control over chain production in the future.[95]

However, at the meeting held on 2 September, despite the economic and moral pressure outlined above, the CMA did not submit unconditionally. It agreed to pay the minimum rates. But it also demanded that the NFWW undertake to support financially all the women who refused to work for less than the rates for the duration of the strike.[96] Essentially, the CMA was asking the NFWW to protect it against the non-associated masters and middlemen. The fourth annual report of the NFWW later described this pact as 'perhaps unique in the annals of Trade Unionism'.[97] The organ of the SDF, *Justice*, was more candid. The CMA, it declared, was urging the workers to strike in order to bring all the masters under one rule. The agreement between the CMA and the NFWW, it stated:

> Is merely an effort of the bigger firms to crush the smaller ones under. They [the CMA] know perfectly well that any alteration in the wages scale would considerably embarrass the smaller firms. Dog eat dog, big capitalist kill small capitalist is the game under this cut-throat system of competition.[98]

Mary Macarthur did not submit to the terms of the CMA's demands without a great deal of consideration. As she told a meeting of the women, 'what the association ought to have done was to have taken the lead at the very beginning, and said "We advise the paying of the price". That however they did not do.'[99] There was also the problem of financing such an extension of the strike. As Charles Sitch, the local NFWW organiser, pointed out, to meet the guarantees demanded by the CMA and to

---

[92] *Ibid.* Government contracts accounted for one third of the factory owners' trade.

[93] *Daily News*, 5 September 1910.

[94] *Midland Evening News*, 12 September 1910.

[95] *Birmingham Evening Despatch*, 10 September 1910; *CA*, 10 September 1910.

[96] *CA*, 10 September 1910. For a list of firms who signed the 'white list' including Noah Hingley and Sons, see *CE*, 24 September 1910.

[97] NFWW, *Fourth Annual Report* (1911), p. 7.

[98] *Justice*, 3 September 1910.

[99] The CMA, despite requests from Macarthur, refrained from contributing to the strike fund: *CE*, 3 September 1910; *CA*, 3 September 1910.

support the non-unionists would require at least £1,000. He counted that about £60 would be needed weekly and, at that time, they had only £300.[100] The subsequent decision of the NFWW to accept the CMA's offer was finally determined by the generosity of the public in subscribing to the women's fund.

Subscriptions in support of the women poured in. By the second week of the strike, grants had been received from over two hundred trade societies in various parts of the country. Collections were made on the women's behalf outside churches, chapels and factories. Gifts were also made in kind, including a collection of old-fashioned jewellery, a vanload of bread produced under the eight-hours system and two hams for a tea for the women.[101] 'High Society', celebrated novelists such as John Galsworthy and members of prominent business families including Lady Mond and the Cadburys also appended their names to the subscription lists.[102]

While the generosity of the public encouraged the women's leaders to accept the CMA's offer, the actions of the middlemen made it absolutely necessary to co-operate with the associated masters. By 7 September reports were received that the middlemen, although ostensibly paying the minimum rates, had been extorting some of the money back.[103] Some women, hitherto the makers of good quality chain, complained that under the new rates the middlemen were compelling them to work on common export chain. They were, therefore, earning very little more than under the old rates while less skilled workers were being forced to 'play'. It had also become a common device of the middlemen to raise by 50 per cent the price of hiring a chain block and tools.[104]

The acceptance of the CMA's terms meant that the middlemen who were resorting to such tactics would be forced out in the open. If their names were not appended to the 'white list' of those employers paying the minimum, they would be dubbed 'sweaters'. If they signed the 'white list' but did not pay the new rates, they were liable to prosecution. From the middlemen's point of view there was only one course of action. They organised themselves and demanded for their services a percentage from the manufacturer above the rate fixed by the board. This, they declared, was a fair reward for the useful function they served in the trade.[105]

The CMA reluctantly conceded that its members should pay the middlemen a margin above the legal minimum.[106] On 19 October, Mary Macarthur announced to the women that 200 had signed the 'white list'. Twelve employers, she explained, had not yet signed but the strike need not be prolonged on their account. Such offenders, she added, could now be dealt with on an individual basis. Officially, the women's

---

[100] *CA*, 3 September 1910. In addition to Macarthur and C.H. Sitch, the leaders of the dispute were Julia Varley, Charles Homer and Helen Stocks: *CE*, 10 September 1910.

[101] *Express and Star* (Wolverhampton), 14 September 1910; *Blackburn Telegraph*, 9 September 1910; *Manchester Evening News*, 8 September 1910; *CE*, 17 September 1910.

[102] For list of contributors to the Cradley Heath fund, see the September issues of the *Daily News*.

[103] *Ibid.*, 7 September 1910.

[104] The cost of hiring a block was normally 3d per week, and for tools and a block, 6d per week: *CE*, 17 September 1910.

[105] *CA*, 24 September 1910.

[106] *CE*, 24 September 1910.

strike was terminated on 22 October 1910.[107] It had lasted eight weeks and the speedy settlement of the dispute had created an excess of funds. Of the £4,156 raised, there was a surplus of £2,730. The women's leaders divided one third of this sum between the WTUL, the NFWW and the NASL. But the bulk of the proceeds were set aside for the building of a workers' institute for the women. The institute, it was hoped, would form a centre of organisation for all the sweated workers in the district and would furnish the means by which to administer a contributory unemployment fund. The intention was to safeguard the older and less efficient workers, those most prone to redundancy consequent upon the establishment of the legal minimum wage.[108]

IV

According to the local press, the women's triumph was 'the first decisive victory in a campaign to abolish poverty by securing for laborious toil a just and reasonable reward'.[109] But the successful settlement of the women's dispute did not entirely end dissension over the chainmakers' legal minimum. The settlement of 1910 only encompassed the hand-hammered section of the industry, mainly employing females. The rates of the men engaged in making dollied and tommied chain were not included in the provisions drawn up for the women. Rates for the former were not established until December 1910 and the three months' waiting period did not elapse until 6 February 1911. Once again, the chain employers, supported by the CMA, approached the male chainmakers with a view to contracting out of the new rates until the six months' waiting period had terminated.[110] When the men refused, the employers locked them out.

George Williams, who spoke on behalf of the CMA, acknowledged that the women had been sweated but denied that the men were the victims of low pay.[111] The men retaliated by declaring a strike on 18 January 1911.[112] Some 330 workers and between 60 and 100 firms were directly affected by their actions.[113] Since the women's strike, some of the dollied and tommied chainmakers had been contributing to a strike fund but, as the time had been so short, they had accumulated only a small amount of money.[114] As with the women chainmakers, appeals were made to the public. At the same time, Thomas Sitch threatened that, if the outworkers' dispute was not immediately settled, he would withdraw the labour of the factory men.[115] This latter threat finally persuaded the CMA to negotiate with the union, twenty-five

---

[107] *Ibid.*, Strikes and Lockouts in 1910, NA, LAB 34/28.
[108] *CA*, 15 April 1911, 29 April 1911. The Countess of Dudley opened the institute in 1912: *Express and Star* (Wolverhampton), 13 August 1912.
[109] *CA*, 22 October 1910.
[110] *CA*, 28 January 1911.
[111] *CE*, 1 January 1911.
[112] Strikes and Lockouts in 1911, NA, LAB34/29.
[113] *Ibid.*
[114] *CA*, 28 January 1911.
[115] *CA*, 11 February 1911.

days after the start of the strike. However, as with the women's dispute, the CMA did not surrender unconditionally.

Representatives of the CMA demanded that, before they recommended their members to sign the 'white list', and prior to bringing pressure to bear on the unassociated masters, at least 75 per cent of the middlemen's names were to be recorded on the list.[116] By 25 February, only eight firms had refused to sign the 'white list' and the number of men involved in the strike had been reduced to 150. Those firms not complying with the request to pay the new rates were now informed by the union that that their female workers would also be called out to support the men.[117] This additional pressure brought the few refractory employers into line and on 3 March 1911 the strike was officially terminated.[118] It had lasted six weeks and two days, and had cost over £500 to support the striking men.[119] Only £40 of this sum had come from the men's own fund; the remainder had been amassed largely from trade union donations, including aid from the women's account.[120]

V

Morris represents trade boards as a product of large employers' desire for social control. She maintains that the legislation was not a concession won by the working class, for 'the organised labour movement did not play a decisive part in the campaign ....'[121] She contends that the over-riding motive of large manufacturers 'was to preserve the existing social order by attempting to eliminate the cancerous phenomenon of unorganised, inefficient and poorly paid workers struggling for survival'.[122] Echoing the Webbs, she concludes:

> The reasoning which won the day for Wages Boards may be summarised thus – fierce competition amongst employers and workers in certain trades dragged down wages to a level at which the health of the worker, and in a wider sense, the health of society, was threatened. In these trades there were 'good employers' who wished to pay adequate wages but were unable because of competition from less sociably responsible employers. The condition of the workers and the fact that most of them were women, prevented trade union organisation from raising wages. It was therefore necessary for the State to step in ... The motivation was a concern with social control ....[123]

---

[116]   *CA*, 25 February 1911.

[117]   *Ibid.*

[118]   Strikes and Lockouts in 1911.

[119]   *CA*, 25 February 1911.

[120]   *CA*, 4 February 1911.

[121]   Morris, *Women Workers*, p. 192. Roberts, Rickard and Harrison also share her opinions: Roberts, *The Trades Union Congress*, pp. 216–17; Rickard, 'The anti-sweating movement', pp. 587–8; B. Harrison, *Not Only the 'Dangerous Trades': Women's Work and Health in Britain, 1880–1914* (London, 1996), p. 158.

[122]   Morris, *Women Workers*, p. 212.

[123]   *Ibid.*, pp. 211–12. For the considerable problems associated with social control theories, see Hay, 'Employers' attitudes to social policy ', pp. 107–25. Hart considers that 'the motivation of social control ... is an undiscriminating theory': *Bound by Our Constitution*, p.

Yet the successful application of the Trade Boards Act to its first industry, chainmaking, had hinged not upon the altruism or enlightened self-interest of the employers but on the insistence of the public and the chainmakers themselves that the Act should be properly implemented. The success of the strikes meant that the principle of trade boards had been vindicated. The mono-causal argument that social reforms like the Trade Boards Act arose simply out of employer pressure is not tenable. Indeed, the actions of the CMA demonstrated the fragility of the Webbs' concept of the 'responsible' employer. Although superficially coherent and uncomplicated, it was riddled with flaws. It neglected entirely change over time and the pragmatic approach adopted by even the most sophisticated of large employers. The Webbs never examined in any detail the internal processes of management in tactical terms, such as the use of internal subcontract. In essence, the Webbs' thesis presumed a certain logic and stability which within the dynamic, competitive capitalist order simply did not exist. As Tomlinson notes for a later period, we need to recognise that enterprises possess diverse practices, policies and actors.[124] Finally, and most importantly, the Webbs' theory of the responsible employer was vague and imprecise. There are considerable problems with defining 'goodness'. As one early welfare worker shrewdly noted:

> In raising the standard of industrial conditions, the influence of the good employer is undoubtedly of great importance. But to determine in any individual case whether an employer may justly be deemed 'good' is a matter of considerable difficulty.[125]

199, n. 67. However Hart, like Roberts and Harrison, mistakenly attributes the narrowness of trade boards to male trade union indifference.

[124] J. Tomlinson, *The Unequal Struggle: British Socialism and the Capitalist Enterprise* (London, 1982), pp. 21–2, 34–5, 98.

[125] E.D. Proud, *Welfare Work: Employers' Experiments for Improving Working Conditions in Factories* (London, 1916), p. 297.

Chapter 6

R.H. Tawney and the Minimum Wage

Theories in support of the 1909 Trade Boards Act had revolved around the principles that sweating was both unethical and uneconomic. NASL supporters as disparate as Arthur Henderson and Viscount Milner had viewed sweating as a national disgrace, an evil that required a drastic legislative solution. In reality, the 1909 Act was manifestly limited and defective. It was limited to four trades, covered only a quarter of a million workers and failed to make an impact on income redistribution. Prior to Churchill's arrival at the Board of Trade, civil servants – with the exception of Askwith – had been unreceptive to trade boards. Even then, Askwith, despite reassurances to the WTUL that the Trade Boards Act would be sympathetically administered, argued against drastic interference by the state in the wages bargain.[1] As he remarked of the Trade Boards Act to Dilke: 'This is a very delicate plant. It appears to offend the canons of many political economists. If it is to be allowed to live, its roots should get firm hold of the soil before many experiments are made.'[2] Board of Trade officials, while wishing to alleviate the social deprivation of low pay, did not want radically to alter the structure of British industry. The 1909 Act, as the trade union organiser Joseph Hallsworth pointed out, was 'marked with caution, and applied to a very limited extent of the whole field of underpaid labour'.[3]

Nevertheless, in view of the trepidation with which the Trade Boards Act was finally placed on the statute book, it was perhaps inevitable that the benefits of the first boards would be eulogised by their supporters. One of the major popularisers of the experiment was Tawney. His interest in anti-sweating legislation had begun in the early years of the twentieth century, when he worked as a volunteer at Toynbee Hall, and in 1906, when he had played a formative role in the establishment of the NASL.[4] In 1912 he was appointed to the directorship of the Ratan Tata Foundation to promote the study and methods of relieving poverty. He ensured that trade

---

[1]   *WTUR*, October 1909, p. 3. Askwith had written to A.G. Hooper pledging that additional trades would not be added without a provisional order: Dudley and District Chamber of Commerce Minute Books, 28 September 1909.

[2]   G. Askwith, *Industrial Problems and Disputes* (London, 1920), p. 293.

[3]   J. Hallsworth, *The Legal Minimum Wage* (London, 1925), p. 8.

[4]   Tawney was a resident of Toynbee Hall between 1903 and 1906, most of 1908 and the spring of 1913. During this time, he worked in close association with influential figures in the anti-sweating movement, in particular, Clement Attlee and Mallon. Mallon later became (1919–1954) the warden of Toynbee Hall. See J. Mallon's introduction to J.A.R. Pimlott, *Toynbee Hall: Fifty Years of Social Progress* (London, 1935), pp. ix–xv; R. Terrill, *R.H. Tawney and His Times: Socialism as Fellowship* (London, 1974), p. 32; S. Meacham, *Toynbee Hall and Social Reform, 1880–1914* (London, 1987), pp. 157–61; A. Briggs and A. Macartney, *Toynbee Hall: The First Hundred Years* (London, 1984), pp. 138–9.

boards were prominent among the topics under investigation. He personally wrote two monographs in the Ratan Tata social research series concerning the chain and tailoring boards, and subsequently sat as an independent member on the Chain Trade Board.[5] Tawney considered his anti-sweating activities to be one of the finest achievements of his career and sincerely believed that the enactment of the 1909 legislation represented a decisive moment in twentieth-century social reform. As he remarked in 1927 at an international conference on low pay, the Act signified: 'One of the most remarkable changes in economic opinion which has taken place in the last hundred years'. He added:

> the historian of the future, who points to the Ten Hours Act of 1847 as a watershed in the social history of the first half of the nineteenth century, will find in the second a not less critical turning-point in the rise of the forces which ultimately produced the Trade Boards Act of 1909. The weight of ignorance and prejudice, as well as reasoned opposition, to be overcome was enormous .... [6]

So important did Tawney believe the 1909 legislation to be that he commented further: 'No one can regard himself as competent to discuss operations of social policy until he has mastered its main lessons.'[7]

Tawney vehemently defended the boards when they faced severe opposition during the inter-war years. Referring to the Cave Committee, established to enquire into the working and effects of trade boards, he pronounced its report 'a landmark in the history of British social policy ...'. The Conservative government, he declared, had not included on the committee any person who had practical experience of trade boards and no-one with an initial bias in their favour. But the committee, despite its prejudices, had been forced to vindicate the boards and to proclaim them a success. Having survived the storms of the 1920s, trade boards, Tawney predicted, could now 'weather anything' and their future was assured. Indeed, he prophesied: 'What will be remembered ten years hence ... will be, not the amendments which this latest committee has proposed, but the general endorsement of the system.'[8]

---

[5]   The Ratan Tata Foundation was established at the LSE between 1912 and 1922 and was funded by the son of a wealthy Bombay iron and steel magnate. Tawney's two monographs were: *Chainmaking Industry* and *Tailoring Industry*. He also wrote the introductions to: Bulkley, *Boxmaking Industry*, and V. de Vesselitsky, *The Homeworker and Her Outlook* (London, 1916). See also J. Harris, 'The Webbs, the Charity Organisation Society and the Ratan Tata Foundation: social policy from the perspective of 1912', in M. Bulmer, J. Lewis and D. Piachaud (eds), *The Goals of Social Policy* (London, 1989).

[6]   Tawney, 'Fixing minimum wages', p. 19. See also, R.H. Tawney, *The British Labor Movement* (New York, 1968; first published 1925), pp. 53–4. As late as the 1950s, Tawney, in a notable review, chided E.H. Phelps Brown for underestimating the determined resistance faced by trade boards. See R.H. Tawney, review of E.H. Phelps Brown, *Economic Growth and Human Welfare*, Delhi, 1953, in *Economica*, 22 (1955), p. 78.

[7]   R.H. Tawney, review of E.M. Burns, *Wages and the State: A Comparative Study*, London, 1926, in *Economica*, 7 (1927), p. 102.

[8]   R.H. Tawney, 'The minimum wage in Great Britain', *New Republic*, 28 June 1922, pp. 125, 127.

Despite the important role which trade boards played in Tawney's life, the reasons for his unstinting support of these bodies remains undocumented. Few today know that two of Tawney's earliest works, written during the formative period of his career, were upon the chain and tailoring boards. Ross Terrill, for example, is perhaps too dismissive of Tawney's outrage against sweating.[9] Other scholarly work by Jay Winter and, more recently, by Anthony Wright, Norman Dennis and A.H. Halsey, only briefly mentions Tawney's trade board interests.[10] Similarly, John Atherton, Hugh Clegg, David Reisman and Schmiechen quickly gloss over Tawney's trade board initiatives. In doing so, these writers unwittingly accept his very favourable view of the operation of this particular piece of anti-sweating legislation.[11] Atherton goes so far as to comment of Tawney's chainmaking book that: 'The impact of industrial poverty, and the effects of its removal, has rarely been more sensitively described.'[12] Yet, as we shall see, Tawney, together with his close friend Mallon, often exaggerated the boards' significance in order to prove that they were models of working efficiency.

Utilising Tawney's material on chainmaking and tailoring, this chapter argues that Tawney felt a promising image was necessary in order to reassure conservatives that boards were not 'thrusting an iron rod into the complicated mechanism of industry'.[13] Moreover, he hoped to convince trade unionists that trade boards would not conflict with traditional, voluntary collective bargaining techniques. At the same time, he wished to deflect demands, spear-headed by the Webbs, for a subsistence-based minimum wage. The CTB, being not only the first wages board but also the most geographically compact and easiest to investigate, gained Tawney's full attention.

I

Tawney praised the CTB for increasing the wages of the chainmakers. Those who benefited the most, he emphasized, were engaged upon the poorest quality of chain and were the least skilled and lowest paid. The minimum, he sought to show, did not become the maximum. Certain workers received wages well above the basic legal rate established by the board.[14] In addition, Tawney concentrated on the improved

---

[9]   Terrill, *Tawney*, p. 98.

[10]   J. Winter, 'R.H. Tawney's early political thought', *Past and Present*, 47 (1970), pp. 71–96; Wright, *Tawney*, p. 9; N. Dennis and A. Halsey, *English Ethical Socialism: Thomas More to R.H. Tawney* (Oxford, 1988), p. 194.

[11]   J.R. Atherton, 'R.H. Tawney as a Christian Socialist moralist', unpublished Ph.D. thesis, University of Manchester, 1979, pp. 434–41; H.A. Clegg, *A History of British Trade Unionism since 1889, Volume 2* (Oxford, 1985), pp. 100–101; D. Reisman, *State and Welfare: Tawney, Galbraith and Adam Smith* (London, 1982), pp. 121–4; Schmiechen, *Sweated Industries*, pp. 174–6.

[12]   Atherton, 'Tawney', p. 437.

[13]   Tawney, 'The minimum wage', p. 125.

[14]   Tawney, *Chainmaking Industry*, pp. 86–7. See also, R.H. Tawney, 'The working of trade boards', *Fabian News*, 14 June 1914, pp. 50–51.

standard of living and security of life brought about by the CTB. He stressed how in 'Cradley Heath ... the effect of the minimum rates is visible to the eye .... The Trade Board has ... forced itself on the notice of classes of people other than workers and employers through the influence it has had upon the general life of the town.'[15] The women, his witnesses averred, seemed different beings from the apathetic people of pre-board days. Employers, teachers and union officials in Cradley Heath also testified to the improved appearance of the chainmakers' children. They were better clothed, fed, and shod.[16] The enhanced living standards of the chainmakers had led to a reduction of arrears and an increase in savings in the locality. The minimum rates had also proved to be a steadying influence on insurance contributions and trade union subscriptions, and 70 per cent of the men and 60 per cent of the women had joined their respective trade societies. He pointed out: 'It is as though a weight which crushed a plant had been removed. The bent stalk gradually straightens, the crushed leaves unfold and the sap begins to circulate through the expanding veins.'[17]

Tawney also claimed that the trade board dramatically improved industrial relations in domestic chainmaking. The effect of the board, he suggested, was to transfer the previous individual bargaining to a general representative body. In this respect, he praised the role of the appointed members, calling them 'the pivot upon which the whole system turns'.[18] Their presence, he insisted, ensured that the machinery for collective bargaining could not break down. The independent members had a casting vote, they brought the two representative sides together and they gave a less partisan and more rational approach to the board's determinations.[19] At the outset, the considerable power of the appointed members was not exercised but as the two representatives' sides came to an agreement, the role of the appointed members became crucial:

> The two [representatives'] sides initiate the proposals which are to be debated, and the appointed members listen. The members of the two sides vote on a motion, and if each side acts as a unit they are equal. The appointed members refrain from voting, and the motion is therefore not carried. The two sides must put forward new motions; each has to consider whether, if it pitches its claim too high, the appointed members may not vote for that of the other side and carry a motion against it .... It is better for the employers to offer a farthing more for fear that the workpeople may offer to accept a farthing less and win the appointed members to their side. It is better for the workpeople to accept less ... rather than to allow the employers, by moderating their demands, to carry the appointed members with them. Their mere presence, therefore, narrows the margin between one party and the other.[20]

---

[15]   Tawney, *Chainmaking Industry*, pp. 99–100.

[16]   *Ibid.*, p. 100. See also, Tawney, 'The working of trade boards', p. 51.

[17]   Tawney, *Chainmaking Industry*, p. 101.

[18]   *Ibid.*, p. 32. J. Stevenson concurs: 'Pivot or pilot? The role of the independent members of wages councils', *Journal of Social Policy*, 9 (1980), pp. 25–48.

[19]   Tawney, *Chainmaking Industry*, pp. 32–3. See also, Tawney, 'The working of trade boards', p. 50.

[20]   Tawney, *Chainmaking Industry*, pp. 32–3.

Finally, although Tawney sensed that the procedures for inspection represented a weakness of the Trade Boards Act, he overcame these doubts in connection with the chain industry:

> The inadequacy of the present staff of investigating officers produces less practical evils in the case of the chain trade than it does in that of tailoring and box-making industries, partly because the concentration of the manufacture of chain in a small area facilitates inspection, partly because, since minimum piece rates and not merely minimum time rates have been fixed by the Trade Board, it is relatively easy for the investigating officers to discover breaches of the determinations .... On the whole, as far as the chain trade is concerned, nearly all the evidence suggests that the Act is being successfully administered.[21]

II

When carefully examined, the benefits, which the CTB conferred, were not as spectacular as Tawney alleged. Moreover, his study was completed too early since the CTB had been functioning for little more than four years. His appeals to the experiences of the board in this short time were premature. More importantly, throughout these four years, the industry had been relatively prosperous. During the inter-war years, when the trade was heavily depressed, the CTB encountered conditions and circumstances which Tawney had not foreseen.

The employers' representatives on the CTB, pleading that a dramatic increase in wage rates would ruin their industry, proceeded with the utmost caution. Hence, the basic trade board rates for chainmaking remained appallingly low. These low rates were only accepted because the workers' representatives on the board curbed their demands in view of the employers' threats to mechanise the trade.[22] As the first industry to set minimum rates, the chain trade, by fixing low rates, undoubtedly established a precedent for the other boards. As Tawney admitted, one of the commonest objections to the wages fixed by the clothing and boxmaking industries was, significantly, that the CTB had fixed a minimum time rate of only 2½d an hour.[23] Even then, as we have seen, the chainmakers, had to strike in 1910 and again in 1911 to secure the application of minimum rates to their industry.

Three years after the establishment of these low minima, the employers still opposed any variation from them despite the substantial rise in the cost of living. The generally moderate local newspaper, the *County Advertiser for Staffordshire and Worcestershire* was moved to comment:

> It is an undoubted fact that the women workers of Cradley Heath despite the laborious nature of their calling are amongst the worst paid in England .... One would like to see the officials go boldly forward irrespective of any considerations for the manufacturing

---

[21] *Ibid.*, pp. 127–9.

[22] Untitled typed sheets, TP, folder 405a, pp. 3–4.

[23] Tawney, *Chainmaking Industry*, pp. 40–41. For details of rates for all the boards scheduled under the 1909 legislation, see Appendix 2.

interest and press for 15s a week, which the trade can well afford to pay. In this event there would be support forthcoming from all parts of the country.[24]

One year later, the *County Advertiser* made similar references to the poor wages of the dollied and tommied male chainmakers. It stated how the low minimum rate of one pound per week received by these workers bore no relation to the physical fitness or training required for such an occupation. In contrast, the newspaper continued, labourers and roadmen in some districts obtained 23s a week for a task which required neither craft skills nor training.[25]

Nor was Tawney able to prove his assertions that wage rates rose above the statutory minimum. On the contrary, his data indicated that at the outset some workers were failing to attain even the minimum itself. In table XIV of his book, for example, examining the hourly rates of women chainmakers during one week in July 1913, he demonstrated that nearly three-quarters of the 588 women interviewed were earning less than the minimum time rate of 2½d per hour.[26] This discrepancy he partly excused on the grounds that women were not totally dependent on their own earnings. They often worked irregular hours and further: 'It must be remembered that many of these women have husbands, fathers and brothers making chain as well as themselves ...'.[27] This argument could not be applied to the all-male dollied and tommied section, yet here, too, workers were falling below the minimum. Tawney's table VII clearly showed that for one week in October 1913, thirty-nine workers (17.5 per cent) out of a total of 222 examined, failed to attain the lowest rate established by the board, 5d per hour.[28] Even Tawney had to confess that: 'it is a little disquieting to find that (according to the facts supplied by themselves) between one-fifth and one-sixth of the men visited were obtaining less than the minimum.'[29] These marked anomalies, and the fact that Tawney only interviewed a minority of the workers in the trade, led one critical observer to state that Tawney's optimistic pronouncements were less than convincing.[30]

The CTB rates were so low that on the declaration of war in 1914 the women chainmakers, attracted by the higher remuneration in munitions factories, flocked to them in their hundreds. In his evidence before the War Cabinet Committee on Women in Industry, J. Bean stated that the exodus of female chainmakers to the Dudley national projectile factory, of which he was managing director, caused domestic chainmaking to be staffed by young girls of 14, 15 and 16 years of age.[31] He also added, significantly, that the better standard of living attained by the women

---

[24]   *CA*, 18 January 1913.

[25]   *Ibid.*, 7 February 1914.

[26]   Tawney, *Chainmaking Industry*, p. 91.

[27]   *Ibid.*, p. 93.

[28]   *Ibid.*, p. 78.

[29]   *Ibid.*, pp. 79–80.

[30]   A.E.R [Randall], ' Views and reviews: making economic history', *New Age*, 30 July 1914, pp. 304–5.

[31]   Ministry of Reconstruction, *Report of War Cabinet Committee on Women in Industry* (oral evidence), NA, LAB 5/1 pt. 1, p. D25.

in munitions work would deter them from returning to their old trade.[32] Labour in the chain trade became so scarce that even the chain manufacturers were forced to raise the women's wages in 1918 from 2¾d to 4d an hour. This new increase yielded, for a fifty-four hour week, a general minimum time rate of only 18s. In contrast, the report of the War Cabinet on Women in Industry gave the rates prescribed for women on men's work in engineering plants in 1918 as 40s for a forty-seven hour week, and 33s as the minimum wage for women on munitions work.[33]

Even if Tawney had been correct in his statement on CTB wages before 1914, the situation was radically altered by the depression in the chain trade during the 1920s and early 1930s. Domestic chainmaking was mainly an export trade before the war. The conflict disrupted trading connections with pre-war customers, several of whom had perfected chainmaking machines. In many respects, continental machine-welded chain was inferior to the English hand-made variety. The former was more subject to corrosion and was less durable and dependable; but it was also a great deal cheaper.[34] As one union official observed, 'machine-made chain ... can be produced at a lower cost than by the old method, thereby displacing many operatives in the staple trade of the Cradley Heath district.'[35] The inter-war slump also deprived the industry of orders in shipping and engineering, its chief source of custom.[36] Following the war, Cradley Heath was one of the five areas of the Black Country that suffered most from trade depression.[37] Evidence from a senior trade board official indicated that the minimum, where it was observed, had become the maximum.[38] After 1921, wages were only marginally advanced and frequently reduced.[39] In 1938 G.D.H. Cole could remark that the wage rate in chainmaking was only 6d an hour, thus preserving the industry's reputation as being 'among the worst paid women's trades'.[40]

The low wages in domestic chainmaking, together with the poor prospects in the trade from the 1920s, effectively deterred the young from entering the craft. As early as 1919, Charles Sitch attributed the dearth of learners in the trade to inadequate wages.[41] In reply to the chain manufacturers' refusal to vote the women an increase in pay that year, he stated: 'Is it not a fact that many [learners] have not only left it

---

[32] *Ibid.*, p. D43.

[33] Ministry of Reconstruction, *Report of War Cabinet Committee on Women in Industry* (PP. 1919, XXXI), pp. 119, 150–51.

[34] *CA*, 4 February 1928; 28 February 1931.

[35] *Ibid.*, 12 March 1932. For further details of foreign competition in the chain trade, see G.C. Allen, *The Industrial Development of Birmingham and the Black Country, 1860–1927* (London, 1929), especially p. 378; *The Victoria County History of Staffordshire, Volume 2* (London, 1967), pp. 263–5.

[36] *CA*, 28 February 1931.

[37] West Midland Group, *Conurbation: A Study of Birmingham and the Black Country* (London, 1948).

[38] Memo on the extent to which employers pay more than trade board rates, NA, LAB 11/716 TB168/2/1927.

[39] CTB minutes, 1917–1929, p. 348, NA, LAB 35/75; CTB minutes, 1930–1939, p. 24, NA, LAB 35/76.

[40] Cole, 'Living wages', p. 23.

[41] *CA*, 18 October 1919.

[the chain trade] for more remunerative occupations but that girls who might, under favourable conditions, be disposed to enter the trade on grounds of heredity, are employed in Birmingham, where higher pay prevails?'[42] That the industry was not attracting young recruits was further indicated by official trade board surveys. On the eve of the First World War, one trade board officer reported that, after random visits to chain shops, 19 per cent of male workers were under twenty years of age and 30 per cent of females were under twenty years.[43] By 1927 a similar investigation conducted by the trade boards office showed that, out of 200 workers interviewed, no more than six (3 per cent) were under twenty years of age.[44]

The unwillingness of the young to enter the trade was reflected in the diminution in the total number of chainmakers. In 1911, the number of women chainmakers had been around 2,000; by 1925 this figure had fallen to barely 500.[45] 1926 saw a slight increase in the women chainmakers' ranks but this was a temporary phenomenon caused by the scarcity of work amongst the male population due to the General Strike and the miners' lockout.[46] Thereafter, decline was resumed. By 1928 those who remained in domestic chainmaking were mainly the old who could not adapt to other trades. On the eve of the Second World War, the *County Advertiser* could comment that the women chainmakers numbered no more than twelve; they could almost be counted on the fingers of two hands.[47] The ranks of the male domestic chainmakers were similarly decreased. At the annual meeting of the Chainmakers' and Strikers' Association in 1925, Sitch stated that fewer than 200 men were engaged in the domestic workshop sector.[48] Tawney's optimism about the high level of the chainmakers' wages under the Trade Boards Act had not been borne out by the facts and, with the passage of time, the numbers of the workers had collapsed.

III

Tawney's statements on the more secure and enhanced standard of living of the chainmakers were as premature as his thesis on the high levels of pay brought about by the board. His account of the improved lifestyle of the chainmakers was based mainly on random observation unsupported by statistical data or detailed case studies. Factors which contradicted his pro-trade board stance were either ignored or glossed over. As to the improved appearance of the chainmakers, he neglected to remark that in 1914 Mary Macarthur regarded Cradley Heath as one of the worst branches affiliated to the NFWW with regard to sickness.[49] The application of trade boards

---

[42]   *Ibid*, 18 October 1909.
[43]   CTB minutes, 1917–1929, p. 118.
[44]   *Ibid.*, p. 299.
[45]   *CA*, 19 March 1925.
[46]   *Ibid.*, 3 July 1926.
[47]   *Ibid.*, 8 July 1939.
[48]   *Ibid.*, 1 August 1925.
[49]   Macarthur found that 25 per cent of the sickness claims made by the women chainmakers arose from tubercular troubles: National Health Insurance Committee, *Report* (PP 1914–1916, XXX), Q. 11,382.

to the chain industry could not instantly improve the inadequate medical facilities of the district nor drastically change the generally poor health of the workers. Such was the prevalence of anaemia among women chainmakers in 1914 that doctors alleged that benefit societies hesitated to give sickness payment in ordinary cases of the illness.[50] Rebecca West sarcastically observed that women chainmakers were far from being 'lotos-eaters':

> Only once have I seen a group of Cradley Heath chain-makers. The course of treatment that they suggested to me was six weeks in a nursing home, a long holiday on the Mediterranean and a large income for the rest of their lives ... poor dears, they have never heard of happiness ... only some miracle from above could repair the injuries they had incurred in their slavery.[51]

Tawney's witnesses attributed much of the increased prosperity of the chainmaking community to the Trade Boards Act, rather than to the improved economic circumstances of the industry following its revival in late 1909–1910. However, the *County Advertiser* stated in 1913 that the factory chainmakers had an extra £400,000 to spend in Cradley Heath as a consequence of the trade's revival.[52] Yet these chainmakers, being factory based, were not associated with the trade board which affected only sweated labour.

Any benefits which the board conferred were soon obliterated by the trade's decline after 1918. The trade board's inspectorate (TBI) left no doubt as to the quality of life of the domestic workers when they commented in 1923 that the chainmakers were very near starvation point. And they observed in 1926 that: 'their homes are hovels; they eat meat but rarely; their washing when displayed on the lines is pathetic....'[53] Descriptions of the chainmaking town during the inter-war years clearly showed that Cradley Heath, despite the trade board, had altered only marginally since 1910. Even the *County Advertiser* with its local patriotism was forced to confess in 1924 that the chainmaking town was: 'One of the few spots that seems to retain the old Black Country atmosphere ...'. [54] In a less restrained vein three years earlier, the journalist Thomas Burke had seen fit to label Cradley Heath, 'the Devil's Allotment':

> It is not a town; it is not a village; it is not a dog-kennel. It has the vilest aspects of all these things .... It is more dreadful than a village devastated by guns and bombs. Their work is usually fully done, but Cradley Heath is only torn and ravelled .... Better perhaps that these hovels and dog-kennels should have been completely destroyed by Zeppelins ....[55]

---

[50]   *CA*, 7 February 1914.

[51]   R. West, 'The sheltered sex', *Clarion*, 4 July 1913 in J. Marcus (ed.), *The Young Rebecca West* (London, 1982), pp. 184–5.

[52]   *CA*, 20 September 1913.

[53]   Prosecution file Messrs. Mole and Bedall, NA, LAB 2/982/TBIA18657.

[54]   *CA*, 21 June 1924.

[55]   *Ibid.*, 23 April 1921. According to some accounts, no doubt apocryphal, German airmen refrained from bombing Cradley Heath because they believed it to be sufficiently derelict (*Ibid.*, 26 June 1915).

The chainmakers, renowned for their high incidence of infant mortality in the 1880s, continued to give medical officers of health cause for concern half a century later. Nor had child labour, as Tawney hoped, been abolished. In 1922 public health officials could comment on the extent to which the health of the chainmakers' children was being ruined by excessive and illegal employment in the domestic workshops.[56] This infraction was only one manifestation of the fact that the TBI, during the industry's decline, proved thoroughly incapable either of upholding the CTB's decisions or protecting the chainmakers' standard of life.

IV

Despite Tawney's faith in the CTB inspectorate, the TBI was notoriously incapable of discharging the duties placed upon it from the outset. Ordinarily, the task of the TBI was an unenviable one. As deputy chief inspector Miss B.M. Power pointed out in 1925, the work was 'carried on under conditions which are strenuous, lonely and uncomfortable, and in addition to a varied technical equipment, calls in a high degree for qualities of judgment, firmness, forbearance and self possession.'[57] The poor and inadequate methods whereby firms maintained their records were a particularly difficult problem.[58] In addition, transport facilities were often inadequate.[59] Working men and women, especially those in closed communities such as Cradley Heath, were either un-co-operative or hostile to the TBI. The physical presence of the inspectors so terrified some chainmakers that they were unable to tell the truth. In the case of Hannah Chater, the inspectorate recorded: 'she was afraid we were going to put her in jail .... We did our best to reassure her ... but we were quite unable to get her to tell the facts of the matter.'[60] On other occasions, the TBI was blamed for the chainmakers' personal misfortunes. The death of one worker who died shortly after being interviewed was attributed by his widow to the TBI's questioning. [61]

These difficulties were compounded by the financial stringency of the Treasury and politicians. When introducing the Trade Boards Bill, Winston Churchill had insisted that the boards would not become a burden on the state.[62] Other ministers followed his parsimonious example. In July 1915, when inspection figures first became available, there were six trade boards covering approximately 500,000 workers employed in 12,000 firms while the staff of inspectors numbered only

---

[56]   *Ibid.*, 27 May 1922.

[57]   Inspection report, December 1925, NA, LAB 2/1170/TB159/1925.

[58]   CTB minutes, 1917–1929, p. 338.

[59]   In 1926, for instance, after one visit to Cradley Heath in constant hail and snow, Senior Inspector Miss M. Darlow informed Chief Inspector Todd that if no official car was provided 'it may shortly be necessary for you to pay either for a cheap wreath or for some spiked chain for a monument'. See prosecution file, Messrs Kendrick and Mole Ltd., NA, LAB 2/1618/TBIA1593 pt. 3.

[60]   See prosecution file, W. Mills and Co., NA, LAB 2/1606/TBIA1350.

[61]   See NA, LAB 2/1119/TB119/3/1928.

[62]   *Hansard* (Commons), 24 May 1909, col. 961.

twelve.[63] Although the position was improved during the ensuing two decades, it remained far from adequate. On the eve of the Second World War, the chain and other trade board establishments were being inspected only once in every five years compared to once in eighteen months for those firms covered by the factory acts.[64]

Inadequate levels of inspection were aggravated by the policy adopted by the factory inspectorate towards trade board infractions. When the Trade Boards Act was passed, it was arranged that the factory inspectorate would assist its enforcement. Accordingly, the Home Office instructed factory inspectors that, during the course of their ordinary duties, they should note whether trade board notices were posted and if they were not to draw the attention of the occupier to the omission and to report the matter. The factory inspectorate was also directed to forward to the trade boards office written complaints received by them, and to report all trade board infringements. Despite the fact that these provisions would have helped to supplement the slender resources of the TBI, they remained virtually a dead letter as factory inspectors chose to ignore them.[65]

Nor were the inadequate resources of the TBI aided by the timid prosecution policy adopted by the Ministry of Labour. It was not until 1925 that increasing the number of prosecutions was seriously considered as a means of supplementing the small percentage of inspections.[66] Up to that date, the main principle that had dictated Trade Board policy towards prosecution had been that cases should only be brought to court when there was a good chance of convicting the offender. This attitude had been largely dictated by the TBI's experience in the early days of trade depression when magistrates had frequently displayed prejudice and hostility.[67] As a consequence the Ministry of Labour had tried to find a compromise with regard to underpayment by differentiating between 'trivial' and 'serious' offences in 1922. Under 'trivial' were grouped all those instances of underpayment which did not amount, in the case of an individual worker, to more that 20 per cent of the total wage and, in the instance of a group of workers, to more than 5 per cent of the total wages due in the workshop concerned. Such 'trivial' offences were to be settled, wherever possible, at the time of inspection. Under 'serious' were classed those violations where a considerable amount of underpayment had occurred. Such cases were vetted for possible prosecution proceedings.[68]

In 1925 Humbert Wolfe, head of the general department and a principal assistant secretary in the Ministry of Labour, considered that this procedure should be reversed for the following reasons:

> The attitude of the Bench throughout the country … has definitely changed, and we have as much chance now as any other department of receiving a sympathetic hearing … I am far from thinking that an unsuccessful prosecution is in itself bad for the Acts. Failure

---

[63]   Sells, *British Trade Boards*, p. 40.

[64]   Sells, *British Wages Boards*, p. 213.

[65]   NA, LAB 2/918/TB251/1925.

[66]   Revised instructions respecting submission of cases for prosecution, NA, LAB 2/2028/TB149/1934.

[67]   *Ibid.*, minute by Humbert Wolfe.

[68]   Suggested modification in present inspection policy, NA, LAB 2/884/TB/4/1921.

on a technical point will still indicate to employers ... that the Department is proceeding actively with the enforcement of the Acts.[69]

Nevertheless, the former policy of settling 'trivial' offences out of court was not discontinued, merely restated. Only if a worker was paid less than 90 per cent of the wages due, compared to 80 per cent previously laid down, was prosecution considered.[70] The Ministry of Labour had not changed its basic policy of utilising criminal proceedings as the ultimate threat to bring only the most recalcitrant employers into line. This was clearly not a satisfactory state of affairs, particularly when the costs of bringing a case to court effectively barred anyone but the Ministry of Labour from instituting proceedings.[71]

Not surprisingly, with the onset of depression in the chain industry in the1920s, accusations were legion that the trade board rates were being evaded. Some of these complaints were in the form of anonymous letters to the Ministry of Labour and were undoubtedly written by chainmakers victimised after refusing to accept below the minimum.[72] Moreover, the TBI frequently made reference to the large extent to which they believed infractions were occurring.[73] Complaints were also forwarded to the Ministry by members of the CTB and by the professional trade unionists for the industry. Both workers' and employers' representatives on the board viewed with alarm the failure of the TBI to prosecute all evasions, especially after 1922 when it was widely known that the minimum was not being paid.[74]

The acceptance of arrears out of Court also caused particular friction between the TBI and union representatives. The chainmakers' unions adopted a policy of non-co-operation with the TBI if they thought that criminal proceedings were not likely to be taken. Following one visit by Charles Sitch to the trade boards office in Birmingham in connection with a possible prosecution case, Kendrick and Mole in 1926, senior inspector Darlow despatched a minute to the Ministry of Labour giving an account of the visit. Sitch, she said, called on her in connection with a complaint but: 'The real object of his visit was, if possible, to secure information as to the evidence in possession of the officers in order that he might press for proceedings.'[75] Six months later, Darlow communicated with chief inspector Todd:

> I saw Mr Sitch again on Thursday with a view to getting from him further information about another large firm of chainmakers, Joseph Griffiths and Son. Mr Sitch told me then that he did not feel inclined to press the case, as he thought the Department had been wrong in accepting the arrears before going to Court. I felt that it was useless to discuss

---

[69]   NA LAB 2/2028/TB149/1934.

[70]   *Ibid.*

[71]   See Sells, *British Trade Boards*, p. 45.

[72]   For examples of anonymous letters, see S. Blackburn, 'Sweated labour and the minimum wage: a case study of the women chainmakers of Cradley Heath, South Staffordshire, 1850–1950', unpublished Ph.D. thesis, University of London, 1984, Appendix IV.

[73]   CTB minutes, 1917–1929, p. 287.

[74]   *Ibid.*, p. 181.

[75]   Prosecution file, Kendrick and Mole Ltd., NA, LAB 2/1618/TBIA1593, pt. 2.

the matter with him, but I thought that you might like to know that little help is anticipated from him.[76]

In his annual report to the Chainmakers' and Strikers' Association sixteen months later, Sitch made a specific issue of the TBI's attitude towards prosecution. He complained of the irregularity of treatment 'meted out by the Ministry of Labour in taking some employers to Court where infractions of the Trade Boards' determinations have taken place, and not proceeding against other guilty employers'.[77]

Nor was Tawney correct to assume that breaches of the CTB's determinations would always be simple to detect. During the 1920s the TBI was forced to concede that CTB evasions were extremely sophisticated. In 1926, for example, G. H. Anderton, a legal advisor to the TBI, drew attention to the numerous evasions in the chain industry, at the same time delineating the devices whereby employers avoided payment of the legal minimum rates. He first described how employers, after paying workers the prescribed rates, insisted that a certain proportion should be refunded. Second, he referred to the falsification of records by employers to show that minimum rates had been paid when, in practice, the workers concerned had received below the minimum. Third, he claimed that manufacturers bought chain from workers that precluded the payment of trade board rates or of a reasonable price for the iron.[78] Finally, he spoke of the device whereby employers contracted with a worker to make a larger size chain for the price of a smaller variety.[79] The problem was only solved in the mid-1930s when the volume of trade and the number of chainmakers had diminished to such an extent that infractions could be considered negligible.[80]

V

While Tawney under-estimated the effectiveness of the TBI, he over-estimated the impartiality of the appointed members. In the middle years of the CTB, the Ministry of Labour admitted that some of the appointed members made no attempt to disguise their pronounced conservative politics. The most notorious were Cécile Matheson, member of the CTB from 1919 to 1954, and Professor Frank Tillyard, chairman of the CTB between 1919 and 1923. Ironically, Tawney, because of his well-known attitudes on labour matters, was carefully vetted by the Ministry of Labour before being appointed to the deputy-chairmanship of the CTB in 1919. He was finally selected on

---

[76] *Ibid.*, pt. 3.

[77] *CA*, 4 February 1928.

[78] Efficient workers usually saved a small quantity of iron on each hundredweight of chain. When trade became slack, they made this accumulated stock of iron into chain and sold it to chain firms on their own account. Such transactions were not subject to the provisions of the Trade Boards Act: 'CTB information', p. 6, NA, LAB 2/1119/TB119/6/1925.

[79] Prosecution file on Messrs. Kendrick and Mole, pt. 3, Good chainmakers were also employed to make inferior chain. These workers were paid at the lowest trade board rate but, in view of their skill, still made fine quality chain. Their employers retailed this chain as superior quality: 'CTB information', p. 31.

[80] Sells, *British Wages Boards*, p. 230.

the grounds that both Tillyard and Matheson were known to hold opposing political convictions to him. Since Tawney only infrequently attended CTB meetings, the latter two virtually dictated CTB policy between 1919–1922.[81] At the end of his three-year term of office, Tawney was not re-appointed.[82]

Tawney's faith in the impartiality of the appointed members was not shared by the trade union world. One of the most vociferous critics was Joseph Hallsworth, General Secretary of the National Union of Distributive and Allied Workers. Hallsworth believed that the appointed members had three major failings that prejudiced their judgements. First, the independent members were drawn not from the working class but from the professional and governing classes: 'However great may be their individual desire to be independent and impartial, it is difficult for them to look at matters from the standpoint other than that of their own class.'[83]

Second, Hallsworth asserted that, although the workers' and employers' representatives were equal on the boards, the former had the hardest task in proving that an increase in wages was both desirable and necessary. Employers' representatives, on the other hand, could always plead that the trade could not bear a wage increase and that a rise in pay would lead to unemployment, considerations which often held significant weight with the appointed members.[84] Third, Hallsworth argued that appointed members, when casting their deciding votes, were too sympathetic to the small master, 'whose cause is often espoused by the larger employers in the hope that the lightening of the small man's burden will also ease their own'.[85] In other words, rather than establishing a decent minimum, they often settled at the level of the least efficient firm.

Not only did Tawney over-estimate the independence of the appointed members, he also credited the chainmakers' unions with too much strength. The male outworkers proved to be only poor trade unionists. In 1914, the same year as Tawney published his chainmaking book, Thomas Sitch could refer to the male outworkers as being weak both financially and numerically.[86] The previous year Charles Bloomer, President of the Chainmakers' and Chain Strikers' Association, had categorically discounted the possibility of one union for the trade since the male outworkers were content to accept pathetically low wages.[87] The women's organisation, although more resilient, was reduced in size by the war.

However, despite the effects of the war, there is little reason to believe that the trade union organisation of the women would have endured for long. The conflict

---

[81]   NA, LAB 2/276/TB10257/1918. During his period of office on the CTB, Tawney underwent a gall-bladder operation which was complicated by his war wounds, twice stood unsuccessfully for Parliament as a Labour candidate, sat on the Sankey Commission to investigate the coal industry and joined the Fabian Society executive (in 1921). In addition, he was reader in economic history at the LSE and, amongst other published works, completed *The Acquisitive Society* (London, 1920): Terrill, *R.H. Tawney*, pp. 62–3.

[82]   NA, LAB 2/928/TBP114.

[83]   J. Hallsworth, *The Legal Minimum Wage* (London, 1925), p. 52.

[84]   *Ibid.*, p. 53.

[85]   *Ibid.*, pp. 53–4.

[86]   *CA*, 25 July 1914.

[87]   *Ibid.*, 19 July 1913.

merely accelerated the inevitable decline. By 1922 the Ministry of Labour could lament that there were no females on the elected workers' side of the CTB although the trade was 'mainly carried on by women'.[88] As Ellen Wilkinson informed her audience, which included Tawney, at a conference on the minimum wage in 1927, the workers in trade board establishments soon became uninterested in trade unionism because the boards sapped the spirit of independence essential for good organisation. Although the establishment of a trade board in chainmaking initially sparked enthusiasm for organisation, this euphoria quickly evaporated and 'as soon as the Trade Board got into working order the opposite tendency took place'.[89]

The final blow to any residual trade union solidarity among the chainmakers was administered by the severe inter-war depression. During this period workers, fearing victimisation, were reluctant to denounce those employers who paid below the minimum.[90] Miss Carter of the TBI clearly understood the situation when she stated in 1923:

> the workers who are in many cases at starvation point would make any statement at the present time rather than be dragged into Court and run the risk of having to make statements against an employer which might lessen their chances of obtaining work .... A warehouse man in a good firm in the trade told me some time ago that out-workers who gave evidence ... found it difficult to obtain work afterwards ....[91]

The collusion of workers with employers became so great that special instructions were issued to the TBI to help them determine whether a chainmaker was telling the truth or not. One of the hints given to inspectors was as follows:

> it should be noted that the workers in this trade are generally illiterate, and obliged to rely largely upon their memories, which, in consequence, are generally found to be good. If, therefore, a worker is able to state the amount per cwt. for chain recently made, and is not able to give the weight of the chain or the amount 'picked up' for it, there is a strong prima facie reason for suspecting the rate paid.[92]

Other advice regarding inspection included the sequence in which interviews should be conducted. In cases of complaint, for example, it was 'generally desirable to carry the inspection of outdoor workers as far as possible before visiting the firm employing them. If the firm is visited first it is not unlikely that a messenger will be despatched to the outworkers warning them ... as to the information they are to furnish.'[93]

With regard to the taking of statements from workers in connection with evasions, the guidelines laid down by the trade board's office were highly significant. Inspectors were advised to take written evidence from workers at all times since 'the workers

---

[88]   Memo on election and nomination of trade board representatives, NA, LAB 2/15/ TB224/1922.

[89]   E. Wilkinson, speech, in League of Nations Union, *Towards Industrial Peace*, p. 43.

[90]   Prosecution file, Mrs Hollingsworth: NA, LAB 2/1604/TBIA12394.

[91]   *Ibid.*

[92]   'CTB information', p. 41.

[93]   *Ibid.*

are likely to be influenced by the employer before the case comes into Court.'[94] The non-compliance of the chainmakers became so great that Senior Inspector Darlow even contemplated taking proceedings against four chainmakers for fabricating particulars. The case of one chainmaker, David Pearce, evidently exasperated Darlow so much that she wrote to the trade boards office in 1927:

> Frequent reference had previously been made to the deplorable lack of veracity amongst workers in this trade. It will be recollected that a very great deal of time has been spent in endeavouring to elicit true information from them, and that practically a deadlock exists at the moment, as from evidence as to current selling prices, a number of employers continue to cook their books and a number of workers to protect them by false statements to inspectors.[95]

Tawney also misjudged the power which the CTB gave to the employers in the trade vis à vis the workers. As G.D.H. Cole pointed out, trade boards 'stimulated organisation, most of all among the employers …'.[96] The chain manufacturers were directly strengthened by the application of the Trade Boards Act to their industry since it simplified collective action by employers. In the years after 1910, the middlemen were gradually squeezed out of the trade and became workers dependent solely on their labour.[97] The divisive effect of the subcontractors was thus largely removed and wage bargaining, in respect of the employers, was thereby rationalised.

The CMA was also prominent in the Employers' (Trade Board) Joint Advisory Committee, a body representing employers in industries encompassed by the Trade Boards Act. This was a powerful pressure group allowing employers to take concerted action over such matters of trade board policy of which they disapproved.[98] There is no doubt that the chainmakers viewed the increasing strength of the CMA with apprehension. In his half-yearly report for 1914, Thomas Sitch explained to the Chainmakers' and Strikers' Association that the manufactures' federation embraced nearly all the chain employers in the trade. While the chain manufactures negotiated as a unified body, the workers bargained separately for the three branches of the trade.[99] The masters, in addition to having a more unified organisation, also held the most potent bargaining weapons on the board: the bogey of foreign competition and the threat to increase mechanisation in the trade if wages were advanced and profits cut.

VI

Tawney's monograph on chainmaking was therefore not a realistic account of trade board performance. This did not prevent him from embarking upon a second study in 1915, embellishing the achievements of the tailoring trade board. Although slightly

---

[94]   *Ibid.*, p. 43.

[95]   NA, LAB 2/1119/TB119/13/1927.

[96]   Cole, 'Living wages', p. 8.

[97]   'Information report on inspection and enforcement for year ending 31 December 1923', CTB minutes, 1917–1929, p. 222.

[98]   NA, LAB 2/15/TB 233/1922.

[99]   *CA*, 25 July 1914.

more cautious than his chainmaking work, Tawney's tailoring inquiry nevertheless praised the tailoring board for raising the wages of the poorest workers while simultaneously encouraging the growth of orderly industrial relations. He declared that 'the earnings of at least 38 per cent of the women piece-workers, and probably more, must have been increased as a result of the Trade Boards' determination ....'[100] On the other hand, he asserted that the increase in male wages, though not as dramatic, was still very significant for 'about a quarter of them must have obtained an advanced in earnings .... In certain districts e.g. Hebden Bridge and Norwich, the proportion affected is much larger.'[101]

Moreover, the minimum rates fixed were free and clear of all deductions and fines, which had in the past seriously oppressed the women, were now illegal.[102] Since the board laid down that workers must not earn less than the minimum rates during the time they were in the factory, the old abuse of keeping the workers waiting for work without pay had been abandoned.[103] Tawney claimed that the result of this regulation was remarkable:

> By establishing this general rule, the Trade Board has removed one of the minor grievances undergone in the past by women workers. The change means at once higher weekly earnings – for since employers must pay all persons upon their premises, whether actually working or not, they take great pains than hitherto to ensure that work passes smoothly from one department to another – and more leisure, for when there is a shortage of work, the workers, instead of wasting their time in the factory, are free to go home.[104]

An incidental effect of the tailoring board was a reduction in the number of hours worked. Some employers, stimulated by the board into improving their work output, could now organise production in a shorter period of time. The masters had, accordingly, voluntarily shortened their working week.[105] Furthermore, Tawney contended that the board had transformed industrial relations. Prior to the trade board, employers in the tailoring industry were mainly unorganised, including the largest section of masters, the factory occupiers. As a direct result of the board, three employers' associations had developed, the two most important ones representing the Jewish subcontractors and the factory owners. In addition, the secretaries of these two latter organisations both had seats on the tailoring board.[106]

The workers for their part, Tawney maintained, also benefited as a result of the board. Although the trade board did not cause the creation of trade unionism amongst the workers, as fifteen societies were previously in existence, it stimulated federation between them. Before the establishment of the trade board, workers' societies had been numerically weak. In consequence of the board, higher pay led directly to increased union membership because many workers, for the first time, could afford to

---

[100]   Tawney, *Tailoring Industry*, p. 253.
[101]   *Ibid.*
[102]   *Ibid.*, pp. 60–61, 95.
[103]   *Ibid.*, pp. 61–2.
[104]   *Ibid.*
[105]   *Ibid.*, p. 63.
[106]   *Ibid.*, p. 32.

pay the trade union subscription.[107] The secretary of the Scottish Tailor's Association reported 'that not only the girls, but their parents are now willing that they should pay contributions to the union.'[108] Tawney stated that these newly augmented unions were, in several parts of the country, securing rates considerably above those fixed by the trade board. Morale amongst the workforce had, as a direct consequence, been raised accordingly.[109] As he pointed out:

> Workers who were till recently convinced that agitation for higher wages was always futile and often dangerous have at last seen the advance for which they did not dare to ask brought about by law, and, now that the incredible has happened, have realised that there is no insuperable barrier in the way of better conditions.[110]

Virtually the only point on which Tawney criticised the tailoring trade board was regarding inspection. Unlike chainmaking where he saw enforcement as simple, he considered that the clothing trades were difficult to inspect because they were embraced by a complex industry which was distributed over the whole country and employed numerous outworkers. These outworkers constantly entered and left the industry and, despite medical officer of health lists, were extremely difficult to trace since they frequently changed their address. This problem was compounded by insufficient inspection. During the six months period between 31 October 1913 and 31 March 1914, only 400 clothing workers were visited. Yet, excluding homeworkers, the total number of tailoring factories and workshops was in the region of 4,200. As Tawney remarked: 'It is evident that at the present rate of inspection it would take about five years for all of them to be visited once.'[111] But Tawney concluded on a positive note: 'This does not mean that wages have not been raised, or that evasion is general.'[112]

VII

Tawney's comments upon the success of the tailoring board, as with the chain industry's minimum wage regulating machinery, do not stand up to even the most cursory examination. The first tailoring trade board's authority was confined to only the wholesale bespoke and ready-made sections of the industry. This catered for clothing worn entirely by males and left untouched the whole field of ladies' tailoring. As one union official declared at the 1915 Trades Union Congress: 'It is manifestly ridiculous that the Trade Boards Act should fix a minimum for the making of clothing for males and allow the manufacturers of female clothing to sweat their victims to their hearts' content.'[113] The limited nature of the first board thus supplied unscrupulous employers

---

[107]   *Ibid.*, p. 103.

[108]   *Ibid.*

[109]   *Ibid.*, p. 92.

[110]   *Ibid.*

[111]   *Ibid.*, pp. 221, 226.

[112]   *Ibid.*, p. 233.

[113]   Gurney Rowlerson, General Secretary of the Amalgamated Society of Tailors (AST) in TUC, *Report of Proceedings: Annual Trades Union Congress, 1915* (London, 1915), p. 298.

with a loophole by which they could avoid paying the legal minimum rates. Unfair masters evaded prosecution by employing girls to make female clothing for three or four days a week and then engaging them to make men's wear for the remaining days. As one representative of the AST remarked: 'Unless the Act is definitely extended to cover the manufacture of female clothing we cannot secure fair conditions for the workers.'[114] Furthermore, the 40,000 operatives in shirt making were not added to the trade board schedule until 1913, while the remainder of the clothing industry did not receive trade board status until after the First World War.[115] As S.P. Dobbs observed: 'There is no doubt that in 1914 there was still much sweating in all branches of the clothing trades where it had existed at the time of the *Daily News* Exhibition'.[116]

Even those workers initially covered by the 1909 Act were not as fortunate as Tawney maintained. The minimum wages fixed were extremely low: so modest that they left the earnings of many workers, especially in the large manufacturing centres, basically untouched. As one employer candidly stated at a conference on the minimum wage:

> Personally I think we started too low with the women's rate .... We set out in 1910 to fix a rate which was to be universal and would not inflict hardship on the areas where they were low. Speaking as a representative from Leeds, I may say at once when the rate was fixed at 3¼d we were not buying labour at 3¼d. We would have preferred to have seen it at 4d. We were paying generally 5d for labour at that time ....[117]

The board established for women a wage of only 13s 6½d on the basis of a fifty hour week. This rate, although considerably higher than that set by the CTB, was well below the subsistence level quoted by 'good' employers such as Cadbury.[118] The men's rate of 25s a week was hardly munificent. Indeed, the trade board rates were so inadequate that they caused considerable dissatisfaction amongst many of the organised workers and the tailoring unions campaigned vigorously against the rates set. At the 1912 TUC, a clothing workers' organiser, W.E. Jansen, declared of the women's wages:

> I would like the delegates to understand that before these workers are entitled to a minimum rate of 3¼d per hour it is necessary for them to serve an apprenticeship of four years, and they only secure this wage when they arrive at the age of 18 years. Now 3¼d per hour is not a sufficient wage for a woman of 18 years and upwards to live upon decently. Moreover, the clothing industry is a seasonal one. The working basis of the Trade Boards Act is a week of 50 hours, but from reliable statistics it has been shown that the average hours of the workers in the clothing trade in any one-year will work out at between 40 and 42. If the worker works a full week she gets 13s 6d, but week in week out she can only earn something like 11s 6d. Now the Trade Board was fixed to prevent sweating, but this rate which has been fixed for women workers is what you might call a legal sweating rate

---

[114] *Ibid.*

[115] Stewart and Hunter, *The Needle is Threaded*, p. 148.

[116] S.P. Dobbs, *The Clothing Workers of Great Britain* (London, 1928), p. 182.

[117] D. Little, Wholesale Clothing Manufacturers' Federation, speech in League of Nations Union, *Towards Industrial Peace*, p. 48.

[118] *CA*, 10 September 1910.

.... [F]or the life of me I cannot understand how it is that in this country a woman, after putting in four years' training and becoming a skilled artisan, should only be entitled to such a low rate as 3¼d per hour.[119]

Jansen also criticised the men's rates declaring that on 6d an hour, and after an eight year apprenticeship, 'it is impossible for the men to discharge their domestic responsibilities ....' Jansen concluded: 'One must feel in the light of these facts that the Trade Boards, instead of being a blessing, are really a handicap to the workers ....'[120] Wages were still so low in 1917, despite rapid changes in the cost of living occasioned by the war, that J. Smith of the National Union of Tailors and Garment Workers could state:

> It has been our contention all along that the Board, instead of abolishing sweating by carrying out the provisions of the Act, has made it worse and localised it. The Board instead of taking into consideration the high cost of living for the purpose of fixing a fair rate of wage has viewed the situation from the point of view of establishing sweated rates of pay.[121]

Tawney also accepted the sexual division of labour in tailoring and condoned the fact that the trade boards established rates lower for women than men.[122] Some might say that this was 'entirely typical of his generation ...'.[123] Yet, at the same time as Tawney was tolerating gendered pay levels, Philip Snowden was advocating equal pay for equal work.[124] Moreover, from 1913, members of the Fabian Women's Group, such as Maud Pember Reeves, argued that trade board rates should be the same for both sexes.[125] A further trade union grievance was that, despite Tawney's assertions, there was a tendency for the minimum to become the maximum. Some trade unionists in the clothing industry, disillusioned with their experiences with trade boards, campaigned instead for a fixed national living income to abolish sweating. As J. Young, General Secretary of the United Garment Workers' Trade Union (UGWTU), told the war cabinet committee on women in industry in 1918: 'The Trade Board has always shirked dealing with the questions of a living wage, and that is why we are dissatisfied with its findings.'[126]

---

[119]   TUC, *Report of Proceedings: Annual Trades Union Congress, 1912* (London, 1912), p. 238.

[120]   *Ibid.*

[121]   TUC, *Report of Proceedings: Annual Trades Union Congress, 1917* (London, 1917), p. 247.

[122]   The old and the infirm could also be issued with certificates allowing the employer to pay them less than the minimum. A further modification occurred when lower rates were set for juveniles and learners.

[123]   Wright, *Tawney*, p. 146.

[124]   P. Snowden, *The Living Wage* (London, 1912), pp. 157–61.

[125]   Pember Reeves reasoned that a system of family endowments would obviate the need for a family wage: M. Pember Reeves, *Round About a Pound a Week* (London, 1913), pp. 216–18.

[126]   Ministry of Reconstruction, *Report of War Cabinet Committee on Women* (oral evidence), NA, LAB 5/1 pt. 2.

As regards the impact of the tailoring trade board in improving industrial relations, Tawney's pronouncements were once more too optimistic. Although the first meeting of the Tailoring Trade Board was convened on 14 December 1910, it took, as one bitter trade unionist pointed out, two years, eighteen months and nineteen days for the wages of the women in the trade to be fixed.[127] A major reason for this delay was the un-co-operative attitude of the large employers' representatives on the board. Time and again they used their voting power to defeat higher rates proposed by the workers' representatives.[128]

Moreover, during the three months waiting period laid down by the act, the employers successfully orchestrated a protest movement to have the rate finally reduced to 3¼d per hour. This action, declared one scornful trade union representative, was justified by the large employers on the grounds that: 'it affords the girls a splendid opportunity for coming into the factories to earn a little pocket money ....'[129] Andrew Conley of the UGWTU pronounced the inadequate rates harmful to the relationship between employer and worker. As he remarked before the Cave committee: 'All who were present at the early meetings of the Tailoring Trade Boards testify to the bitterness which characterised the long debates on the subject of equitable rates for men and women.'[130] Even employers conceded that, during the early years of the board, the masters and the workers differed more than they agreed.[131] One Leeds employer with a seat on the board recalled in 1927: 'The first year or two of our Trade Board was very nearly a bear garden. An employer had only to make a statement to have someone on the other side get up and tell him, not always politely, that he is not speaking the truth.'[132] As late as 1928, Dobbs could declare in his survey of the clothing workers that the Wholesale Clothing Manufacturers' Federation, the association of the large clothing employers, was 'regarded with considerable hostility by the trade unions, with whom it conducts negotiations outside as well as within the Trade Board'.[133]

Nor was the growth of trade unionism following the enactment of the tailoring trade board as clear-cut as Tawney claimed. As he was forced to admit, unionisation made little headway in the case of the homeworkers, for 'it seems hopeless to expect that Trade Unionism will ever flourish among the most helpless section of the women.'[134] And although there is no doubt that the board initially stimulated organisation among the factory workforce, it is debatable whether this trend was long-term. A far greater influence upon union membership, particularly among women, was the First World War. The war produced a labour shortage which reacted favourably to the regularity of employment of the workers. But as Dobbs points out, the high level of union membership was not maintained after the war and a large

---

[127]   TUC, *Report of Proceedings: Annual TUC, 1912*, p. 238.

[128]   Morris, *Women Workers*, p. 230.

[129]   TUC, *Report of Proceedings: Annual TUC, 1912*, p. 238.

[130]   *Report to the Minister of Labour of the Committee Appointed to Enquire into the Workings and Effects of the Trade Boards Act* (PP 1922, X), p. 632.

[131]   D. Little, speech, pp. 50–51.

[132]   *Ibid.*

[133]   Dobbs, *Clothing Workers*, p. 159.

[134]   Tawney, *Tailoring Industry*, p. 221.

proportion of the newly recruited women deserted the union.[135] Significantly, Conley could state in written evidence to the Cave committee in 1922 that the scattered nature of the trade made it extremely difficult to unionise the work force.[136]

A major factor in reducing union membership was trade board policy itself. When the inter-war slump occurred, the boards dealing with the clothing trades decided on reductions in the minimum rates. Although union representatives had fought against lowering pay, they were out-voted and the decision became that of the board as a whole.[137] As Hunter and Stewart observed:

> However powerful the economic arguments may have been, this cut in money wages after 1921 did not commend itself to the workers on whom it was imposed. Even those who were prepared to distinguish between real wages and money wages saw little point in the argument that since prices were falling, less money would buy the same amount of goods. They did not accept that they had reached an ideal state in 1918 and that their standard of living should be pegged at that level for evermore. On the contrary, they felt justified in seeking a higher standard.[138]

In addition to membership loss due to unemployment, the unions faced resignations in the 1920s from those still in work but who felt disillusioned with the boards. The largest union, the Tailors' and Garment Workers', suffered the highest fall in members from a peak of 102,000 in 1919 to 55,000 in 1923.[139]

In addition, Tawney's cautious sentiments on trade board inspection were not shared by the tailoring trade unions. Virtually from the inception of the first tailoring board, union resolutions condemning the inadequacy of inspection and the consequent evasion became widespread. Such resolutions were, as one speaker remarked, something of a hardy annual at trade union conferences.[140] Tawney's study, completed as it was in 1915, was also too early to witness the major evasions of the inter-war years. The most common complaints, in addition to non-payment of the legal rates, were that notices of the rates were not posted and adequate wage records were not kept. Evasions of the tailoring rates during these years included abusing the waiting time much vaunted by Tawney. Under this system, workers would be told to 'clock-out' after being employed for several hours. After waiting for more work to turn up, they would 'clock-in' again but they were only paid for the actual hours worked. As Dobbs concluded: 'This is a very difficult practice to check, as the workers are strongly tempted to connive at it in fear that otherwise they will lose the chance of getting any work that may be available.'[141]

Other employers abused the apprenticeship system by employing young girls upon one basic process and, when they reached the adult trade board rate at eighteen,

---

[135]   Dobbs, *Clothing Workers*, p. 184.

[136]   *Committee Appointed to Enquire into the Workings and Effects of the Trade Boards Act*, p. 633.

[137]   Stewart and Hunter, *The Needle is Threaded*, p. 180.

[138]   *Ibid.*

[139]   *Ibid.*

[140]   TUC, *Report of Proceedings: Annual TUC, 1915*, p. 65.

[141]   Dobbs, *Clothing Workers*, pp. 123–4.

dismissing them.[142] Possibly the most worrying offence, as Bernard Sullivan pointed out at the 1931 TUC, was that of waiving the right of workers to be paid the full amount of wage arrears. He told Congress that the TBI often compromised with those employers who pleaded that to pay all the outstanding sum would bankrupt their business and cause unemployment amongst the workforce. The employers' association representatives on the trade boards, he alleged, 'frequently intervened on behalf of poor employers who are found to be under-paying'.[143]

VIII

Tawney's observations upon the operation of the chain and tailoring boards do not survive close scrutiny. They shared one major defect with all the Ratan Tata surveys (excluding *Livelihood and Poverty*) in that, as Harris remarks: 'empirical data was used not merely to reach conclusions but to demonstrate certain preconceived committed beliefs ....'[144] Nevertheless, Tawney's highly favourable portrayal of the effects of the boards was uncritically accepted by many.[145] His findings were immediately seized upon by contemporary reformers. In particular, Tawney's pronouncements set the seal on propaganda literature published by the NASL's secretary, J.J. Mallon. Unlike Tawney's monographs, Mallon's contributions were not professionally researched texts but were essentially propagandist pamphlets. Less concerned than Tawney with meticulous detail, Mallon chose to emphasis immediate impressions. Nevertheless, his broad statements were consistent with Tawney's findings, if slightly more exaggerated.[146] More importantly, Tawney's studies confirmed the views of influential sociologists such as Leonard Hobhouse and encouraged the latter 'to

---

[142] *Ibid.*, p. 171.

[143] TUC, *Report of Proceedings: Annual TUC, 1931* (London, 1931), p. 326.

[144] Harris, 'The Webbs', p. 53. Unlike Tawney, Bowley and Burnett-Hurst utilised advanced statistical methods: A. Bowley and A.R. Burnett-Hurst, *Livelihood and Poverty* (London, 1915).

[145] For very favourable reviews of Tawney's trade boards material, see *Journal of the Royal Statistical Society*, 78 (1915), pp. 630–31 (tailoring review by BLH [utchins]); *Journal of Political Economy*, 25 (1917), pp. 212–13 (tailoring review by Anon.); *American Economic Review*, 5 (1915), pp. 868–70 (tailoring review by John A. Ryan). See also, *Fabian News*, December 1914, p. 7 (chainmaking review by CML); *Fabian News*, September 1915, p. 63 (tailoring review by WSS). See also, W. Graham, *The Wages of Labour* (London, 1921), esp. pp. 78–81.

[146] Mallon's publications included: *The Minimum Wage in Practice* (London, 1914); 'Trade Boards Act extension', *WTUR*, April 1914, pp. 12–17; J.J. Mallon and E.C.T. Lascalles, *Poverty Yesterday and Today* (London, 1930), pp. 66–9; 'The trade boards', in F.E. Gannett and B.F. Catherwood (eds.), *Industrial and Labour Relations in Great Britain* (New York, 1939), pp. 74–88; 'Industry and a minimum wage', in British Institute of Management, (ed.), *Industry and a Minimum Wage* (London, 1950), pp. 5–7. In 1977, Field and Winyard, leading figures in Britain's anti-low pay movement, declared that the only comprehensive studies on the impact of minimum wages were still those carried out by Tawney at the turn of the twentieth century: F. Field and S. Winyard, 'The effects of the Trade Board Act', in F. Field (ed.), *Are Low Wages Inevitable?* (Nottingham, 1977), pp. 61–5.

emphasise the importance of legal rates of wages in appropriate trades'. Hobhouse's evidence (drawing very much on Tawney's surveys), 'constituted the main defence of the work of the Boards before the Cave Committee'.[147]

If the 1909 Trade Boards Act left much to be desired, why did Tawney exaggerate the good aspects of the boards while at the same time glossing over those features which detracted from the favourable image he presented? The answer lies in Tawney's over-riding desire to reassure conservatives that trade boards were neither the embodiment of economic folly nor an oppressive use of the power of the state. Tawney also hoped to reassure trade unionists that trade boards would not impede voluntary collective bargaining methods. Above all, he wished to undermine the campaign for a subsistence minimum wage popularised by the Webbs since 1897.

First, Tawney felt it necessary to project a positive image of trade boards in order to refute orthodox economists' belief that minimum wage regulation was an unwarrantable intrusion by the state in the wages bargaining process. When writing his chain and tailoring monographs, Tawney was acutely aware that such economic analysts viewed the boards with the greatest of suspicion.[148] Tawney recalled that as a young graduate he had been rash enough to advance the idea that increased pay could end sweating. He was told in no uncertain terms that 'each man was paid what he was worth, and that what mattered was, not the amount of wages he received, but the manner in which he spent them'.[149]

Tawney considered such arguments to be 'curiously remote from reality' and, by eulogising the boards, sought to demonstrate that state intervention could be exceedingly beneficial. In his classic account of Elizabethan wage regulation under the Statute of Artificers of 1563, he pointed out that the withdrawal of the state from the regulation of wages had been a comparatively recent event. The last remnants of state intervention in Britain had been removed as recently as 1824 with the repeal of the Spitalfields Act. Modification of the old economic theories, Tawney declared, had been brought about because Parliament recognised that state regulation could act as a brake on unwelcome individualistic tendencies.[150] State intervention such as

---

[147] Testimony by Mallon in J.A. Hobson and M. Ginsberg, *L.T. Hobhouse: His Life and Work* (London, 1931), p. 55. Hobhouse was honorary director of the Ratan Tata Foundation when Tawney completed his studies. Hobhouse had been associated with trade boards since their inception, and became the chairman of many of them (ten by 1922). He was widely praised for his success in this role. (Ibid., pp. 55–8.) See also Freeden's comment that Terrill does not recognise the closeness of Tawney's views to contemporary radical-liberal ones: M. Freeden, *Liberalism Divided: A Study in British Political Thought, 1914–39* (Oxford, 1986), p. 314. Cf J. Tomlinson, 'The limits of Tawney's ethical socialism: a historical perspective on the Labour Party and the market', *Contemporary British History*, 16 (2002), pp. 1–16. The latter argues that Tawney (and other Fabians), unlike Hobson, rejected the market and traditional economics.

[148] For an excellent, short summary of conservative economic doctrines on trade boards, see H.B. Lees Smith, 'Economic theory and proposals for a legal minimum wage', *Economic Journal*, 17 (1907), pp. 504–12.

[149] Tawney, 'Fixing minimum wages', p. 21.

[150] R.H. Tawney, 'The assessment of wages in England by the justices of the peace', in J.M. Winter (ed.), *R.H. Tawney: The American Labour Movement and Other Essays* (Sussex, 1979), pp. 129–86.

the Trade Boards Act could significantly strengthen the 'economic resisting power of the workers'. In answer to those who reiterated the well-worn argument that the labouring poor could rise through their own individual efforts, he tartly replied: '"Sweating" does not disappear from our towns because a certain number of those who are sweated become, as they do, sweaters in their turn, any more than tadpoles disappear from our ponds because a large number of them are annually converted into frogs ....'[151] A legal minimum wage, he maintained, should not be viewed as economic heresy but as a logical extension of factory legislation controlling a maximum working day and minimum sanitary conditions.[152]

By extolling the virtues of the boards, Tawney wished to demonstrate that high wage rates did not necessarily lead to increases in production costs. Far from being an excessive burden on industry, trade boards exemplified the validity of the 'economy of high wages'. The boards had proven the critics wrong by improved management techniques, reorganisation of processes and, ultimately, higher output by the work force. As a result, prices had not been raised to the consumer nor had significant unemployment occurred.[153] Many years later, Tawney asserted: 'the subtlety of human nature – in particular that of the employers and workmen – greatly exceeds the subtlety of the human mind – in particular that of economists ....'[154]

Whilst acclaiming the alleged achievements of the boards, Tawney was also anxious to prove that the fixing of minimum wages by law was not an oppressive use of the power of the state. Although the state played a vital part in minimum rate fixing, he argued, its role was relatively unobtrusive. The state brought the boards into existence, confirmed the minimum rates, provided the inspectorate and, in exceptional cases, the prosecution facilities. But the settlement of the rates and day-to-day administration of the industry concerned were in the hands of those 'who have an intimate knowledge of its technicalities and the more direct interest in regulating it in such a way as not to impair its efficiency'.[155] Tawney further noted that, 'each trade virtually regulates itself, subject to cautious criticism by the chairman and appointed members ....'[156] He was thus eager to show that the boards settled wages not by coercion but by rational arguments based on good-natured debates, which took into account both the interests of the industry and the wider community. As he pointed out in his tailoring survey:

> What actually happens is that the Board crawls to an agreement along a path of which the milestones are one-sixteenth of a penny, and that its ultimate decision represents a compromise between the employers; instincts of what the trade will bear, and the desire

---

[151] R.H. Tawney, *Poverty as an Industrial Problem* (London, 1913), p. 12.

[152] See, for example, Tawney, 'Fixing minimum wages', p. 25; Tawney 'The minimum wage', p. 127; and Tawney 'The abolition of economic controls, 1918–21', *EHR*, 13 (1943), p. 25.

[153] Tawney, 'Fixing minimum wages', pp. 27–8; 'Poverty as an industrial problem', p. 16.

[154] Tawney, 'Poverty as an industrial problem', p. 27.

[155] Tawney, 'The minimum wage', p. 126.

[156] Tawney, 'Fixing minimum wages', p. 27.

of the workers and appointed members to establish a 'living wage' .... The elements of economic strength, bluff and skill in bargaining are not ruled out .... [157]

Tawney hoped that his studies would belie the old maxim that wages must not be settled by anything but the number of labourers compared with the demand.

Tawney's second motive in endorsing the boards was to reassure the organised labour movement that the system would not impinge upon traditional trade union functions. Prior to, and following the passage of the 1909 Act, some trade unionists had been anxious that workers in the scheduled industries, once their wages were settled by the state, would become apathetic towards trade union membership.[158] In praising the boards, Tawney hoped to convince trade unionists that practical investigation proved such fears to be groundless. Sweated workers, because their economic position had been strengthened by the state, were more likely to respond to the appeal of trade union organisers and ultimately, he postulated, this would lead to the attainment of standard rates of pay well in excess of the minimum.[159]

More generally, Tawney sincerely believed that trade boards would contribute to a new moral order – one in which productivity and industry were geared to the service of society and the requirements of the workers. While the Webbs campaigned for a minimum wage on efficiency grounds and envisaged that it would be administered by a professional élite, Tawney cared passionately that trade boards would allow workers to extend their control over the labour process.[160] On his account, the boards helped 'to create in badly organised industries, a rudimentary industrial conscience and morale'. They served as 'a genuine ... organ of industrial self-government ...'.[161]

Finally, Tawney hoped that his propitious trade board studies would help to restrain the demand for a subsistence minimum wage popularised most notably by the Webbs and like-minded Fabians such as Hutchins and Sanders.[162] Although by 1913 the Webbs believed that to 'fix a national minimum wage of 30s a week applicable to all adult workers in this country is an attractive proposal, and, given a thoroughly enlightened public opinion ... might be practicable', they eventually concluded that, since the cost of living varied widely in different areas, then a national but versatile measure was necessary to ensure that individual districts

---

[157] Tawney, *Tailoring Industry*, p. 35.

[158] These fears were eloquently voiced by Wilkinson. See, speech, pp. 41–6.

[159] Tawney, *Tailoring Industry*, pp. 90–92.

[160] Tawney, although he had joined the Fabian Society in 1906, castigated Fabian arguments on efficiency as 'the shallowest of claptrap'. See J.M. Winter and D.M. Joslin (eds), *R.H. Tawney's Commonplace Book* (Cambridge, 1972), p. 40. At this time, Tawney was an unorthodox member of guild socialism. The latter cut across the Webbs' collectivism as well as syndicalist solutions. See Wright, *Tawney*, pp. 69–70.

[161] Tawney, 'The minimum wage', p. 126. See also Tawney, 'Fixing minimum wages', p. 27 and R.H. Tawney, 'Recent thought on the government of industry', in P. Alden *et al.*, *Labour and Industry: A Series of Lectures* (Manchester, 1920), p. 198.

[162] B. Webb, B.L. Hutchins and the Fabian Society, *Socialism and National Minimum*, especially, pp. 82–9. These pages are virtually a re-print from Sanders' earlier, 1906 pamphlet.

could not undercut each other.[163] Under their scheme, the country would be divided into appropriate regions, each of which would be assigned a fixed physiological minimum along the lines recommended by Rowntree.[164] A commission especially established for the purpose, or the Labour Department of the Board of Trade, would be responsible for inquiring into working-class budgets and county, borough and urban councils with a population exceeding 50,000 would administer the system.[165] It followed, therefore, that the Webbs' minimum would 'be calculated on what the worker requires for physical health and efficiency, and not on what the trade will bear'.[166] To Tawney, the establishment of such a minimum wage was little short of barbaric. He declared, 'it means that people are not paid what they are worth, but what is necessary to keep them working. That is how a horse or slave is paid'.[167]

Tawney asserted that it was fundamentally wrong to draw a sharp line between a minimum based upon subsistence and all rates above that point. A subsistence minimum, he argued, was totally impracticable since no one would agree on which principles it should be established. He dismissed the concept of a subsistence minimum as 'so vague as to be almost worthless as a guide to action'.[168] He indicated that in the chain trade a very modest estimate of 'subsistence' would have trebled wages and consequently unemployment would have ensued. But, he noted, to the credit of the CTB, wage rates were only gradually increased thus allowing the industry to adjust over time to the higher wages bill. On the other hand, contrary to the Webbs, he considered that those industries which could pay above a subsistence level should be legally forced to do so. For Tawney, the strength of the boards lay in the fact that they reached their conclusions by a process of trial and error rather than by sharply defined principles. As he pointed out some years after the passage of the 1909 legislation:

> the refusal to prescribe by law a definite standard upon which minimum rates must be based has been a wise one. The empiricism of the British method has its disadvantages. But, compared with proposals which would require the rates to be such as to yield forthwith a

---

[163] NCPD, *The Case for the National Minimum*, pp. 11–14.

[164] They envisaged a minimum wage graded into areas with a low, an intermediate and a high cost of living. Assuming that the low wage areas would be sparsely populated, and those with a high wage, densely populated, they believed that employers in overcrowded areas would seek to lower their wages bills by migrating to less dense centres: Webb *et al.*, *Socialism and National Minimum* pp. 82–4.

[165] *Ibid*, pp. 82–8; NCPD, *Case for the National Minimum*, pp. 12–14.

[166] Webb *et al.*, *Socialism and National Minimum*, p. 75. See also S. and B. Webb, *Industrial Democracy*, pp. 774–5.

[167] Winter and Joslin, *R.H. Tawney's Commonplace Book*, p. 48. Tawney's criticism of a subsistence minimum had, no doubt, been fashioned by a reading of Hobson's work on the 'living wage'. But, unlike Hobson, Tawney viewed a living wage as unattainable. See Freeden, *Liberalism Divided*, p. 313.

[168] Tawney, 'The minimum wage', p. 127. Fellow Fabian Socialist, R.C.K. Ensor (1887–1958) also argued for a rate which the trade could bear: R.C.K. Ensor, 'The practical case for a legal minimum wage', *Nineteenth Century*, 72 (1912), p. 269.

wage based on the cost of living, it has the merit of making possible progressive advances as the trade is capable of bearing them.[169]

However, Tawney never entered into a direct exchange of views with the Webbs over the best machinery to combat low pay. There were several possible explanations for his reticence. He remained a lifelong friend of the Webbs and it was on their recommendation that he became director of the Ratan Tata Foundation.[170] Moreover, at the time of his appointment, the Webbs had become extremely unpopular.[171] As Margaret Cole remarked, during this period, 'they were attacked heartily from both left and right.'[172] In these circumstances, although he criticised the Webbs in private, Tawney always took great care when discussing the Webbs' work in public to assert that the 'conventional portrait of the pair as bureaucratic energumens, conspiring to submit every human activity to the centralised control of an omni-competent state, is a caracature' [*sic*].[173] As Wright comments, even though Tawney was a very different kind of socialist, he always held the 'firm of Webb' in great regard and affection and dedicated *Equality* to them, paid fulsome tribute to their industry, admired their respect for evidence and argument and applauded the 'civic temper' of a lifetime spent toiling away at the machinery of democracy on behalf of a multitude of social and economic reformers.[174]

Tawney also felt obliged to praise the Webbs for being amongst the first to bring the scandal of low pay to the attention of the public. As he said of them: 'They have not done the job for us, but they have given us some of the tools, both intellectual and moral, with which to do it.'[175] If nothing else, in his opinion, the Webbs had 'converted the legal minimum wage from an heresy into something like an axiom'.[176] For their part, although they continued to campaign for a subsistence minimum wage, the Webbs supported Tawney's studies, and welcomed trade board expansion as a stepping stone.[177]

We may speculate that a further important consideration was Tawney's position as director of the Ratan Tata Foundation. In 1912, the COS' School of Sociology and the Ratan Tata poverty research unit had been merged to form the Department of Social

---

[169] Tawney, 'Fixing minimum wages', p. 28.

[170] See Atherton, 'Tawney', p. 59.

[171] The latter's position in the Fabian Society had been seriously challenged, first by H.G. Wells and later by Guild Socialists such as the young G.D.H. Cole. By 1913, too, the Webb's pressure group to break up the poor law, the NCPD, had been forced to disband: McBriar, *An Edwardian Mixed Doubles*, pp. 334–9.

[172] M. Cole, *Beatrice Webb* (London, 1945), p. 122.

[173] R.H. Tawney, *The Webbs in Perspective* (London, 1953), p. 8.

[174] A. Wright, 'Tawneyism revisited: equality, welfare and socialism', in B. Pimlott (ed.), *Fabian Essays* (London, 1984), p. 85.

[175] R.H. Tawney, 'The Webbs and their work', in *The Attack and Other Papers* (London, 1953), p. 143.

[176] Tawney, 'Fixing minimum wages', p. 24.

[177] See McBriar, *Fabian Socialism*, p. 261. See also S. and B. Webb, *English Local Government,* pp. 559–65.

Science and Administration at the LSE.[178] Although key figures in the COS such as Helen and Bernard Bosanquet were not as un-progressive as is commonly assumed, they were highly critical of both the Webbs' policy on a subsistence minimum wage and Tawney's pro-trade board publications.[179] Understandably, Tawney appears to have found it prudent not to strengthen the COS' case by embarking on a potential course of open conflict with the Webbs.

IX

Tawney was, according to Beatrice Webb: 'A scholar, a saint, and a social reformer ...'.[180] To Hugh Gaitskell he was the 'Democratic socialist par excellence ...'.[181] Tawney has been placed alongside G.D.H. Cole and Harold Laski as one of the most important contributors to British socialist thought in the twentieth century.[182] His writings have become socialist classics and, nearly forty years after his death, Tawney's works still exercise a wide influence over British social analysis and policy. Indeed, since the 1980s, Tawney's ideas appear to have witnessed something of a renaissance.[183] While we now know a great deal about certain aspects of his work, such as that on education, his endeavours to eradicate low pay in Britain have received little attention. Yet Tawney himself considered his anti-sweating ventures to be one of the crucial phases of his

---

[178] Harris, 'The Webbs', p. 128.

[179] J. Lewis, *Women and Social Action in Victorian and Edwardian England* (Aldershot, 1991), pp. 172–3. COS literature, although it praised Tawney's meticulous research, also faulted it for not connecting unemployment to trade board legislation: *Charity Organisation Society Review*, 36 (1914), pp. 336–7; *Charity Organisation Society Review*, 38 (1915), pp. 351–4. In his inaugural lecture as director of the Ratan Tata Foundation, Tawney made a scathing attack on charity work which, like that of the COS, gave priority to individual failings rather than to the problems of the economic system: Tawney, *Poverty as an Industrial Problem*, pp. 10–12.

[180] N. and J. Mackenzie (eds), *The Diary of Beatrice Webb, Volume, 4* (London, 1985), p. 360.

[181] H. Gaitskell, 'An appreciation', in R.H. Tawney, *The Radical Tradition*, (ed.), R. Hinden (London, 1964), p. 212.

[182] A. Wright, *R.H. Tawney* (Manchester, 1987), p. vii.

[183] When the founders of the Social Democratic Party (SDP) seceded from the Labour Party in 1981, they established a Tawney Society as an equivalent to the socialist Fabian Society. At the same time, Raphael Samuel castigated the SDP for claiming to be the heirs of Tawney's brand of socialism. (*Guardian*, 29 March 1982). Similarly, in the new foreword to Tawney's *The Attack and Other Papers* (Nottingham, 1981), Tony Benn praised Tawney for maintaining his socialist convictions. Tawney figures prominently in Neil Kinnock's 'The future of socialism', *Fabian Tract*, 509 (1986), and in Roy Hattersley's *Choose Freedom: The Future for Democratic Socialism* (London, 1987). Tawney has also been honoured in Christian Socialist Movement literature. See D. Ormrod (ed.), *Fellowship, Freedom and Equality: Lectures in Memory of R.H. Tawney* (London, 1990), and J. Smith *et al*, *Reclaiming the Ground: Christianity and Socialism* (London, 1993). The latter volume contains a foreword by Tony Blair. A 1994 survey found that Tawney's work was still a key literary influence for Labour politicians: *New Statesman and Society*, 30 September 1994. See also the *Guardian* survey of ninety-eight Labour MPs, 4 April 2005: 'Tawney is ... the most influential intellectual among Labour MPs, along with the Italian Marxist Antonio Gramsci ....'

life's achievements. The Trade Boards Act of 1909, he argued, was a landmark in social policy history.

By supporting such a modest reform as the 1909 legislation, Tawney appears to have been led astray by pragmatic considerations. His studies of chainmaking and tailoring show him to be more concerned with moderate – in his estimation, workable – policies than with radical ideas. It could be argued that what was required to end low pay was not industry-based trade boards but a national minimum wage based on an agreed living income target; a minimum which, as Hobson pointed out as early as 1896, took into consideration (unlike the Fabians' version) 'a margin ... of leisure, of material means, the needful conditions of the growth of new physical, intellectual, and moral needs'.[184] While Tawney condemned the Webbs' national minimum wage for being too subsistence based, he also dismissed a more generous minimum if it was considered to be above what the individual trade could bear. His opinions were so well received by contemporaries that they dominated propagandist literature for the subsequent decades, most notably that produced by the founders of the powerful anti-sweating group, the NASL. His premises also attracted the attention of academics such as Hobhouse, one of the major figures of twentieth century social thought in Britain.

Increased awareness of Tawney's role in the campaign for trade boards should also make us wary of accepting Davidson's thesis that civil servants at the Board of Trade were singularly responsible for restricting Britain's low pay machinery.[185] Such a view overlooks the limiting role of central activists such as Tawney and Mallon. Some might argue that Tawney's unstinting support for trade boards was simply youthful inexperience. Yet while he adopted this policy of social legislation in the formative period of his career, he defended it well into his old age. Indeed, he became agitated in his final years when the anti-sweating campaigns to achieve trade boards were largely forgotten.[186] As Wright remarks, Tawney's basic outlook and political orientation was shaped early in his life and were not greatly altered after the First World War.[187] Although often regarded as one of this country's greatest socialist thinkers, in the area of trade boards, he was disappointingly circumspect and conventional. Consequently he should be regarded as a poor guide to the solution of the problem of low pay in the twentieth century. On the issue of minimum wages, he was a very moderate socialist indeed. As John Saville appositely remarks:

---

[184] Hobson, 'A living wage', pp. 128–9. Some would go further and have recommended the establishment of a basic income – irrespective of whether the recipient is working or not: A.B. Atkinson, *Incomes and the Welfare State: Essays on Britain and Europe* (Cambridge, 1995), esp. ch. 15.

[185] Davidson, for instance, comments that Llewellyn Smith and his colleagues were so suspicious of state intervention that they obstructed the establishment of a national minimum wage for the more modest trade boards. The prime objective of these officials, he concludes, was the alleviation of poverty wages, but not at the price of drastically altering the status quo, nor at the risk of rendering British exports uncompetitive by raising labour costs: Davidson, 'Sir Hubert Llewellyn Smith and labour policy', esp. pp. 197–224. The same point is made in Davidson, *Whitehall and the Labour Problem*, pp. 269–73.

[186] L. Jeger, 'Ideas and the man', *Tribune*, 26 January 1962.

[187] Wright, *Tawney*, p. 23.

The struggle for any particular reform has always in this country aroused so much opposition that when it is achieved it is at least understandable that those who spent half a lifetime on its behalf too easily believe that with its enactment a new period in social history is beginning ... when it comes, its results are usually exaggerated and its significance grossly overestimated.[188]

---

[188] J. Saville, 'The welfare state: an historical approach', *New Reasoner*, 1 (1957–1958), p. 17.

Chapter 7

The Persistent Problem of Low Pay

The pro-trade board sentiments of social reformers like Tawney were rewarded when, in 1913, the system was extended to five more industries.[1] Tawney's optimism was not completely shared by the trade union movement. In 1910, the secretary of the General Federation of Trade Unions, W.A. Appleton could remark that the Trade Boards Act demonstrated the futility of attempting to achieve the millennium simply through acts of Parliament.[2] From 1911, the TUC and the Labour Party, concerned with rising prices and rents, agitated for a universal minimum wage. Will Crooks introduced a bill in the Commons proposing a general legal minimum of thirty shillings a week for all adult workers.[3] The motion was subjected to trenchant criticism, most notably by Arthur Steel-Maitland, for being crude and unworkable.[4] When the national miners' strike of 1912 prompted further interest in a living wage, Crooks renewed his campaign. Beatrice Webb confided smugly in her diary: 'The ordinary Trade Unionist has got the National Minimum theory well fixed in his slow solid head.'[5]

In 1913 Crooks modified his living wage programme. He still insisted that all adult government workers should receive a thirty shillings minimum. But he also suggested a different minimum for the urban and country worker, and envisaged that this could be achieved via the extension of trade boards.[6] His proposal was rejected as absurd by civil servants. As one Trade Board official scoffed:

---

[1]   These were sugar confectionery and food preserving, shirtmaking, hollowware and tin-box making. The cotton and linen embroidery board was restricted to Ireland.

[2]   Cited in C. Watney and J.A. Little, *Industrial Warfare: The Aims of Capital and Labour* (London, 1912), p. 236.

[3]   The motion had the support of the Labour Party and two million trade unionists: *Hansard* (Commons), 26 April 1911, cols 1,882, 1,893. Money insisted that a minimum wage of thirty shillings would only add £900,000,000 a year to the country's wages bill: *ibid.*, col. 1,913.

[4]   *Ibid.*, esp. cols 1,897–907. The member for East Birmingham, Steel-Maitland was a former secretary to Viscount Milner. A Tariff Reformer with a social conscience, an expert on imperial, social and economic questions, he became the first chair of the Conservative Party in September 1911.

[5]   Diary entry, 5 September 1912, in M. Cole (ed.), *Beatrice Webb's Diaries, 1912–1924* (London, 1952), p. 5. The miners' campaign led to the Coal Mines (Minimum Wage) Act, 1912. This was an *ad hoc* measure passed by the government to end an impasse over wages between two well-organised groups: the mine owners and the coal miners. It was unconnected with the anti-sweating campaign that led to the establishment of trade boards. The Webbs disapproved of the Act because rates were only enforceable via civil, not criminal proceedings: S. and B. Webb, *English Local Government*, p. 561.

[6]   *Hansard* (Commons), 9 April 1913, esp. cols 1,280–90.

We ask for about £12,000 a year to run Trade Boards in four trades. If *all* workers in the country are to be covered the number of Trade Boards would be enormous and the cost would be a great burden. Mr Crooks is not proposing to 'extend' the Trade Board Act but to tear it up and substitute a universal minimum wage Act. He suggests no difference in the rates for men and women and treats all trades alike, but the Trade Boards themselves have fixed different rates for men and women and the rates are *not* the same in all trades.[7]

The Times sneered that: 'The terms of the motion and the tone of the speeches made in support of it have not the ring of reality.'[8] Unhappy that Crooks, an avowedly right-wing Fabian who prided himself on working closely with the Liberals, should have his 'moderate' submission so debased, the *New Statesman* responded that he 'was supported by the best economic science of to-day'. Evidently exasperated by the incapacity of the 'weak-kneed' Liberal Government, it asserted: 'True to the tradition of Liberalism, it does not really want to prevent them [low wages] at any inconvenience to the employers.'[9] H.V. Emy contends that on the eve of the First World War, the Liberals were on the verge of considering a programme that had the legal minimum as a key component.[10] Yet even advanced Liberals such as Rowntree, who advocated the general principle of a subsistence wage for every worker and the extension of wages boards to agriculture, held that there were limits beyond which wages could not be increased without creating unemployment.[11] In 1914 Hobson argued:

apart from the great bulk of casual workers in all less skilled trades, there are a large strata of skilled and trained adult labour in the staple trades of the country which are not paid a full subsistence wage. Such are the large bodies of women employed in factories and workshops and in retail trade, at wages varying between eight and fourteen shillings. Indeed, it may safely be asserted that the average wage of an adult working woman in this country, not in domestic service, is a sweating wage .... The same statement holds true of the wage of agricultural labour in most districts of the middle and southern counties of England.[12]

During the First World War, minimum wages were guaranteed to other categories of workers, notably in munitions in 1916 and in agriculture in 1917.[13] For eighteen months after the War great strides were made towards ending low pay in Britain.

---

7   NA, LAB11/150/L/1913.

8   *The Times*, 10 April 1913.

9   'Thirty Shillings a Week', *New Statesman*, 12 April 1913, p. 7.

10   Emy, *Liberals, Radicals and Social Politics*, esp. pp. 271–5. Tanner also cites Liberal progressivism on wages: D. Tanner, *Political Change and the Labour Party, 1900–1918* (Cambridge, 1990), pp. 65–70, 75, 209–11.

11   B.S. Rowntree, 'The effects of minimum wage legislation upon British industry', *Financial Review of Reviews*, July 1914, p. 745. See also B.S. Rowntree, *The Human Factor in Business* (London, 1922), p. 2.

12   J.A. Hobson, *Work and Wealth: A Human Valuation* (London, 1914), p. 179.

13   In return for guaranteed prices for wheat and oats, the Corn Production Act (1917) required farmers to pay their adult, male workforce a weekly minimum of twenty-five shillings. A central board with district boards operating in an advisory capacity determined rates. When the Act was repealed in 1920, the minimum weekly minimum had risen to forty-

Under the 1918 Temporary Regulation Act, virtually the entire working class was given the protection of a minimum wage. At the same time, the Labour Party published its *Labour and the New Social Order*. Largely written by Sidney Webb, it advanced, among other things, the enforcement of a universal national minimum wage. The state, the Ministry of Labour retorted, could not set a universal minimum rate and, besides, the experience of trade boards had clearly proven the need to handle wage issues industry by industry.[14] The recommendations of the War Cabinet Committee on Women in Industry that a national minimum wage be instituted similarly received short shrift.[15] The proposal of the National Industrial Conference (NIC) of 1919 that legal minimum time rates should be introduced and a national minimum wage commission be appointed to investigate how they should be fixed, was also rebuffed.[16]

Instead, in a bid to counteract the calls for a universal minimum wage and following the recommendations of the Whitley Committee, the Government passed

---

six shillings: R. Gowers and T. Hatton, 'The origins and early impact of the minimum wage in agriculture', *EHR*, 50 (1997), p. 83.

[14]   NA, LAB 11/166/ML/1658/2/1918

[15]   Ministry of Reconstruction, *Report of the War Cabinet Committee on Women in Industry*, p. 274; The majority recommended a fixed, subsistence rate for single women in all occupations (excluding domestic service) not covered by trade boards or industrial councils. Women working in London and large towns were to receive an additional supplement to compensate for the higher cost of living. Rates were to be adjusted at intervals to meet cost of living variations. Mothers' pensions, widows'/deserted wives' allowances and maternity benefits were recommended. All the members with the exception of Sir William Mackenzie and Beatrice Webb signed the majority report. The former insisted that the way forward was via trade boards/industrial councils rather than one national minimum. Webb produced an eighty-page minority report, later reproduced as *The Wages of Men and Women – Should They Be Equal?* (London, 1919). She argued for a national, subsistence minimum wage based on occupational or standard rates applicable to all irrespective of sex, creed or race. Wages above the national minimum, for which a definite standard of efficiency would be required, were to be determined by the circumstances of individual occupations. She rejected the popular formula of equal pay for equal work, and the principle that wages should be determined by family obligations, but accepted family endowment.

[16]   On 27 February 1919, the National Industrial Conference (NIC) delegated thirty employers' representatives and thirty representative trade unionists to form a provisional joint committee (PJC). On 4 April, the PJC members presented a unanimous report recommending, in addition to a national minimum wage, trade board expansion. The Ministry of Labour never seriously contemplated the former. On 19 July the PJC resigned. A Minimum Wage (Commission) Bill was moved on 18 August 1919. It failed to secure a second reading. A major sticking point was one of jurisdiction. The PJC wanted the Minimum Wage Commission to set the rates, not simply to enquire into the basis on which the rates might be set. The government found this unacceptable: see A. Salter's ILP pamphlet, *A Living Wage for All* (London, 1923), esp. pp. 6–8; R. Charles, *The Development of Industrial Relations in Britain, 1911–1939* (London, 1973), esp. pp. 229–57. See also, R. Lowe, 'The erosion of state intervention in Britain, 1917–24', *EHR*, 31 (1978), esp. pp. 274–5; R. Lowe, 'The failure of consensus in Britain: the national industrial conference, 1919–21', *Historical Journal*, 21 (1978), esp. pp. 656–66; R. Lowe, *Adjusting to Democracy: The Role of the Ministry of Labour in British Politics, 1916–1939* (Oxford, 1986), esp, p. 99.

the 1918 Trade Boards (Amendment) Act.[17] The legislation empowered the Minister of Labour to create additional boards without the lengthy procedure of a provisional order. It abolished the controversial six months' waiting period and reduced to two months the time allowed for objections. The Act permitted the establishment of boards not only where pay was exceptionally low but also where no adequate collective bargaining machinery existed. It was anticipated that, when collective bargaining mechanisms had become sufficiently developed, the boards would transform themselves into Joint Industrial Councils (JICs).[18]

Under the guise of an amending act, Parliament had thus advanced beyond a concern for sweating to viewing the boards as forerunners of voluntary collective bargaining. According to the legal theorist Otto Kahn-Freund, the legislation signified a crucial change in British statutory wage regulating policy. An old institution was given a new and significantly different social purpose, but without essentially changing its legal structure.[19] In the years immediately following the passage of the amending Act, the Ministry of Labour expended considerable time in rapidly expanding the board system. By 1921, sixty-three boards had been created covering some three million workers, and plans were announced to extend the system to additional industries further encompassing two million employees.[20]

I

Following the onset of the inter-war recession in the spring and early summer of 1920, a large section of employers became highly critical of the system.[21] While employers had found that trade boards had sheltered them from excessive pay settlements during the period of post-war boom and inflation, they now felt that the boards retarded downward wage adjustments. Wage reductions were deemed to be vital by the business community, especially in the labour-intensive industries dominated by trade boards. The subject was debated at the annual meetings of the Association of British Chambers of Commerce with the result that local chambers of commerce were advised to amass evidence demonstrating the deleterious effect of trade boards. The intention was to co-ordinate a strong case by the Association

---

[17] Chaired by John Henry Whitley, then Speaker of the House of Commons, the Whitley Committee had been appointed by the Ministry of Reconstruction in 1916 to enquire into the relations between employers and employees: *Relations Between Employers and Employed Second Report* (PP 1918, X).

[18] Unlike trade boards, JICs did not include independent members, and their decisions were not legally binding. Tawney contemptuously referred to these bodies as ineffective 'tea-parties': *Equality* (London, 1964; first published 1931), p. 179.

[19] O. Kahn-Freund, 'Minimum wage legislation in Great Britain', *University of Pennsylvania Law Review*, 97 (1948–1949), p. 787.

[20] *Report of the Committee Appointed to Enquire into the Working and Effects of the Trade Boards Acts*, p. 10. Consequent on the Anglo-Irish agreement of December 1921, the nineteen Irish boards (covering approximately 1,500,000 workers) established independent systems.

[21] By May 1921, unemployment had leapt to over 22 per cent of the insured population, peaking at 2.4 million: D.H. Aldcroft, *The British Economy, Volume 1: The Years of Turmoil, 1920–1951* (Brighton, 1986), pp. 5–6.

against the system.[22] More significantly, the Treasury, which had always disapproved of the extension of trade boards beyond sweated industries, encouraged like-minded employers to complain.[23]

Antagonism towards the boards culminated in the establishment of a distinctively conservative committee of inquiry headed by Viscount Cave.[24] The Cave Committee reported that the primary intention of trade boards was to prevent sweating and not to compensate for lack of voluntary collective bargaining machinery. It adjudged that the 1918 amending Act amounted to unjustifiable intrusion by the state in wage settlements and, on these grounds, recommended its repeal.[25] The report, in effect, advocated the burial of the 1918 Act before its consequences had come to fruition. The Government accepted this recommendation.[26] Tawney lamented that the committee, 'presumably of set purpose, did not include … any person who had practical experience of the procedure of the trade boards' and that the report was a 'somewhat amateurish document, replete with general statements unsupported by the all-important facts …'.[27] Trade unions, which had previously been distrustful of the board system, had come to view them as a buffer against unemployment. They pressed for their retention and expansion as well as better inspection and enforcement of their rates.[28]

The advent of a minority Labour Government ensured that the Cave reforms were never fully implemented. But the process of extending trade boards to other industries was virtually halted. The most important exception was in agriculture where, in 1924, the Labour Government passed the Agricultural Wages Act. Even here, the state was only permitted to uphold rates that varied according to the different localities.[29] The Fabian socialist and veteran of the NIC, G.D.H. Cole, regretted that:

---

[22] The Drapers' Chamber of Trade, according to Mallon, spearheaded the attack: *The Times*, 19 September 1921.

[23] The Treasury had long been incensed by what it perceived to be the financial extravagance of the Ministry of Labour. A grant to create a hundred boards had been used up with only thirty-six established. When the Labour department of the Board of Trade (previously responsible for trade boards) was absorbed into the new Ministry of Labour in 1916, the innovative qualities of the old department rapidly diminished: R. Davidson and R. Lowe, 'Bureaucracy and innovation in British welfare policy, 1870–1945', in W.J. Mommsen (ed.), *The Emergence of the Welfare State in Britain and Germany* (London, 1981), pp. 263–95. See also, R. Lowe, 'The Ministry of Labour, 1916–1924: a graveyard of social reform?', *Public Administration*, 52 (1974), esp. pp. 423–36; Lowe, 'The erosion of state intervention in Britain, 1917–24', esp. pp. 277–86; Lowe, *Adjusting to Democracy*, esp, pp. 60–61, 101–3.

[24] *The Times*, 20 September 1921.

[25] *Report of the Committee Appointed to Enquire into the Working and Effects of the Trade Boards Acts*, p. 27. The Committee's rebuttal of a national minimum wage received warm support from A.C. Pigou: 'Trade boards and the Cave Committee', *Economic Journal*, 32 (1922), p. 324.

[26] Ministry of Labour, *Statement of the Government's Policy in the Administration of the Trade Boards Acts* (PP 1922, XVII).

[27] Tawney, 'The minimum wage', p. 195.

[28] TUC, *Report of Proceedings: Annual TUC*, 1921 (London, 1921), esp. pp. 290–94.

[29] The 1924 legislation re-established agricultural wages boards for England and Wales (Scotland was excluded until 1937): Sells, *British Wages Boards*, pp. 35, 37–8. Gower and

The Agricultural Wages Bill, designed to restore the minimum wage that had been taken away in 1921, was mutilated by depriving the new Central Wages Boards of power to over-ride the decisions of the Agricultural Wages County Committees, and the Board was thus prevented from enforcing a national minimum wage ... The Labour view, right or wrong, was that, in view of the uncertainty of living costs, it was better to have no definite figure laid down by statute, as any figure thus given legal sanction might easily become a standard rather than a minimum.[30]

The Times agreed with the Government, observing that: 'Parliament has consistently and wisely refused to commit itself to a definition of a fair wage, or even of a minimum wage.'[31]

Disappointed with the lack of progress on low pay, the ILP, which now included Hobson amongst its advisors, renewed the living wage campaign. In March 1923, Alfred Salter introduced a motion in the Commons calling for a living wage.[32] Charles Sitch seconded it. In support, William Graham drew on Tawney's 'distinguished' trade board studies which, he urged, had 'proved that not only had the health of the workers very greatly improved, and not only had their remuneration been increased, but the cost of production, and the general efficiency of the industry as a whole, had been very greatly improved.'[33] The motion was defeated by a narrow majority of thirteen, 189 votes to 176.[34]

Three years later, in a report submitted to the National Administrative Council of the ILP, H.N. Brailsford, Hobson, A. Creech Jones and E.F. Wise proposed a living wage supplemented by family allowances.[35] It constituted the core of *Socialism in Our Time* – a policy approved by the ILP conference in April 1926, advocating nationalisation of public utilities, public ownership of banks and agricultural re-

---

Hatton maintain that the 1924 legislation raised wages but caused high unemployment: 'The origins and early impact of the minimum wage in agriculture', pp. 82–103. See also, T. Hatton, 'Trade boards and minimum wages, 1909–1939', *Economic Affairs*, 17 (1997), pp. 22–8. However, since agricultural labourers were not eligible to claim unemployment insurance before 1936, the available statistics are unreliable. Unemployment could also be the result of unprogressive management: G. Savage, 'Friend to the worker: social policy at the Ministry of Agriculture between the wars', *Albion*, 19 (1987), esp. p. 208. Rowntree, made much the same point: B.S. Rowntree. *The Human Needs of Labour* (London, 1937), p. 132.

[30]   G.D.H. Cole, *A History of the Labour Party from 1914* (London, 1948), p. 162.

[31]   *The Times*, 9 July 1924.

[32]   *Hansard* (Commons), 7 March 1923, cols. 627–76. See also Salter, *A Living Wage for All*. Salter was Labour MP for Bermondsey West.

[33]   *Hansard* (Commons), 7 March 1923, col. 650. A future president of the Board of Trade, Graham was an ILP member and Labour MP for Central Edinburgh. The author of *The Wages of Labour*, he was unseated at the October 1931 election.

[34]   *Hansard* (Commons), 7 March 1923, cols. 673–6.

[35]   H.N. Brailsford, J.A. Hobson, A. Creech Jones and E.F. Wise, *The Living Wage* (London, 1926). The state was not to impose the living wage, but merely to 'make the conditions' in which unions could successfully negotiate for its implementation (p. 35). Although the authors thanked Beatrice Webb for her 'valuable criticisms', they added 'she dissents from some of our proposals.' (*Ibid.*, p. 55).

organisation.[36] The basic rationale was the now familiar under-consumption thesis that, by improving wages and purchasing power, production would increase whilst unemployment would fall. Although the level of the actual living wage was not specified, the intimation was that it should be set at double the annual average working-class income.[37] Alan Booth considers that the living wage report was 'an enormously impressive ... pamphlet which addressed both the immediate problem of unemployment and the longer-run principles of economic policy under socialism.'[38] To David Marquand it was: 'a milestone in the history of the British left ... [It] pointed the way to the managed welfare capitalism which was to transform most of the western world after 1945 .... [I]t offered the Labour movement ... the basis of a reformist alternative, both to revolutionary Marxism and to its existing unhappy mixture of utopian aspiration and fiscal orthodoxy.'[39]

However, no agreement was reached on what might constitute a living wage. Some believed that the amount of the living wage should be determined by what could be skimmed off from individual profits, without causing long-term economic damage.[40] Others, like Brailsford, based their version of the living wage not upon what industry could pay but upon the minimum nutritional requirements of a man and wife plus family allowances.[41] The living wage concept was also rejected by the trade union movement and by Labour leaders, and it increased the rift between them and the ILP. Ernest Bevin, General Secretary of the Transport and General Workers' Union (TGWU), believed that a living wage was illusory and that it would enmesh unions within irrelevant political wrangles. He remained a fervent supporter of JICs and free collective bargaining.[42] Male trade unionists were particularly wary of family allowances.[43] Some held that family allowances would be used to justify wage cuts – especially since Eleanor Rathbone, its major proponent, was prepared to advocate payment of the allowance by employers in a deal combining wage reductions for childless workers.[44]

---

[36] However, Dowse considers that many ILPers balked at using it as a strategy in Parliament: R.E. Dowse, *Left in the Centre: The Independent Labour Party, 1893–1940* (London, 1966), pp. 121, 212–15.

[37] Brailsford *et al*, *The Living Wage*, p. 32.

[38] A. Booth, 'The Labour Party and economics', *Bulletin of the Society for the Study of Labour History*, 47 (1983), p. 37.

[39] Marquand, *Ramsay MacDonald*, p. 432.

[40] ILP, *The Living Income* (London, nd, 1929?), p. 4. See also J. Macnicol, *The Movement for Family Allowances* (London, 1980), p. 139.

[41] H.N. Brailsford, *Socialism for Today* (London, 1925), p. 77.

[42] A. Bullock, *The Life and Times of Ernest Bevin, Volume 1: Trade Union Leader, 1881–1940* (London, 1960), pp. 389–91.

[43] The General Council did not change its opposition until early 1942. It was not 'a wholehearted conversion': S. Pedersen, *Family Dependence and the Origins of the Welfare State: Britain and France, 1914–1945* (Cambridge, 1993), esp. pp. 331–5.

[44] F.M. Leventhal, *The Last Dissenter: H.N. Brailsford and His World* (Oxford, 1985), p.193. For Rathbone's exposition of family endowment and a living wage see, *The Disinherited Family* (London, 1924), esp. ch. 2.

Ramsay MacDonald thought that, if adopted, the ILP's 'Socialism in Our Time' programme would make Labour unelectable. In his view, the most enthusiastic ILP advocates of a living wage, such as James Maxton, wished to destroy capitalism, not to reform it. In private, Hobson informed MacDonald that he shared some of the latter's misgivings.[45] Fabian socialists also contended that the ILP's plan to nationalise those industries that were not able to pay the living wage would saddle governments with inefficient enterprises.[46] The Labour Party's answer to 'Socialism in Our Time', *Labour and the Nation* (1927), was written with Tawney's assistance. Significantly, it neglected to mention either family allowances or minimum wages. In this respect, according to Cole, it was more moderate than Webb's 1918 programme, which it replaced.[47] When Maxton introduced a Living Wage Bill, as a private Member on behalf of the ILP in February 1931, Margaret Bondfield, Minister of Labour, dismissed it as impractical.[48] A living wage was also bitterly opposed by R. Palme Dutt, the principal theoretician of the Communist Party of Great Britain. He condemned the concept as pallid reformism designed to rationalise capitalism and to distract workers from the real issues of the class struggle.[49] Orthodox economists refused to countenance the living wage scheme. So far as they were concerned, the only solution to Britain's economic problems was wage cuts leading to lower production costs and to more competitive exports.[50]

Opposition to the boards lessened following the onset of trade revival after 1934. Ethical employers, frustrated by wage under-cutting during the worst years of the slump, sanctioned the resumption of trade board growth. It is also arguable that many employers, following the implementation of Tariff Reform in 1931, found state intervention in the economy not only more acceptable but also conducive to an increased sense of business confidence.[51] Where a special case could be made – as in baking or road haulage – a modest expansion of government responsibility for wages was deemed acceptable.[52] The following years up until 1939 thus witnessed the creation of seven new trade boards plus the Road Haulage Wages Board, covering

---

[45]   Marquand, *Ramsay MacDonald*, p. 455.

[46]   Dowse, *Left in the Centre*, pp. 133–5. For Cole's antipathy to the ILP's living wage, see N. Riddell, '"The Age of Cole?" G.D.H. Cole and the British labour movement, 1929–1933', *Historical Journal*, 38 (1995), pp. 937, 942.

[47]   See Cole, *A History of the Labour Party*, p. 198.

[48]   J. Maxton, *A Living Wage for All* (London, 1931). See also, *The Times*, 7 February 1931. For further details, see W. Knox, *James Maxton* (Manchester, 1987), pp. 61–4, 78–80. See also, G. Brown, *Maxton* (Edinburgh, 1986), ch. 24. The Bill made no mention of family allowances: S. Pedersen, *Eleanor Rathbone and the Politics of Conscience* (New Haven, CT, 2004) p. 230. Pedersen feels that the ILP modified Rathbone's scheme to privilege class-centred rather than gender-based redistribution: Pedersen, *Family Dependence*, pp. 179–80. The ILP disaffiliated from the Labour Party in 1932.

[49]   R.P. Dutt, *Socialism and the Living Wage* (London, 1927).

[50]   Macnicol, *The Movement for Family Allowances*, pp. 139–40.

[51]   F.J. Bayliss, *British Wages Councils* (Oxford, 1962), esp. ch. 3.

[52]   K. Ewing, 'The state and industrial relations: "collective laissez-faire" revisited', *HSIR*, 5 (1998), pp. 26–7.

one and a half million workers in total.[53] At the same time, the Holidays With Pay Act (1938) empowered statutory wage-regulating authorities to make provision for paid time off.[54] Extension of the trade boards system, however, was no longer to be dependent on the initiative of the Minister for Labour but on the joint request of employers and workers in the industry concerned. This change of emphasis was most certainly a device to prevent a rapid growth of the scheme for, at the time, there were still many industries where both low pay and lack of collective bargaining facilities existed. Indeed, on this basis, virtually the whole of British industry would have been eligible, at some point during the 1930s, for trade board status.

Some reformers remained decidedly sceptical. Writing in 1938, Cole insisted:

> It is plain that the Trade Boards Acts as they stand, are not enough. It is highly desirable to maintain the Trade Board system, and to show renewed energy in applying it to additional trades ... But not even the widest extension of the Trade Board system will suffice to prevent the continuance of gross instances of underpayment over a wide range of miscellaneous occupations and small-scattered trades.[55]

He recommended that insured workers not encompassed by trade boards or the Agricultural Wages Act of 1924, should have a basic minimum wage established for them by a General Minimum Wage Commission.[56] The latter would proceed industry by industry, along lines similar to those established for trade boards. The Commission would be able to fix either uniform national or regional rates. These would become law when ratified by the Ministry of Labour. In addition, he considered that the state should fund a system of family allowances paid for out of general taxation.[57] In the same year, the future Conservative Prime Minister, Harold Macmillan in his *The Middle Way* proposed a national minimum wage for the employed, and subsistence benefits for the jobless.[58] According to Alan Booth and Melvyn Pack, this work was

---

[53]   Bevin was a key participant in securing the legislation that led to the Road Haulage Wages Board: Bullock, *The Life and Times of Ernest Bevin, Volume 1*, pp. 389–91, 601, 618–19. See also, A. Bullock, *The Life and Times of Ernest Bevin, Volume 2: Minister of Labour, 1940–1945* (1967), p. 93. The Road Haulage Act made provision for a central wages board and a number of area boards, the former being able, following consultation with the latter to submit proposals to the Minister for ratification regarding wages and holidays with pay: P. Smith, 'The road haulage industry, 1918–1940: the process of unionisation, employers' control and statutory regulation', *HSIR*, 3 (1997), pp. 49–80. See also, P. Smith, *Unionization and Union Leadership: The Road Haulage Industry* (London, 2001).

[54]   Bayliss, *British Wages Councils*, p. 42. See also, S. Jones, 'Trade union policy between the wars: the case of holidays with pay in Britain', *IRSH*, 31 (1986), p. 44.

[55]   G.D.H. Cole, 'Living wages', p. 13. Cole had aired similar ideas, briefly, in his *The Next Ten Years in British Social and Economic Policy* (London, 1929). They were developed in Cole's, *Fabian Socialism* (London, 1943), esp. pp. 83–7.

[56]   He suggested, for urban workers a maximum working week of forty-eight hours, and fifty shillings for adult men, and thirty shillings for women over eighteen: 'Living wages', pp. 20, 24–6.

[57]   *Ibid.*, pp. 25–30.

[58]   The debates in Macmillan's, *The Middle Way* (London, 1938) had developed from his participation in the Next Five Years Group. A broad coalition formed to combat unemployment,

the most sophisticated of all the radical programmes of the 1930s.[59] Nevertheless, at the outbreak of war, the direct responsibility of the state for wages matters remained limited.

II

The implementation of compulsory arbitration during the Second World War decreased the role of trade boards. In the main, board industries were not of vital importance to the war effort and a great deal of board labour was re-deployed to more essential war work such as munitions production.[60] Towards the end of the conflict, the boards acquired more significance and formed part of a post-war strategy on re-construction. Ernest Bevin, as Minister of Labour in the wartime coalition, urged that statutory wage regulating machinery was of paramount importance if Britain was to avoid the destructive effects of unemployment and disruption of collective bargaining machinery which had followed the First World War. Like Arthur Deakin, his successor as leader of the TGWU, and the General Council of the TUC, he ruled out a statutory national minimum wage.[61] So, too, did the Government, which viewed family allowances as an expedient method of minimising interference in the labour market without directly addressing the problem of low pay.[62] Equal pay legislation was also discounted on the grounds that it was likely to cause inflation and that it would subvert the principle of voluntary collective bargaining.[63]

Instead, the problem was addressed piecemeal. Catering remained one of the largest industries in the country in which wages, hours and conditions of work were uncontrolled by collective agreement or statutory regulation. Accordingly, the 1944 Catering Wages Act was passed, encompassing half a million people.[64] Under a

---

it included Eleanor Rathbone, Rowntree, Hobson and G.D.H. Cole: W.H. Greenleaf, *The British Political Tradition, Volume 2: The Ideological Heritage* (London, 1983), pp. 245–54. Marwick emphasises 'middle opinion' growth before the war: A. Marwick, 'Middle opinion in the thirties: planning, progress and political "agreement"', *English Historical Review*, 79 (1964), pp. 285–98.

[59]   A. Booth and M. Pack, *Employment, Capital and Economic Policy: Great Britain, 1918–39* (Oxford, 1985), p. 67.

[60]   Gazeley argues that gender pay inequality in munitions was considerably reduced during the war: I. Gazeley, 'The levelling of pay in Britain during the Second World War', *European Review of Economic History*, 10 (2006), pp. 175–204.

[61]   Bullock, *Life and Times of Ernest Bevin, Volume 2*, p. 194.

[62]   Family Endowment Society arguments such as encouraging the birth-rate and raising the social and economic status of women played little part in securing the Family Allowances Act of 1945: Macnicol, *The Movement for Family Allowances*, esp. p. 202; Pedersen, *Family Dependence and the Origins of the Welfare State*, p. 351.

[63]   Royal Commission on Equal Pay, *Report* (PP 1945–1946, IX). Three of the four female members signed a minority report disagreeing with the main recommendations: P. Thane, 'Towards equal opportunities? Women in Britain since 1945', in T. Gourvish and A. O'Day (eds), *Britain Since 1945* (London, 1991), pp. 189, 191.

[64]   The legislation was strongly attacked by the powerful Hotel and Restaurant Association, and many backbench Conservative MPs: Bullock, *Life and Times of Ernest Bevin, Volume 2*,

further Act of 1945, trade boards were re-named wages councils.[65] The new title signified both a return to the principles of 1918 which emphasised lack of collective bargaining, and a desire to cast off the old stigma associated with sweating.[66] The wages council system was subsequently extended to a number of trades, mainly in the retail sector and largely where a high proportion of the labour was female. The result of the 1945 Act was to increase the number of workers covered by legal wage regulating machinery to approximately three and a half million, a total which excluded the three-quarters of a million workers protected by Agricultural Wages Boards.[67]

The new legislation, by sheer weight of the numbers encompassed, thus transformed Britain's statutory wage fixing machinery. The *Economist* was moved to remark that the new law was 'one of the most important pieces of legislation ever laid before Parliament'.[68] The Act was widely regarded as a personal achievement for Bevin. At the time of his death in 1951, the number of wages councils had been increased to sixty.[69] Yet, as one critical observer commented: 'What does not exist is any clear minimum standard, even a rough one, which is regarded as a first charge on industry and which is embodied in any way in the decisions of Wages Councils ....'[70] Some trade unionists supported a universal, adult minimum wage at the 1946 TUC on the grounds that: 'there must be a new approach to wages.' However, General Council speakers condemned the proposal as unworldly and unworkable: the motion was lost by the comparatively narrow margin of 3,522,000 votes to 2,657,000.[71] The closeness of the vote in part reflected support for the measure in unions where Communist Party influence had grown during the war. But the Communist Party's temporary commitment to building the post-war social democratic consensus did not

---

pp. 220–24. But Bevin forged ahead, variously advising employers they could 'go to hell', or that the new board would afford protection to the 'good' employer: K. Jefferys (ed.), *Labour and the Wartime Coalition: From the Diary of James Chuter Ede, 1941–1945* (London, 1987), p. 113. See also, *Hansard* (Commons), 1 April 1943, cols 366–461.

[65]   Catering required a separate act because it was not technically a trade. In 1959, both sets of wages councils were consolidated.

[66]   Significantly, this legislation did not face the hostility, which had threatened to wreck the Catering Wages Bill two years previously. This was probably due to Bevin's growing authority and to the fact that, wages councils were accepted as a logical progression of Churchill's 1909 legislation: *The Times*, 17 January 1945. See also, Bullock, *Life and Times of Ernest Bevin, Volume 2*, p. 351.

[67]   Bayliss, *British Wages Councils*, pp. 72–3. The Fair wages resolution of 1946 was also passed.

[68]   *Economist*, 13 January 1945, p. 37.

[69]   Bullock, *Life and Times of Ernest Bevin, Volume 2*, pp. 353–4.

[70]   M. Heinemann, *Wages Front* (London, 1947), p. 48.

[71]   R.H. Edwards (National Union of Vehicle Builders) moved the resolution. J.R. Scott (Amalgamated Engineering Union) seconded it. Deakin and Joseph Hallsworth (General Council) opposed it: TUC, *Report of Proceedings: Annual Trades Union Congress, 1946* (London, 1946), pp. 417–24. See also, A. Campbell, N. Fishman and J. McIlroy, 'The post-war compromise: mapping industrial politics, 1945–64', in A. Campbell, N. Fishman and J. McIlroy (eds), *British Trade Unions and Industrial Politics, Volume 1: The Post-War Compromise, 1945–64* (Aldershot, 1999), pp. 77–8.

survive the onset of the Cold War. When the prospect of a national minimum wage resurfaced at the 1953 annual TUC, it was resoundingly rejected on the General Council's advice by a margin of almost two million votes.[72]

III

Under post-war conditions of full-employment, a widespread belief existed that low waged poverty had been conquered by the welfare state. This viewpoint appeared to be borne out by Rowntree's third survey in 1950, which concluded that low pay in York accounted for only 1 per cent of families below the poverty line compared with 52 per cent in 1899 and 42 per cent in 1936.[73] The subsequent decade and a half of apparent economic growth led many to question the wisdom of expanding the statutory wage regulating machinery. Chief amongst these critics was Fred Bayliss. Bayliss predicted that full employment was to be a permanent feature of British society and that the new economic circumstances rendered wages councils obsolete. He asserted that the system inhibited free collective bargaining and that steps should be taken to ensure that 'unnecessary' councils could be abolished more speedily.[74] His sentiments were shared not only by the trade union world but were also reflected in the report of the Royal Commission on Trade Unions' and Employers' Associations (the Donovan Commission) and by the National Board for Prices and Incomes (NBPI).[75]

The evidence of the Ministry of Labour before the Donovan Commission was particularly significant. It marked a crucial change in the department's post-war support for statutory wage-bargaining machinery. Future policy, the minister argued, would be directed towards the removal of wages councils as soon as the industry proved itself capable of sustaining voluntary collective bargaining.[76] With even the Ministry of Labour declaring that the dismantling of the councils would create few problems, it was scarcely surprising that the Commission on Industrial Relations (CIR), established by the Labour Government in 1969 could, after examining thirty councils, recommend that five should be eliminated.[77]

---

[72] TUC, *Report of Proceedings: Annual Trades Union Congress, 1953* (London, 1953), pp. 360–68. The minimum wage motion was lost by 4,767,000 to 2,883,000.

[73] B.S. Rowntree and G.R. Lavers, *Poverty and the Welfare State* (London, 1951), p. 35. See also, K. Coates and R. Silburn, *Poverty: The Forgotten Englishman* (Harmondsworth, 1970), p. 34.

[74] He also considered that large employers were using the councils to drive out smaller businesses, and that unions found councils a convenient scapegoat for recruitment inertia: Bayliss, *British Wages Councils*, esp. ch. 9.

[75] National Board for Prices and Incomes (NBPI), *General Problems of Low Pay*, Report no. 169 (London, 1971), p. 66. See also, Royal Commission on Trade Unions and Employers' Associations, 1965–1968, *Report* (London, 1968), p. 66.

[76] Royal Commission on Trade Unions and Employers' Associations 1965–1968, *Report*, esp. paragraphs 262–3.

[77] H.A. Clegg, *The Changing System of Industrial Relations in Great Britain* (Oxford, 1979), p. 425. The Commission on Industrial Relation (CIR) reports underestimated the number of low paid workers: See C. Craig *et al.*, *Labour Market Structure, Industrial Organization and*

The Labour Government of 1974–1979 continued this strategy.[78] As a result, between 1969 and 1979, fourteen councils were abolished.[79] Few mourned their passing. Academic researchers in the 1970s were quick to castigate wages councils. Jim Kincaid viewed wages councils as anachronisms with amusing titles such as the Ostrich and Fancy Feather and Artificial Flower Wages Council. He considered them to be a cumbersome and slow method of pay bargaining. As he pointed out:

> The employers are able to stretch out negotiations over a much longer period of time than is the case in other forms of wage bargaining. Thus workers covered by Wages Councils receive pay increases at much less frequent intervals than most groups of workers. Furthermore, when Wage Councils do eventually make pay awards, the percentage increase is almost always lower than the going rate for workers able to use normal methods of wage bargaining. The combination of lower increases less frequently awarded tends to leave wages council workers further and further behind in a period of rapid inflation.[80]

The labour economist Nick Bosanquet similarly criticised wages councils for having little impact on levels of pay:

> In general the Wages Councils have not been effective guardians of the lower paid. There were two main reasons for this failure. First, too much responsibility was on Government and on the independent members of the Councils. They were being asked to take rather fundamental decisions of politics – about raising the earnings of the lower paid relatively faster without proper guidance from the Government .... Secondly, the Wages Councils are too close to the circumstances of individual industries. They have given more weight to the possible difficulties of employers than to the injustices to workers implied by very low rates of pay.[81]

Few trade unionists, with the possible exception of those in clothing or retailing, thought the wages councils were worth retaining. Union leaders were antagonistic towards the system for several reasons. They believed that the councils institutionalised low pay and discouraged the labour force from seeking union membership.[82] A frequent complaint was that the workers were mainly engaged in small, scattered

---

Low Pay (Cambridge, 1982), pp. 152, 158. Armstrong's study of Birmingham demonstrated that low pay was not incompatible with full employment, especially if the demand for labour draws vulnerable or disadvantaged workers into the economy: E.G.A. Armstrong, 'Minimum wages in a fully employed city', *British Journal of Industrial Relations (BJIR)*, 4 (1966), pp. 22–38.

[78] The Conservative Government's Industrial Relations Act of 1971 also facilitated wages council removal. It jettisoned the requirement that adequate collective bargaining machinery should exist prior to a council's abolition: P. Davies and M. Freedland, *Labour Legislation and Public Policy: A Contemporary History* (Oxford, 1993), p. 190.

[79] Only ten councils had been abolished in the previous twenty-four years (1945 to 1968). See Clegg, *Changing System of Industrial Relations*, p. 424. The Employment Protection Act 1975, passed by the Labour Government, permitted wages councils to be transformed into SJICs.

[80] J.C. Kincaid, *Poverty and Equality in Britain* (Harmondsworth, 1973), pp. 189–90.

[81] N. Bosanquet, 'The real low pay problem', in F. Field (ed.), *Low Pay* (London, 1973), p. 31.

[82] S. Keevash, 'Wages councils: an examination of trade union and Conservative government misconceptions about the effect of statutory wage fixing', *Industrial Law Journal*, 14 (1985), esp. pp. 220–22.

establishments with a high turnover of employees. It followed, therefore, that the cost to the unions of serving the councils was too expensive.[83]

IV

Disillusionment with wages councils and the 're-discovery' of poverty from the 1960s meant that the notion of a national minimum wage once more demanded serious attention.[84] Interest grew further when, between 1964 and 1970, the Labour Government attempted to control incomes. TUC concern for the low paid was reflected in a resolution at its 1966 annual Congress. In return for supporting Labour's income policies, trade unions sought favourable consideration of a national minimum wage. Soon after, the Royal Commission on Trade Unions' and Employers' Associations (1968) recommended government examination of the idea.[85]

The Labour Party, following an inter-departmental working party report on a national minimum wage in 1969, preferred to legislate for equal pay.[86] It was argued that, since the majority of the low paid were female, then the Equal Pay Act of 1970 would be more beneficial than a national minimum wage. The fact that women were likely to be low paid not only because of discrimination but also as a result of occupational segregation, was brushed aside.[87] The TUC responded with its report on *Low Pay* in 1970. [88] However, in accordance with its traditional stance on free

---

[83]   R. Moore, 'Can't unions do more?', in F. Field (ed.), *Are Low Wages Inevitable?* (Nottingham, 1977), esp. pp. 114–17. See also, L. Bisset and E. McLennan, 'Britain's minimum wage system: the wages councils', in F. Field (ed.), *Policies Against Low Pay: An International Perspective* (London, 1984), p. 19.

[84]   Abel-Smith and Townsend demonstrated that, in 1960, three million lived in households where the head was in full-time work but had either relatively low wages or several children, or both: B. Abel-Smith and P. Townsend, *The Poor and the Poorest* (London, 1965). Further reports substantiated these findings. The most significant of these was the Ministry of Social Security's, *The Circumstances of Families* (London, 1967). A key development was the advent of the Department of Employment and Productivity's, New Earnings Survey (NES). Carried out annually from 1970, the surveys provided detailed knowledge of the nature and extent of low pay. From 1971, Family Income Supplement (FIS, later Family Credit) was introduced to improve the resources of those earning very low wages. Recipients of FIS were also eligible for a range of other means-tested benefits such as free school meals, rent and rate rebates. Take-up rates were very unsatisfactory and the new benefit created a 'poverty-trap' – if a claimant's take-home pay was increased, then the benefits were reduced or lost altogether: Kincaid, *Poverty and Equality in Britain*, pp. 119–24. In response, the poverty lobby, which had previously concentrated on the need for better social security for the low paid, turned to more direct action on low pay itself.

[85]   Royal Commission on Trade Unions and Employers' Associations, *Report*, p. 71, paragraph 280. See also, C. Duncan, *Low Pay: Its Cause, and the Post-War Trade Union Response* (Chichester, 1981), pp. 84–92.

[86]   Department of Employment and Productivity, *A National Minimum Wage* (London, 1969).

[87]   T. Rees, *Women and the Labour Market* (London, 1992), p. 22.

[88]   As a guideline for low pay negotiations, the General Council suggested a figure of about two-thirds of average male earnings to be adjusted in line with increases in average earnings.

collective bargaining, the TUC recommended that a national minimum wage should only be voluntary. The major problem of a legally enforceable minimum wage, it contended, was that the trade union movement had no guarantee that governments would either introduce or establish a minimum at a level acceptable to the unions.[89]

The year 1970 thus saw the TUC welcoming the Equal Pay Act, though criticising it for not proceeding with sufficient expedition, while at the same time shying away from a *statutory* minimum wage. This attitude set the seal on trade union opinion for the rest of the decade, with the conspicuous exception of the National Union of Public Employees (NUPE, now part of Unison). Although highly organised, many of NUPE's members were low paid.[90] NUPE thus demanded not a trade union solution to low pay but political action via a legal minimum wage.[91] NUPE's campaign fell on deaf ears. The traditional trade union view, with its emphasis on recruitment and the extension of free collective bargaining to end low pay, remained paramount. Despite NUPE's efforts, interest in a national minimum wage waned.

V

In the new, more challenging context of the early 1980s, the trade union consensus on state control of low pay shifted from negative to positive. In April 1982 the TUC wrote to the Secretary of State for Employment expressing its opposition to any further reductions in the number of wages councils.[92] This about-turn was due primarily to three factors. First, the experience in those trades where the councils had been withdrawn had not been reassuring. Researchers reported that few benefits had accrued to workers as a result of abolition while many were 'probably in a worse position'.[93] Similarly, the Advisory, Conciliation and Arbitration Service (ACAS), when examining the evidence for abolition of several wages councils, intimated that if the councils were terminated then significant sectors of the labour force would be exposed to low pay.[94]

Second, trade unions reacted to new and adverse economic conditions. The TUC, confronted by recession, declining trade union density, and more 'flexible' working practices, was now forced to accept that free collective bargaining backed up by strong trade union organisation was no longer a permanent feature of the economy. It acknowledged that when unions were threatened by a growing element of unorganised, part-time, temporary or subcontracted employees, then a fresh and

---

[89] TUC, *Low Pay: General Council Discussion Document* (London, 1970), esp. paragraph 69.

[90] NBPI, *The Pay and Conditions of Manual Workers in Local Authorities, the National Health Service, Gas and Water Supply*, Report no. 29 (London, 1967).

[91] A. Fisher and B. Dix, *Low Pay and How to End It* (London, 1974), ch. 4.

[92] Keevash, 'Wages councils', p. 224.

[93] C. Craig, J. Rubery, R. Tarling and F. Wilkinson, *After the Wages Councils: Industrial and Staff Canteens* (Cambridge, 1980), p. 108. See also, C. Craig *et al., Abolition and After: The Paper Box Wages Council* (Cambridge, 1981).

[94] C. Pond, 'Wages councils, the unorganised and the low paid', in G.S. Bain (ed.), *Industrial Relations in Britain* (Oxford, 1983), p. 199.

more comprehensive policy towards low pay was required. The situation which Bevin had feared after the Second World War, of an unorganised and marginalised group of workers under-cutting the pay and conditions of the organised sector, had become uncomfortably real.[95]

Third, and most importantly, trade unions reacted to the Conservative government's attack on the traditional statutory wage-fixing machinery. The composition of wages councils, with their tripartite structure and legally enforceable minimum rates, did not commend them to the new, free-market Conservatism. To the Thatcherite right, wages councils were an interference with the freedom of employers to offer, and job seekers to accept, work which would otherwise be welcome. The system created rigidities in the labour market and caused unemployment. Conservative economists such as Patrick Minford attributed the failure of many small businesses to wages council awards. The councils, he maintained, evinced no concern for employers' ability to pay. Pay awards were often retrospective and difficult to interpret. This made financial planning virtually impossible. Minford declared: 'In short, if a Wages Council comes to be regarded as effective, it is ... harmful; if it is looked upon as ineffective, it is therefore otiose and useless.'[96]

Initially, the Conservative Party intended to abolish wages councils outright by withdrawing the United Kingdom, in 1985, from the International Labour Organisation agreement requiring signatory governments to maintain some form of protective wage machinery for low-paid workers. Yet, while the Institute of Directors and the National Federation of Self-Employed and Small Businesses spearheaded the movement to abolish the councils, the Confederation of British Industry (CBI), Chambers of Commerce and the Institute of Personnel Management (IPM now Chartered Institute of Personnel and Development), saw some merit in the system. The CBI argued that many employers, rather than relying on the vagaries of free collective bargaining, preferred to negotiate through wages councils. Additionally, the CBI feared that abolition, instead of modification, would lead to worsening industrial relations, a movement of the workforce to more militant trade unionism and to price-cutting by disreputable firms. Above all, the CBI was concerned that the emasculation of wages councils would galvanise trade union support for a statutory national minimum wage.[97]

The British Chamber of Commerce and the IPM took a similar stance, stating that abolition would neither stimulate business nor reduce unemployment.[98] The *Economist* pointed out that the operations of wages councils were similar to the much-vaunted system of pendulum arbitration abroad, viewed by many at the time as the great hope for the future of collective bargaining.[99] Mindful of these comments, the Conservative government reformed rather than abolished the system

---

[95]   TUC, *Fair Wages Strategy: National Minimum Wage* (London, 1986), p. 6.

[96]   P. Minford *et al.*, *Unemployment: Cause and Cure* (Oxford, 1983), p. 122.

[97]   CBI, *News Bulletin*, 29 June 1984. See also, S. Winyard, 'Low pay', in D. Bell (ed.), *The Conservative Government, 1979–84: An Interim Report* (London, 1985), pp. 57–8.

[98]   IPM, *The Future of Wages Councils* (London, 1982). See also, remarks by Lords McCarthy and Graham in *Hansard* (Lords), 6 June 1986, col. 1,223 and 8 July 1986, col. 238.

[99]   *Economist*, 1 June 1985, p. 30.

in 1986. Each council was only permitted to set one adult minimum hourly rate and a single minimum overtime rate, regardless of skill. In addition, the procedure for the abolition of councils was simplified and young workers, those under twenty-one, were removed from wages council protection on the grounds that this would improve their job opportunities. At the same time, the 1946 Fair Wages Resolution was rescinded.[100]

Opponents of the 1986 legislation proposed alternative strategies to solve the problems of wages councils. Chris Pond, then director of the Low Pay Unit (LPU), recommended improved co-ordination between the councils; rationalisation of their structure; and increased provision for research, publicity and dissemination of information. He also believed that many councils could be transformed into SJICs with reliance upon final settlement by ACAS, thereby obviating the need for independent representatives. Most importantly, supporters of the councils insisted that there was an urgent need to improve the level of enforcement, which had remained a major weakness of the system from its inception.[101]

Rather than choosing to reform wages councils, the Major government abolished them in 1993.[102] The removal of the remaining twenty-six councils withdrew pay protection from an estimated 2.5 million workers, the bulk of whom were women or members of ethnic minorities.[103] According to the TGWU, abolition of the councils caused pay levels to fall and the gap between men's and women's pay to increase.[104] Against such claims, the government argued that the system was introduced in a very different economic and social climate: Victorian and Edwardian sweatshops were a thing of the past; workers were now better organised; there was extensive legislation to protect workers' rights; and the welfare state provided comprehensive social security. As a result, wages councils ceased to be relevant to modern employment conditions.[105] The government, on the same reasoning, seriously considered abolishing the Agricultural Wages Boards, despite support for the boards from both sides of the industry.[106]

---

[100] Davies and Freedland, *Labour Legislation and Public Policy*, p. 541.

[101] C. Pond, 'No return to sweatshops! Government economic strategy and the wages councils', *Low Pay Unit (LPU) Pamphlet*, 37 (1985); C. Pond, 'The great pay robbery', *LPU Pamphlet*, 50 (1988). See also, LPU, 'Who needs wages councils?', *LPU Pamphlet*, 24 (1983); A. Bryson, 'Undervalued, underpaid and undercut: the future of wages councils', *LPU Pamphlet* 53 (1989).

[102] Employers' support had waned because of the difficulties wages councils placed on Sunday retail trading. As Rubery notes 'employers came to favour abolition for reasons other than that the councils set too high wages': J. Rubery, 'The low paid and the unorganized', in P. Edwards (ed.) *Industrial Relations: Theory and Practice in Britain* (Oxford, 1995), p. 559. See also, *Financial Times*, 20 February 1988.

[103] LPU, 'Keep your councils', *New Review*, 18 (1992), p. iv.

[104] TGWU, *In Place of Fear: The Future of the Welfare State* (London, 1994).

[105] Minford *et al.*, *Unemployment: Cause and Cure*, pp. 122, 124, 127.

[106] TGWU, *In Place of Fear*, p. 20. Agricultural Wages Boards encompass about 200,000 farm workers.

VI

The demise of the wages council system, as the CBI predicted, strengthened the national minimum wage lobby. Advocates of a national minimum wage urged that low wages not only caused hardship, injustice and higher property crime, but also contended that the community paid dearly in economic terms for inefficiency and lower productivity.[107] Like the Webbs, they promoted the concept of the 'good' employer to reassure big business that a national minimum wage was practicable, worthwhile and to the latter's economic advantage. Responsible employers, it was suggested, realised that effective management should hinge on a well-designed, quality product expertly manufactured – rather than on rapacious under-cutting. A national minimum wage would also boost tax and national insurance contributions while simultaneously reducing social security spending by removing around 300,000 families from dependence on benefits such as family credit. Echoing the sentiments of Hobson, it was argued that a minimum wage would be a vital reflationary step – workers would have more to spend and this would increase purchasing power.[108] Several economists, drawing extensively from the experience of the USA and Canada, where the practical consequences of the minimum wage were already visible, and employing a monopsonistic model of the labour market, emphasised that such a policy generated jobs.[109]

A key turning point for the labour movement occurred in 1986 at the annual TUC Congress. The decision to support a statutory minimum wage was heralded as the most important pronouncement of the proceedings.[110] Rodney Bickerstaffe, then general secretary of NUPE, informed delegates that their decision was historic, not just for the poor but for the entire trade union world.[111] However, supporters of a universal minimum failed to overcome the traditional hostility of the TGWU and of the electricians' union. The latter anticipated that, should a minimum wage be placed on the statute book, they would be urged not to press for excessive pay rises for fear of jeopardising the position of the low waged. A statutory policy with legal

---

[107] S. Machin and C. Meghir, 'Does crime pay better?', *Centrepiece*, 4 (1999), pp. 25–7.

[108] C. Pond and S. Winyard, 'The case for a national minimum wage', *LPU Pamphlet*, 23 (1983) pp. 1–63; P. Brosnan and F. Wilkinson, 'Cheap labour: Britain's false economy', *LPU Pamphlet*, 45 (1987), pp. 1–44; P. Brosnan and F. Wilkinson, 'A national statutory minimum wage and economic efficiency,' *Contributions to Political Economy*, 7 (1988), pp. 1–48.

[109] When Card and Krueger investigated the impact of the 1992 rise in New Jersey's state-specific minimum wage, they found that employment in the state's fast food sector increased at a swifter rate than that in neighbouring Pennsylvania. Moreover, low-wage restaurant workers in New Jersey (those most exposed to change), saw their employment opportunities improve relative to those in higher-waged restaurants: D. Card and A. Krueger, *Myth and Measurement* (Princeton, N.J., 1995). For criticisms of Card and Krueger, see D. Neumark and W. Wascher, 'The effects of New Jersey's minimum wage on fast food employment: a re-evaluation using payroll data', National Bureau of Economic Research, *Working Paper*, 5224 (1995).

[110] *Labour Weekly*, 5 September 1986.

[111] TUC, *Report of Proceedings: Annual Trades Union Congress, 1986* (London, 1986), pp. 559–60.

enforcement was viewed by these unions as the slippery road to a rigid incomes policy.[112]

Nevertheless, as a result of the Congress resolution, the TUC was committed to consolidating its talks with the Labour Party on a joint wages policy. Labour Party thinking had moved a long way since the 1960s. In that decade, Harold Wilson had declared that, without greater economic growth, a minimum wage would be disastrous for Britain.[113] Twenty years later, Labour proposed that a minimum wage, if set at a reasonable level, would not dislocate the economy and was realisable almost immediately.[114] By 1994, Labour's Commission on Social Justice which produced the Borrie Report concluded: 'We firmly believe that a national minimum hourly wage is essential.'[115] Initially, the details on both the statutory level and the eventual target for the minimum were left deliberately vague. However, in defiance of the Labour Party leadership and its own general secretary, John Monks, the TUC in September 1996 placed a precise amount on a minimum. After much heart-searching and following a heated debate, the conference agreed to a call from amongst others, Rodney Bickerstaffe and Arthur Scargill, leader of the National Union of Mineworkers, for a national minimum wage of £4.26 an hour equal to £162 a week or £8,400 a year. This was equivalent to half-median male earnings. An estimated 5.4 million workers would have benefited, of whom 70 per cent would be women, most of them working part-time.[116]

The Labour Party preferred not to fix a definite amount until after the outcome of the 1997 election was known. It considered that the nature of the minimum should be the subject of negotiations between the union movement, employers and the government: the minimum could not be imposed unilaterally by the state. The Labour Party proposed that a Low Pay Commission (LPC) involving 'social partners' and independent nominees should examine the economic and employment implications as well as considerations of social justice before fixing the level. Such a body would scrutinize all suggestions made by the 'social partners'. In other words, the Labour leadership viewed union support for £4.26 an hour as merely one bid amongst many: the proposed commission would also receive submissions from the CBI and other organisations.[117]

Opponents of a statutory national minimum wage declared that, if it was set above market equilibrium levels, unemployment would occur, particularly amongst the young and unskilled. It would also decrease on-the-job training possibilities.[118] The Conservative Party argued that 750,000 jobs would vanish if a minimum wage

---

[112] *Ibid.*, pp. 561–7.

[113] M. Barrett-Brown, 'The welfare state in Britain', in R. Miliband and J. Saville (eds), *Socialist Register* (London, 1971), p. 204.

[114] Hattersley, *Choose Freedom*, pp. 245–9; R. Hattersley, *Economic Priorities for a Labour Government* (London, 1987), pp. 180–85. See also, TUC/Labour Party, *Low Pay: Policies and Priorities* (London, 1986), esp. pp. 10–20.

[115] Commission on Social Justice, *Social Justice: Strategies for National Renewal* (London, 1994), p. 204.

[116] TGWU, *In Place of Fear*, p. 107.

[117] D. Metcalf, 'The British national minimum wage', *BJIR*, 37 (1999), pp. 174–8.

[118] D. Forrest, 'Low pay or no pay?' *Hobart Paper*, 101 (1984).

equal to half male median wages was introduced and two million workers would lose out if a minimum was set at two-thirds of median male earnings.[119] Furthermore, a minimum wage would not significantly reduce poverty for the single reason that many households had no income from work at all. Poverty and low wages were not clearly correlated and, as a result, a minimum wage was a very blunt instrument for solving this particular problem. Conversely, many workers who were low paid tended to be supplementary wage earners, such as the young still living at home, the old, or married women who augmented the principal source of family income.[120] It was asserted that minimum wage legislation was only popular because it pandered to certain powerful interest groups. These include organised labour determined to uphold union negotiated pay levels from being undercut by the unorganised; high waged areas anxious to forestall industry relocation to lower-waged ones; and established employers eager to stave off competitors by harnessing new firms to a high legal 'going rate'.[121] It was also argued that a minimum wage would have a serious impact upon the pay structure. If other groups of workers sought to restore differentials, inflation would increase. Deepak Lal, one of the chief critics of a minimum wage, thus concluded that it was 'an inefficient, well-intentioned but inexpert interference with the mechanisms of supply and demand …'.[122]

In response, Stephen Bazan, using Family Expenditure Survey (FES) data, estimated that a minimum set at half or two-thirds of male median hourly rates would only reduce employment, at the most, by 250,000 and 885,000 respectively. There would be a time lag of several years before the full consequences would be felt. The impact would be localised in three sectors: clothing, distribution and miscellaneous services.[123] The CBI, too, conceded that a minimum set at £4 would lead only to the loss of about 150,000 jobs.[124] Others contended that most successful companies were already content to pay in the region of £4 an hour.[125] As for any narrowing of differentials and consequent inflationary pressures, supporters of a minimum wage maintained that, since the low paid were concentrated in particular sectors, there could be no direct link through pay bargaining structures with more highly paid groups.[126] The claim that the working poor shared households with wealthier wage earners was also contested. It was pointed out that such a proposition assumed that

---

[119] L. Simpson and I. Paterson, 'A national minimum wage for Britain?' *Economics*, 28 (1992), pp. 12–18.

[120] D. Lal, 'The minimum wage: no way to help the poor', *Institute of Economic Affairs Occasional Paper*, 95 (1995), pp. 12–13. See also, the *Economist*, 9 September 1995, p. 30.

[121] Forest, 'Low pay or no pay?', *passim*.

[122] Lal, 'The minimum wage: no way to help the poor', p. 31.

[123] S. Bazen, 'On the employment effects of introducing a national minimum wage in the UK', *BJIR*, 28 (1990), pp. 215–26. The Expenditure and Food Survey replaced the Family Expenditure Survey (FES) in April 2001. For criticisms of Bazen, see S. Fernie and D. Metcalf, *Low Pay and Minimum Wages: The British Evidence* (London, 1996), p. 18.

[124] LPU, 'Why £4?', *New Review*, 35 (1995), p. 6.

[125] P. Bassett, 'Please sir, can I have some more?', *New Statesman*, 21 June 1996, p. 22.

[126] Pond and Winyard, 'The case for a national minimum wage', esp. pp. 54–7. See also, LPU, *New Review* (1994), p. 12; J. Hughes, 'The realities of a national minimum wage', in TUC (ed.), *Arguments for a National Minimum Wage* (London, 1995), pp. 71–2.

household incomes were always pooled. Moreover, rising wage inequality in the 1980s and 1990s had resulted in a firm link between low pay and low household income.[127]

Finally, supporters of reform argued that a national minimum wage was not necessarily a very revolutionary measure. A number of western European countries had possessed such a floor to their wage bargaining agreements since the Second World War.[128] To allay fears that the minimum might have adverse economic effects, wages had often been fixed at 'safety-net' levels'. As one observer noted: '... in most cases minimum wages do not appear to have a great impact on income distribution, in large part because they are set rather low – at molehill levels.'[129] Such problems led several to comment that, alongside the minimum wage, there was a need for other mechanisms to be deployed. These included strengthening equal pay and sex discrimination legislation, fair wages measures, greater child-care provision, improved access to arbitration as well as a complete overhaul of the tax and social security system to nullify the poverty trap.[130] Some even suggested that if Britain was entirely to remove its historic tradition of low pay, it must also be prepared to institute maximum income limits as well as minimum wages.[131] These were contentious proposals but supporters insisted that the costs must be weighed against the penalties of not introducing such legislation – in terms of social justice or economic efficiency.[132]

---

[127] TUC, *Campaigning for a National Minimum Wage* (London, 1996), p. 8. See also, J. Goode, R. Lister and C. Callender, 'Whose money is it anyway', *New Review*, 50 (1998), pp. 14–17; R. Dickens and S. Machin, ' Minimum wages in Britain: issues involved in setting a minimum wage', in TUC, *Arguments for a National Minimum Wage*, pp. 56–7; R. Dickens, 'The national minimum wage', in R. Dickens, *et al, The State of Working Britain: Update 2001* (London, 2001), pp. 51–3.

[128] Luxembourg introduced a national minimum wage in 1944. France (1950), Spain (1963), the Netherlands (1969) and Portugal (1974) followed. Some, like Austria, Belgium, Denmark and Germany set a minimum wage through legally binding industry level collective agreements: LPU, 'Minimum wages in Europe', *New Review*, 29 (1994), pp. 8–12.

[129] R. Freeman, 'National minimum wage: making mountains out of molehills', in Field, *Policies Against Low Pay*, p. 145.

[130] LPU, *Submission to the Low Pay Commission on the National Minimum Wage* (London, 1997), esp. pp. 28–30. See also, Fernie and Metcalf, *Low Pay and Minimum Wages: The British Evidence*, pp. 20–24.

[131] P. Townsend, 'An alternative anti-poverty programme', *New Society*, 7 October (1982), pp. 22–3. See also, A. Simms, 'Now for a maximum wage', *Guardian*, 6 August 2003. The Borrie Report dismissed a maximum income on the grounds that 'high-earners would simply move to other ... countries ....': Commission on Social Justice, *Social Justice*, p. 207.

[132] Brosnan and Wilkinson, 'Cheap labour', esp. pp. 19–28; Brosnan and Wilkinson, 'A national statutory minimum wage', esp. pp. 19–32.

VII

Following its landslide victory in 1997, Labour fulfilled its election promise and set up the LPC.[133] The National Minimum Wage Bill was introduced in the Commons on 26 November 1997 and received Royal assent on 31 July 1998. In April 1999 the minimum was set at £3.60 an hour for adults and at £3.00 for those aged between 18 and 21.[134] According to George Bain, the LPC's first chair, the initiative was a triumph for the unprotected worker, a cause for celebration and a landmark in the battle against low pay.[135] To Rodney Bickerstaffe it was an 'historic victory for the low paid'.[136] David Metcalf, an LPC member, predicted that, although initially very modest, the minimum rates would raise the pay of around three million by roughly one third. This would be attained at a direct cost of adding only 0.6 per cent to the total national wages bill. Since the minimum wage formed part of a wider strategy directed at 'making work pay', including Working Families Tax Credit (WFTC), it was unlikely to have adverse overall consequences.[137] Borrowing the words of Harold Spender, he insisted the national minimum wage (NMW) is a 'labour market plimsoll line for the whole nation. More than 9 in 10 workers will be paid above the NMW but the exploitation of those at the bottom of the pay distribution will be drastically reduced and, hopefully, completely eliminated'. [138]

Others have been less enthusiastic and view Labour's national minimum wage as a missed opportunity to end poverty pay.[139] Four major criticisms have been put forward: the rates set are inadequate; large numbers are excluded; 'rogue' employers are being subsidised via in-work benefits; and, most important of all, governments

---

[133] A small civil service secretariat and eight commissioners representing the interests of unions, employers, and the academic community assist the Low Pay Commission's (LPC) chair. The representatives sit as individuals, not as delegates. Initially, responsibility for enforcement was assigned to a special compliance unit within the Inland Revenue. Since April 2006, HM Revenue and Customs have assumed this task.

[134] Hourly rates in October 2006 were: adults, £5.35; 18–21 year olds, £4.45 and those aged 16–17, £3.30. The minimum rate for the adult standard worker covered by the Agricultural Wages Board for England and Wales was higher at £5.74.

[135] G. Bain, 'The national minimum wage: further reflections', *Employee Relations*, 21 (1999), pp. 22–3.

[136] *Guardian*, 29 March 1999.

[137] D. Metcalf, 'The Low Pay Commission and the national minimum wage', *Economic Journal*, 109 (1999), p. 65. In 1999, Working Families Tax Credit (WFTC) replaced Family Credit. Payment was via the wage packet to the main child carer. As a tax credit, rather than a means-tested benefit like Family Credit, it was hoped that WFCT would reduce the stigma associated with claiming benefits. In 2002, WFTC was split into two new tax credits: Child Tax Credit (CTC) and Working Tax Credit (WTC). The intention of the CTC was to minimise the impact of unemployment and the poverty trap by creating a seamless system of financial support for parents whether they were in or out of work. The WTC encompassed households without children. It was payable to those over twenty-five working at least thirty hours a week.

[138] Metcalf, 'The Low Pay Commission and the national minimum wage', p. 65. See also Spender's introduction to Snowden's, *The Living Wage*, p. x.

[139] N. Burkitt, C. O 'Donnell and B. Patel, 'George Bain and a "mechanistic formula": the purpose and politics of £3.60', *Industrial Relations Journal*, 30 (1999), pp. 178–83.

can disregard the LPC's recommendations. First, it is suggested that the national minimum wage has had minimal impact on UK wage inequality because the legislation only tackles the most extreme cases of exploitation.[140] Social explorers such as Fran Abrams and Polly Toynbee have revealed how difficult it is for single people to survive on the minimum wage, especially in London.[141] The LPC has moved cautiously and, as Metcalf candidly admits, its decisions are based not on matters of principle but on pragmatism.[142] The LPC's initial optimistic estimate of coverage encompassing two million has been revised downwards. It is now thought that only one million, 4.4 per cent of the workforce, have benefited.[143] Some place the figure as low as 800,000 – far fewer than the two and a half million encompassed by wages councils when they were abolished in 1993.[144]

Second, coverage is not universal and leaves much to be desired. Certain groups, such as au pairs, family members working in family businesses and share fishermen, fall outside the ambit of the legislation.[145] Although young workers aged 16–17 have been included since 2004, rates for those under 21 are lower than for adults.[146] This raises the possibility that cheaper, teenage labour might be substituted for older employees. These exceptions, it is argued, undermine the simplicity of a single, national minimum and possibly impinge on compliance. Workers and employers are confused regarding their legal entitlements and obligations.[147] Lack of clarity, despite rigorous enforcement, also encourages unscrupulous employers to find ways around paying the minimum wage, for example by methods such as cutting hours or by making illegal deductions.[148]

---

[140] R. Dickens and A. Manning, 'Spikes and spillovers: the impact of the national minimum wage on the wage distribution in a low-wage sector', *Economic Journal*, 114 (2004), pp. 95–101.

[141] F. Abrams, *Below the Breadline: Living on the Minimum Wage* (London, 2002); P. Toynbee, *Hard Work: Life in Low Pay Britain* (London, 2003).

[142] Metcalf, 'The Low Pay Commission', p. 51.

[143] LPC, *National Minimum Wage Report, 2005* (London, 2005), p. 4; B. Simpson, 'The national minimum wage five years on: reflections on some general issues', *Industrial Law Journal*, 33 (2004), p. 24.

[144] Estimating coverage is problematic since many of the low paid possess more than a job. See R. Dickens and A. Manning, 'Minimum wage, minimum impact', in R. Dickens *et al.* (eds), *The Labour Market Under New Labour* (London, 2003).

[145] B. Simpson, 'Implementing the national minimum wage: the 1999 regulations', *Industrial Law Journal*, 28 (1999), pp. 171–82. Employers are also legally entitled to make deductions from the minimum wage for accommodation and transport costs: LPC, *National Minimum Wage Report, 2006* (London, 2006), esp. pp. 120, 125. See also, TUC, *Below the Minimum: Agency Workers and the Minimum Wage* (London, 2005).

[146] Apprentices aged 16–17, and those on pre-apprenticeship programmes continue to be excluded from the national minimum wage.

[147] Simpson, 'The national minimum wage five years on', esp. pp. 25, 28.

[148] Abrams catalogues how hours were 'lost' when employers calculated wages. One employer compelled his workers to attend an unpaid 'training day'. Others made illegal deductions for protective clothing required by health and safety regulations: *Below the Breadline*, esp. pp. 12, 72. Employers are not obliged to maintain detailed records as originally

Third, it is claimed that tax credits are being used as an indirect subsidy to employers, that the state is funding a low-pay culture. The New Policy Institute argues that tax credits not only encourage the persistence of low pay but that they act as disincentives for employers to become more efficient. Moreover, for low-income earners in receipt of tax credits, a rise in the minimum wage produces only a small increase in net household income. As research in America demonstrates, tax credits are unlikely to succeed unless accompanied by measures to boost jobs that pay sufficient to remove working families out of poverty.[149]

Finally, establishing the level of the minimum is a political decision. Since there is no automatic up-rating mechanism, increases are arbitrary and unpredictable.[150] Governments can disregard the findings of the LPC.[151] It has also been suggested that the LPC is not an exemplar of social partnership in other ways: for example, there is little input from the unions.[152] According to Bob Simpson, the LPC is far removed from the old system of wages councils. The latter's tripartite composition had a semblance of joint regulation. Employers' and workers' representatives came together to agree where the floor under wages should be established, and wage rates could only be referred back to the council by government, not modified.[153] Indeed, while recent writers have suggested that Tawney was an early precursor of New Labour thinking, it is doubtful whether a minimum wage which can be altered according to the whims of politicians or the vagaries of elections, would have commended itself to him.[154]

Disappointment with the low rates set and the 'making work pay' strategy has rekindled enthusiasm for the concept of 'a living wage'. In their joint submission to the LPC in 2002, both Unison and the LPU argued that the national minimum wage should be converted into a living income, that earnings rather than benefits should become the major route out of poverty.[155] Inspired by the living wage movement in America and the activities of the East London Communities Organisation (TELCO),

---

suggested. They are obliged to keep 'sufficient records' only: LPU, 'A star is born. How brightly will the new minimum shine?', *New Review*, 56 (1999), p. 12.

[149] New Policy Institute, *Why Worry Any More About Low Pay?* (London, 2004), esp. pp. 14–18, 20.

[150] See LPC, *National Minimum Wage Report, 2005*, p. 2, where it is accepted that the timing and implementation of the rates depends 'both on Government intentions and the Parliamentary schedule'. For employers' concerns, see: CBI Evidence to the LPC, *Reviewing the National Minimum Wage* (London, 2004), p. 51 esp. sections 126–8.

[151] The LPC recommended in its first report a £3.20 youth rate for 18–20 year olds. The Government reduced the rate to £3.00 and increased the age limit to 21: Metcalf, 'The Low Pay Commission', p. 49.

[152] LPU, 'Can't pay, won't pay?', *New Review*, 51 (1998), p. 6.

[153] Agricultural wages Boards have retained their tripartite composition: B. Simpson, 'A milestone in the legal regulation of pay: the National Minimum Wage Act 1998', *Industrial Law Journal*, 28 (1999), p. 31.

[154] For Tawney as an intellectual inspiration for Labour's 'third way', see B. Clift and J. Tomlinson, 'Tawney and the third way', *Journal of Political Ideology*, 7 (2002), pp. 315–31.

[155] Unison/LPU, *Justice, Not Charity. Why Workers Need a Living Wage* (London, 2002). Due to financial difficulties, the LPU ceased to exist in 2003.

Ken Livingstone pledged in his mayoral campaign to establish a living wage unit at the Greater London Authority.[156] In April 2006, the unit's second report recommended an adult living wage of £7.05 an hour, slightly below two-thirds of median London earnings but higher than the then national minimum adult rate of £5.05.[157] The intention was to compensate low-paid workers for the higher costs of living in the capital and to establish 'a fair day's pay for a hard day's work' for all metropolitan government and contract employees. The campaign attracted the backing of unions, churches, mosques and other community groups.

As in the past, the living wage movement has not been free of criticisms. First, the most extreme critics, echoing Palme Dutt in the 1920s, have suggested that a living wage, like a national minimum wage, merely bolsters capitalism.[158] Living wage arguments have become embroiled in conflicts about globalisation and the feasibility of implementing wage controls in one country when international corporations compete across borders.[159] Second, it is asserted that the living wage principle is based on how much is required to sustain the 'average' family and that this is a rather antiquated and androcentric view of British household structure. Critics feel that it is too closely connected to the concept of the family wage and the male breadwinner norm.[160] Third, it is maintained that the campaign for a living wage undermines the LPC and will result in consigning its successful partnership into oblivion. The LPC states that its remit is to establish a floor to wages to prevent exploitation, not to establish an income sufficient for a family to live on. The tax credit system has been introduced to achieve the latter goal.[161]

Finally, it is argued that, if a living wage is to be successful, it must take into account regional differences in the cost of living and local economic circumstances.[162] Against this view, the CBI claims that differences can be greater within a region than between regions. Local living costs are only one part of the equation. While

---

[156] Since 1994, living wage laws have been implemented in over one hundred American cities or other local government entities: D. Fairris and M. Reich, 'The impacts of living wage policies', *Industrial Relations*, 44 (2005), p. 1. D. Figart, E. Mutari and M. Power, *Living Wages, Equal Wages: Gender and Labor Market Policies in the United States* (London, 2002); TELCO, *Mapping Low Pay in East London* (London, 2001). TELCO is a broad alliance of faith groups, student organisations, union branches and charities spanning five East London boroughs.

[157] The living adult wage was first calculated at £6.70 in April 2005. The youth/apprenticeship living wage was set at £6. See Living Wage Unit, *A Fairer London: The Living Wage in London. Second Annual Report* (London, 2006). In April 2007, the London living wage was increased to £7.20 an hour. The publication of a separate youth living wage was discontinued as a result of the European Employment Directive outlawing unjustified age discrimination in employment or vocational training: Living Wage Unit, *A Fairer London: The Living Wage in London. Third Annual Report* (London, 2007).

[158] C. Grover, 'Living wages and the "making work pay" strategy', *Critical Social Policy*, 25 (2005), pp. 23–4.

[159] Figart, Mutari and Power, *Living Wages, passim*.

[160] Grover, 'Living wages', pp.16–18.

[161] LPC, *National Minimum Wage Report, 2005*, p. 9 esp. section 7.28.

[162] Grover, 'Living wages', pp. 20–21.

Londoners might feel they need a higher rate to cover the costs of housing, rural seasonal workers could argue they require a higher minimum to compensate for much short-time working. As far as the CBI is concerned, housing accommodation costs should not be passed onto the employer but should be dealt with via social policy legislation. The CBI is also adamant that a regional living wage would be too difficult to monitor and enforce. A single national rate is superior because it is less bureaucratic and more easily understood.[163]

Such problems have led Polly Toynbee to suggest that if the government wishes to raise the minimum to the maximum sustainable, it should bring back wages councils, setting different rates to fit not only different industries but different areas, with an extra weighting for the south-east. They could fix a far higher 'living wage' rate for all state employees and those jobs contracted out to the state.[164] The long debate through the twentieth century on mechanisms to end poverty wages in Britain has once more turned full circle.

---

[163] CBI, *Evidence to the Low Pay Commission: Reviewing the National Minimum Wage*, esp. p. 52. The LPU expounded much the same case, while adding that there will 'always be those who live in one area but work in another': LPU, *Submission to the Low Pay Commission on the National Minimum Wage* (London, 1997), p. 12. However, the British Apparel and Textiles Federation, and the Federation of Small Businesses believe there is a strong case for a regional minimum wage: LPC, *National Minimum Wage Report, 2005*, (London, 2005), p. 9, section 7.28.

[164] P. Toynbee, 'Mean Britain', *Guardian*, 17 January 2003.

Conclusion

> It will be an interesting study for the future historian of the Social Reform movement in the early years of the twentieth century to explain the rapid acclimatisation in England of the idea of the Legal Minimum Wage.
>
> *Women's Industrial News*, 18 (1914), p. 285

By the end of the twentieth century, the explanation of sweating as comprising part of the wider issue of poverty had changed considerably from the narrow definition of sweated labour dating back to the 1840s. Initially this identified needlewomen and male artisans in declining trades as the chief objects of sweating. Jews later featured stereotypically as both exploiters and exploited. By the 1890s, women homeworkers were simultaneously foregrounded as passive victims as well as perpetuators of a degenerate sweated 'underclass'. From 1906, those depicted plying their trade in sensational exhibitions of sweated labour were no longer designated as isolated 'white slaves' but as exploited citizens denied a fair day's pay for a fair day's work. They were also perceived as a danger to national efficiency.

Numerous remedies to solve sweating, such as emigration, the restriction of female labour, more stringent inspection of domestic workshops, better education for all and co-operative production, had all been variously advanced but subsequently found wanting. Eventually, Edwardians sanctioned one cautious measure that they thought might curb sweating at its root: the 1909 Trade Boards Act. When seeking to explain the intractability of nineteenth and early-twentieth century sweating, historians have emphasised women homeworkers' disadvantaged industrial position and the sexual discrimination practised towards them. Yet if sweating is equated with low pay, both males and females were its victims. In recognition of this, the legislation was gender neutral and covered homeworkers as well as factory hands.

An active participant in the tortuous struggle to attain the Trade Boards Act, Tawney heralded it as one of the most successful pieces of social legislation in the first quarter of the twentieth century.[1] His surveys on chainmaking and tailoring pointed to the considerable advantages of the boards. Researchers have suggested that although the 'substance of these studies has never been challenged by any empirical investigation, there is no need to question them ....'[2] But Tawney's material should be treated with caution. Intent on according the boards a positive image, he embellished his findings. The Act was a very tentative measure and encompassed less than a quarter of a million workers. As Winston Churchill candidly acknowledged in 1909, if earnings of less than one pound a week were 'sweated', then one-third of the British workforce suffered from the complaint. Influenced by the Webbs, Churchill

---

[1]   Tawney, 'Fixing minimum wages', p. 19.

[2]   R. Bowlby, 'Union policy toward minimum wage legislation in post-war Britain', *Industrial and Labor Relations Review*, 11 (1957), p. 81.

had initially declared his willingness 'to drawn a line below which we will not allow persons to live and labour'.[3] In its final form, the Act applied to only four trades and made no attempt to establish what the desired minimum should be. It did little to correct the imbalance of incomes between the rich and the poor in Edwardian Britain. Prior to 1918, additional industries could only be granted trade board status by means of a provisional order, a time-consuming process requiring parliamentary approval. Trade board inspection, too, left much to be desired.

The significance of the1909 Trade Boards Act lay more in heralding a break in economic and social thought than in its practical ability to combat sweating. New theories had to be fashioned in order to dethrone orthodox economic thinking that state intervention in the wages contract would be ruinous for the British economy. Contrary to Schmiechen's belief, the challenge to the old laissez-faire assumptions came, not in the 1880s, but essentially in the mid-1890s. Even then, there was a time lag between the new theories being advocated and them becoming more widely accepted. Policy makers were not converted to state control of low pay until after 1906. Although reformers were quite content to use the rhetoric of Hobson and the Webbs, they shied away from sanctioning either a minimum wage or a living income. The legitimacy of state interference had been acknowledged but the suspicion of state intervention remained so powerful that the state itself was not empowered to settle the actual amount of wages. The state's role was minimised and the 1909 Act left the settlement of rates to representatives of the trades concerned and independent members, with the state only using its authority to enforce the decisions of the boards.

However, it is misleading to suggest that the limitations of Britain's early low pay machinery can be solely ascribed to the hostility of organised labour or to the machinations of cautious Board of Trade officials, in particular, Llewellyn Smith. Nor is it correct to assume that the boards were merely the handiwork of employers craving for social control. The key pressure group, the NASL, was also largely responsible for restraining the role of minimum wage legislation in Britain. Mallon remained adamant that a universal minimum wage would 'render sterile' the good works of Britain's selective statutory wage fixing machinery.[4] Both Tawney and Mallon vehemently rejected the Webbs' concept of a subsistence minimum wage; they praised the boards for allowing rates to be settled by those who had a strong grasp of the industry and a personal stake in ensuring that the productivity of the occupation would not be impaired.

Tawney anticipated that the boards would be harbingers of industrial democracy and that they would inject an element of just rewards and fair competition into British manufacturing. In reality, trade boards and their modern counterparts, wages councils, were prisoners of their collective laissez-faire origins. On their own, they were incapable of remedying poverty pay. Many poor workers, including those in the public sector, fell outside the scope of the system. When wages councils were abolished in 1993, they covered only two and a half million employees, some ten per cent of the workforce. The removal of the last vestiges of traditional wage fixing by the Conservative government inadvertently facilitated the implementation of a national

---

[3]   W.S. Churchill, *Liberalism and the Social Problem* (London, 1909), p. 82.

[4]   Mallon, 'Industry and a minimum wage,' p. 7.

minimum wage. The retention of wages councils, as Bayliss observes, would have defeated the purpose of introducing a comprehensive, national minimum wage.[5]

Taking a long view, the history of minimum wage legislation in Britain is one of continuity, discontinuity and tergiversation. Still central to the case for legislation is a fine calculus between social justice and economic efficiency. The arguments of minimum wage proponents at the present time bear a remarkable similarity to those propounded by Hobson and the Webbs over a century ago. Many of the 'good employer' arguments recently deployed to convert the business lobby are neither new nor radical. Even the concept of the Victorian 'sweatshop' is still in common usage as a derogatory term for low-paying, exploitative firms. Notwithstanding their flaws, wages councils continue to have their champions who insist that the system should be re-introduced in a refurbished form. The recent heated debates over a national minimum wage indicate that orthodox neo-classical theory has lost little of its tenacity. Low pay is persistently linked with socially undervalued jobs and with those accorded low labour market status.

There have also been new departures. Supporters of a national minimum wage can now claim that its implementation is hardly a leap in the dark. Since 1944, a number of western European countries have established such a floor to their wage bargain agreements. The recent overwhelming acceptance of a statutory national minimum wage by the British labour movement also signifies a fundamental change of strategy. After the Second World War and until the early 1980s, most trade unionists preferred to deal with the issue of poverty pay through a strategy based on voluntary collective bargaining underpinned by a regularly upgraded target wage. The rapid expansion of the service sector, the spread of part-time working and the decline of trade union membership have caused unions fundamentally to reassess what state intervention can achieve. This has been heightened by the TUC's belief that the future of British trade unionism presently lies in a deepening of its close involvement in the social chapter of the European Union.[6]

There have also been setbacks for minimum wage supporters. The initial rates suggested by the Low Pay Commission were extremely low, coverage is not comprehensive and there is no mechanism for ensuring annual upgrading. These defects have led Wilkinson and Deakin to insist that, despite the national legal minimum wage and the adoption of the European Community's Working Time Directive, regulation of work in Britain remains partial and selective. In their view, the principle of collective laissez-faire still remains triumphant over the Webbs' alternative conception of a comprehensive labour code.[7] There are also many who predict that if Britain is to finally end its historic tradition of low pay, she must be prepared to institute maximum income limits as well as minimum wages. As Peter Townsend has long contended: 'A policy for the poor will not work unless it is also one for the rich'.[8]

---

[5] F. Bayliss, 'Making a minimum wage work', *Fabian Pamphlet* 545 (1991), p. 21.

[6] L. Dickens and M. Hall, 'The state, labour law and industrial relations', in Edwards, *Industrial Relations*, esp. p. 294.

[7] Deakin and Wilkinson, *Law of the Labour Market*, pp. 271, 342

[8] Townsend, 'An alternative anti-poverty programme', p. 22.

Appendix 1

Committee of the National Anti-Sweating League, 1907
President:
Mr George Cadbury
Vice Presidents:

The Rt. Hon. Sir Charles W. Dilke, Bart, MP
Earl of Dunraven
The Rt Hon. Herbert Gladstone, MP
Mr J.C. Gray (The Co-operative Union)
Mr Keir Hardie, MP
Canon Scott Holland
Dr Horton
Miss Irwin (Scottish Council for Women's Trades)

Earl of Lytton
Rev. J. Scott Lidgett, MA
Mr Wm Maxwell (Co-operative Wholesale Society, Scotch)
The Chief Rabbi
The Hon. W. Pember Reeves
Bishop of Ripon
Mr and Mrs Sydney [sic] Webb
Mr H.G. Wells
Mr Henry Vivian, MP

Hon. Treasurer:
Earl Beauchamp

Executive Committee

Chairman:
Mr A.G. Gardiner

Mr George N. Barnes, MP
Miss Clementina Black
Mr Herbert Burrows
Mrs M.A. Gasson*
Mrs Herbert Gladstone
Miss M.R. Macarthur*
Mr L.G.C. Money, MP*
Mrs W. Pember Reeves

Mr George Shann, MA*
Mrs Bernard Shaw
Mrs H.J. Tennant
The Rev. Peter Thompson
Miss Gertrude Tuckwell*
Mr Fabian A.G. Ware
Rev. J.E. Watts-Ditchfield
Rev. H. Russell Wakefield

* Members of the General Purposes Committee

Secretary:

Mr Jas J. Mallon

Source: NASL, *Second Annual Report Adopted at the Annual Meeting Held 21 July 1908* (London, 1909), p. 3.

Appendix 2

Minimum rates in the first four trades covered by the Trade Boards Act, 1909

Trade	Weekly hours in trade used by Trade Board for basis	Initial Trade Board Rates					
		Per hour		Per week on basis of normal number of hours			
		Male d	Female d	Male s	d	Female s	d
Chain	54	5	2½	22	6	11	3
Lace finishing (home-workers)	52	–	2¾	–		11	11
Paper box	52	6	3	26	0	13	0
Ready-made tailoring	50	6	3¼	25	0	13	6

Source: D. Sells, *The British Trade Boards System* (London, 1923), p. 80.

Select Bibliography

Details of archival sources and published sources of a primary nature are contained in the notes. Place of publication is London unless otherwise stated.

Books

Abel-Smith, B., and P. Townsend, *The Poor and the Poorest* (1965).

Abrams, F., *Below the Breadline: Living on the Minimum Wage* (2002).

Adrian, A.A., *Mark Lemon: First Editor of Punch* (1966).

Aldcroft, D.H., *The British Economy, Volume 1: The Years of Turmoil, 1920–1951* (Brighton, 1986).

Alexander, L., *Women, Work and Representation: Needlewomen in Victorian Art and Literature* (Athens, Ohio, 2003).

Atkinson, A.B., *Incomes and the Welfare State: Essays on Britain and Europe* (Cambridge, 1995).

Auerbach, J., *The Great Exhibition of 1851: A Nation on Display* (New Haven, CT, 1990).

Bayliss, F.J., *British Wages Councils* (Oxford, 1962).

Beales, H.L., *The Making of British Social Policy* (Oxford, 1946).

Bercusson, B., *Fair Wages Resolutions* (1978).

Black, J., *The English Press, 1621–1861* (Stroud, 2001).

Booth A., and M. Pack, *Employment, Capital and Economic Policy: Great Britain, 1918–39* (Oxford, 1985).

Briggs, A., *Social Thought and Social Action: A Study of the Work of Seebohm Rowntree, 1871–1954* (1961).

Briggs, A., and A. Macartney, *Toynbee Hall: The First Hundred Years* (1984).

Brown, G., *Maxton* (Edinburgh, 1986).

Buckman, J., *Immigrants and the Class Struggle: The Jewish Immigrant in Leeds, 1880–1914* (Manchester, 1983).

Bullock, A., *The Life and Times of Ernest Bevin, Volume 1: Trade Union leader, 1881–1940* (1960).

Bullock, A., *The Life and Times of Ernest Bevin, Volume 2: Minister of Labour, 1940–1945* (1967).

Bythell, D., *The Sweated Trades: Outwork in Nineteenth Century Britain* (1978).

Caine, B., *Victorian Feminists* (Oxford, 1992).

Card, D., and A. Krueger, *Myth and Measurement* (Princeton, N.J., 1995).

Charles, R., *The Development of Industrial Relations in Britain, 1911–1939* (1973).

Chitty, S., *The Beast and the Monk: A Life of Charles Kingsley* (1974).

Christensen, T., *Origin and History of Christian Socialism, 1848–54* (Aarhus, 1962).

Clegg, H.A., *The Changing System of Industrial Relations in Great Britain* (Oxford, 1979).

Clegg, H.A., *A History of British Trade Unionism since 1889, Volume 2* (Oxford, 1985).

Clubbe, J., *Victorian Forerunner: The Later Career of Thomas Hood* (Durham, N.C., 1968).

Coates, K., and R. Silburn, *Poverty: The Forgotten Englishman* (Harmondsworth, 1970).

Cole, G.D.H., *Fabian Socialism* (1971; first published 1943).

Cole, G.D.H., *A History of the Labour Party From 1914* (1948).

Cole, M., *Beatrice Webb* (1945).

Collette, C., *For Labour and for Women: The Women's Labour League, 1906–1918* (Manchester, 1989).

Craig, C., et al., *After the Wages Councils: Industrial and Staff Canteens* (Cambridge, 1980).

Craig, C., et al., *Abolition and After: The Paper Box Wages Council* (Cambridge, 1981).

Craig, C., et al., *Labour Market Structure, Industrial Organization and Low Pay* (Cambridge, 1982).

Davidson, R., *Whitehall and the Labour Problem in Late-Victorian and Edwardian Britain* (1985).

Davies, J.R., *The Great Exhibition* (Stroud, 1999).

Davies, P., and M. Freedland, *Labour Legislation and Public Policy: A Contemporary History* (Oxford, 1993).

Deakin, S., and F. Wilkinson, *The Law of the Labour Market: Industrialization, Employment and Legal Evolution* (Oxford, 2005).

Dennis, N., and A. Halsey, *English Ethical Socialism: Thomas More to R.H. Tawney* (Oxford, 1988).

Dowse, R.E., *Left in the Centre: The Independent Labour Party, 1893–1940* (1966).

Drummond, D., *Crewe: Railway Town, Company and People, 1840–1914* (Aldershot, 1995).

Duncan, C., *Low Pay: Its Cause, and the Post-War Trade Union Response* (Chichester, 1981).

Emy, H.V., *Liberals, Radicals and Social Politics, 1892–1914* (Cambridge, 1973).

Englander, D., and R. O'Day (eds), *Retrieved Riches: Social Investigation in Britain, 1840–1914* (Aldershot, 1995).

Feldman, D., and G.S. Jones (eds), *Metropolis London: Histories and Representations since 1800* (1989).

Feldman, D., *Englishmen and Jews: Social Relations and Political Culture, 1840–1914* (New Haven, CT, 1994).

Fernie, S., and D. Metcalf, *Low Pay and Minimum Wages: The British Evidence* (1996).

Figart, D., E. Mutari and M. Power, *Living Wages, Equal Wages: Gender and Labor Market Policies in the United States* (2002).

Fisher, A. and B. Dix, *Low Pay and How to End It* (1974).

Fishman, W.J., *East End Jewish Radicals, 1875–1914* (1975).

Fitzgerald, R., *British Labour Management and Industrial Welfare, 1846–1939* (Beckenham, 1988).

Fitzgerald, R., *Rowntree and the Marketing Revolution, 1862–1969* (Cambridge, 1995).

Freeden, M., *Liberalism Divided: A Study in British Political Thought, 1914–39* (Oxford, 1986).

Fried, A., and R. Elman (eds), *Charles Booth's London* (Harmondsworth, 1971).

Gainer, B., *The Alien Invasion: The Origins of the Aliens Act of 1905* (1972).

Gartner, L.P., *The Jewish Immigrant in England, 1870–1914* (1973).

George, D., *London Life in the Eighteenth Century* (Harmondsworth, 1966).

Gray, R., *The Factory Question and Industrial England, 1830–1860* (Cambridge, 1996).

Green, D.R., *From Artisans to Paupers: Economic Change and Poverty in London, 1790–1870* (1995).

Greenleaf, W.H., *The British Political Tradition, Volume 2: The Ideological Heritage* (1983).

Hamilton, M.A., *Arthur Henderson: A Biography* (1938).

Hamilton, M.A., *Mary Macarthur: A Biographical Sketch* (1925).

Hammerton, A.J., *Emigrant Gentlewomen: Genteel Poverty and Female Emigration, 1830–1914* (1979).

Hannam, J., *Isabella Ford* (Oxford, 1989).

Harris, B., (ed.), *Famine and Fashion: Needlewomen in the Nineteenth Century* (Aldershot, 2005).

Harrison, B., *Not Only the 'Dangerous Trades': Women's Work and Health in Britain, 1880–1914* (1996).

Harrison, J.F.C., *Early Victorian Britain, 1832-51* (1988; first published 1971).

Harrison, R., *Life and Times of Sidney and Beatrice Webb, 1858-1905: The Formative Years* (2000).

Hart, V., *Bound By Our Constitution: Women Workers and the Minimum Wage* (Princeton, N.J., 1994).

Hartley, A.J., *The Novels of Charles Kingsley: A Christian Social Interpretation* (Folkestone, 1977).

Hattersley, R., *Economic Priorities for a Labour Government* (1987).

Hattersley, R., *Choose Freedom: The Future for Democratic Socialism* (1987).

Hattersley, R., *Blood and Fire: William and Catherine Booth and Their Salvation Army* (1999).

Hay, J.R., *The Development of the British Welfare State, 1880–1975* (1978).

Haywood, I., *The Literature of Struggle: An Anthology of Chartist Fiction* (Aldershot, 1995).

Haywood, I., (ed.), *Chartist Fiction, Volume Two* (Aldershot, 2001).

Himmelfarb, G., *The Idea of Poverty: England in the Early Industrial Age* (1984).

Honeyman, K., *Well Suited: A History of the Leeds Clothing Industry, 1850–1990* (Oxford, 2000).

Humpherys, A., *Travels Into the Poor Man's Country: The Work of Henry Mayhew* (Athens, GA, 1977).

Huneault, K., *Difficult Subjects: Working Women and Visual Culture, Britain, 1880–1914* (Aldershot, 2002).

Jenkins, R., *Sir Charles Dilke: A Victorian Tragedy* (1958).

John, A.V. (ed.), *Unequal Opportunities: Women's Employment in England, 1800–1918* (Oxford, 1986).

Jones, G.S., *Outcast London* (Oxford, 1971).

Joyce, P., *Work, Politics and Society: The Culture of the Factory in Later Victorian England* (Brighton, 1980).

Kincaid, J.C., *Poverty and Equality in Britain* (Harmondsworth, 1973).

Knox, W., *James Maxton* (Manchester, 1987).

Koot, G.M., *English Historical Economics, 1870-1926: The Rise of Economic History and Neomercantilism* (Cambridge, 1987).

Koss, S., *Fleet Street Radical: A.G. Gardiner and the Daily News* (1973).

Leventhal, F.M., *The Last Dissenter: H.N. Brailsford and His World* (Oxford, 1985).

Lewis, J., *Women and Social Action in Victorian and Edwardian England* (Aldershot, 1991).

Lipman, V., *A History of the Jews in Britain Since 1858* (Leicester, 1990).

Lowe, R., *Adjusting to Democracy: The Role of the Ministry of Labour in British Politics, 1916–1939* (Oxford, 1986).

Lunn, K., (ed.), *Hosts, immigrants and Minorities: Historical Responses to Newcomers in British Society, 1870–1914* (Folkestone, 1980).

McBriar, A.M., *Fabian Socialism and English Politics, 1884–1918* (Cambridge, 1962).

McBriar, A.M., *An Edwardian Mixed Doubles: The Bosanquets versus the Webbs* (Oxford, 1987).

McIvor, A. J., *Organised Capital, Employers' Associations and Industrial Relations in Northern England, 1880–1939* (Cambridge, 1996).

Macnicol, J., *The Movement for Family Allowances* (1980).

Macnicol, J., *The Politics of Retirement in Britain, 1878–1948* (Cambridge, 1998).

Mappen, E., *Helping Women at Work: The Women's Industrial Council, 1889–1914* (1985).

Marquand, D., *Ramsay MacDonald* (1977).

Meacham, S., *Toynbee Hall and Social Reform, 1880–1914* (1987).

Mess, H.A., *Factory Legislation and its Administration, 1891–1924* (1926).

Minford, P., *et al.*, *Unemployment: Cause and Cure* (Oxford, 1983).

Morgan, C., *Woman Workers and Gender Identities, 1835-1913* (2001).

Morris, J., *Women Workers and the Sweated Trades* (Aldershot, 1986).

Mowat, C. L., *The Charity Organisation Society, 1869–1913: Its Ideas and Work* (1961).

Neff, W., *Victorian Working Women* (1966; first published 1929).

Norman, E., *The Victorian Christian Socialists* (Cambridge, 1987).

Ormrod, D., (ed.), *Fellowship, Freedom and Equality: Lectures in Memory of R.H. Tawney* (1990).

Pedersen, S., *Family Dependence and the Origins of the Welfare State: Britain and France, 1914–1945* (Cambridge, 1993).

Pedersen, S., *Eleanor Rathbone and the Politics of Conscience* (New Haven, CT, 2004).

Pelling, H., *A History of British Trade Unionism* (Harmondsworth, 1973; first published 1963).

Pennington, S., and B. Westover, *A Hidden Workforce: Homeworkers in England, 1850–1985* (Basingstoke, 1989).

Phelps Brown, E.H., *The Growth of British Industrial Relations* (1959).

Pope-Hennessy, U., *Canon Charles Kingsley* (1948).

Rees, T., *Women and the Labour Market* (1992).

Reid, J.C., *Thomas Hood* (1963).

Reisman, D., *State and Welfare: Tawney, Galbraith and Adam Smith* (1982).

Richards, T., *The Commodity Culture of Victorian England: Advertising and Spectacle, 1851–1914* (Stanford, CA, 1990).

Roberts, B.C., *The Trades Union Congress, 1868–1921* (1958).

Rule, J., *The Experience of Labour in Eighteenth-Century Industry* (1981).

Schmiechen, J., *Sweated Industries and Sweated Labor: The London Clothing Trades, 1860–1914* (1984).

Schwarz, L.D., *London in the Age of Industrialisation: Entrepreneurs, Labour Force and Living Conditions, 1700–1850* (Cambridge, 1992).

Searle, G., *The Quest for National Efficiency* (Oxford, 1971).

Shinwell, M., *Lead With the Left: My First Ninety-Six Years* (1981).

Simey, T.S. and M.B., *Charles Booth: Social Scientist* (Oxford, 1960).

Smith, P., *Unionization and Union Leadership: The Road Haulage Industry* (2001).

Staples, W. and C., *Power, Profits and Patriarchy: The Social Organization of Work at a British Metal Firm, 1791–1922* (Lanham, MD, 2001).

Stewart, M., and L. Hunter, *The Needle is Threaded* (Southampton, 1964).

Taithe, B., (ed.), *The Essential Mayhew: Representing and Communicating the Poor* (1996).

Tanner, D., *Political Change and the Labour Party, 1900–1918* (Cambridge, 1990).

Taylor, M., *Ernest Jones, Chartism and the Romance of Politics, 1819–69* (Oxford, 2003).

Terrill, R., *R.H. Tawney and His Times: Socialism as Fellowship* (1974).

Thompson, E.P., *William Morris: Romantic and Revolutionary* (1955).

Thompson, E.P., *The Making of the English Working Class* (1963).

Thompson, N., *The Real Rights of Man: Political Economics For the Working Class, 1775–1850* (1998).

Thorp, M., *Charles Kingsley* (New York, 1969; first published 1937).

Tickner, L., *The Spectacle of Women: Imagery of the Suffrage Campaign, 1907–14* (1988).

Tomlinson, J., *The Unequal Struggle: British Socialism and the Capitalist Enterprise* (1982).

Toynbee, P., *Hard Work: Life in Low Pay Britain* (2003).

Trainor, R., *Black Country Élites: The Exercise of Authority in an Industrialized Area, 1830–1914* (Oxford, 1993).

Williams, K., *From Pauperism to Poverty* (1981).

Williams, R., *Culture and Society, 1780–1950* (1967).

Wright, A., *R.H. Tawney* (Manchester, 1987).

Yeo, E., *The Contest for Social Science: Relations and Representations of Gender and Class* (1996).

Articles and Essays

Armstrong, E.G.A., 'Minimum wages in a fully employed city', *British Journal of Industrial Relations*, 4 (1966).

Bailey, V., '"In darkest England and the way out": the Salvation Army, social reform and the labour movement, 1885–1910', *International Review of Social History*, 29 (1984).

Bain, G., 'The national minimum wage: further reflections', *Employee Relations*, 21 (1999).

Barrett-Brown, M., 'The welfare state in Britain', in R. Miliband and J. Saville (eds), *Socialist Register 1971* (1971).

Bazen, S., 'On the employment effects of introducing a national minimum wage in the UK', *British Journal of Industrial Relations*, 28 (1990).

Bender, D., 'Sweatshop subjectivity and the politics of definition and exhibition', *International Labor and Working Class History*, 61 (2002).

Biagini, E., 'British trade unions and popular political economy, 1860–1880', *Historical Journal*, 30 (1987).

Bisset L., and E. McLennan, 'Britain's minimum wage system: the wages councils', in F. Field (ed.), *Policies Against Low Pay: An International Perspective* (1984).

Blackburn, S., 'Working-class attitudes to social reform: Black Country chainmakers and anti-sweating legislation, 1880–1930', *International Review of Social History*, 33 (1988).

Blackburn, S., 'Gender, work and labour history: a response to Carol Morgan', *Women's History Review*, 10 (2001).

Booth, A., 'The Labour Party and economics', *Bulletin of the Society for the Study of Labour History*, 47 (1983).

Bosanquet, N., 'The real low pay problem', in F. Field (ed.), *Low Pay* (1973).

Bowlby, R., 'Union policy toward minimum wage legislation in post-war Britain', *Industrial and Labor Relations Review*, 11 (1957).

Bowley, A.L., 'Earners and dependants in English towns in 1911', *Economica*, 1 (1921).

Brosnan, P., and F. Wilkinson, 'A national statutory minimum wage and economic efficiency,' *Contributions to Political Economy*, 7 (1988).

Burkitt, N., C. O'Donnell and B. Patel, 'George Bain and a 'mechanistic formula': the purpose and politics of £3.60', *Industrial Relations Journal*, 30 (1999).

Caine, B., 'Beatrice Webb and the "woman question"', *History Workshop Journal*, 14 (1982).

Caldwell, J. M., 'The genesis of the Ministry of Labour', *Public Administration*, 37 (1959).

Campbell, A., N. Fishman and J. McIlroy, 'The post-war compromise: mapping industrial politics, 1945–64', in A. Campbell, N. Fishman and J. McIlroy (eds), *British Trade Unions and Industrial Politics, Volume I: The Post-War Compromise, 1945–64* (Aldershot, 1999).

Cassidy, H., 'The emergence of the free labour contract in England', *American Economic Review*, 18 (1928).

Casteras, S., '"The gulf of destitution on whose brink they hang": images of life on the streets in Victorian art', in J. Treuherz (ed.), *Hard Times: Social Realism in Victorian Art* (1987).

Casteras, S., '"Weary stitches": illustrations and paintings for Thomas Hood's *Song of the Shirt* and other poems', in Harris, *Famine and Fashion*.

Chimes, J., '"Wanted: 1000 spirited young milliners": the fund for promoting female emigration', in Harris, *Famine and Fashion*.

Clapham, J., 'The Spitalfields Acts, 1773–1824', *Economic Journal*, 20 (1916).

Clark, A., 'The new poor law and the breadwinner wage: contrasting assumptions', *Journal of Social History*, 34 (2000).

Clift, B., and J. Tomlinson, 'Tawney and the third way', *Journal of Political Ideology*, 7 (2002).

Clubbe, J., 'Introduction', in J. Clubbe (ed.), *Selected Poems of Thomas Hood* (Cambridge, Mass.).

Copelman, D.M., 'The gendered metropolis: fin-de-siècle London', *Radical History Review*, 60 (1994).

Davidson, R., 'Llewellyn Smith, the labour department and government growth, 1886–1909', in G. Sutherland (ed.), *Studies in the Growth of Nineteenth Century Government* (1972).

Davidson, R., and R. Lowe, 'Bureaucracy and innovation in British welfare policy, 1870–1945', in W.J. Mommsen (ed.), *The Emergence of the Welfare State in Britain and Germany* (1981).

Dellheim, C., 'The creation of company culture: Cadburys, 1861–1931, *American Historical Review*, 93 (1987).

Derry, T., 'The repeal of the apprenticeship clauses of the Statute of Artificers', *Economic History Review,* 3 (1931).

Dickens, R., 'The national minimum wage', in R. Dickens, *et al, The State of Working Britain: Update 2001* (2001).

Dickens R., and A. Manning, 'Minimum wage, minimum impact', in R. Dickens *et al.* (eds), *The Labour Market Under New Labour* (2003).

Dickens, R., and A. Manning, 'Spikes and spillovers: the impact of the national minimum wage on the wage distribution in a low-wage sector', *Economic Journal*, 114 (2004).

Dzelzainis, E., 'Chartism and gender politics in Ernest Jones's *The Young Milliner*' in Harris, *Famine and Fashion*.

Edelstein, T J., 'They Sang "The Song Of the Shirt"', *Victorian Studies*, 23 (1980).

Englander, D., 'Booth's Jews: The presentation of Jews and Judaism in *Life and Labour of the People in London*', *Victorian Studies*, 32 (1989).

Englander, D., 'Comparisons and contrasts: Henry Mayhew and Charles Booth as social investigators', in Englander and O'Day, *Retrieved Riches.*

Ewing, K., 'The state and industrial relations: "collective laissez-faire" revisited', *Historical Studies in Industrial Relations*, 5 (1998).

Fairris, D., and M. Reich, 'The impacts of living wage policies', *Industrial Relations*, 44 (2005).

Feldman, D., 'Migrants, immigrants and welfare from the Old Poor Law to the welfare state', *Transactions of the Royal Historical Society*, 13 (2003).

Feldman, D., 'The importance of being English: Jewish immigration and the decay of liberal England', in Feldman and Stedman Jones, *Metropolis London.*

Feltes, N., 'Misery or the production of misery: defining sweated labour in 1890', *Social History*, 17 (1992).

Field, F., and S. Winyard, 'The effects of the Trade Board Act', in F. Field (ed.), *Are Low Wages Inevitable?* (Nottingham, 1977).

Freeden, M., 'J.A. Hobson as a New Liberal theorist', *Journal of History of Ideas*, 34 (1973).

Gazeley, I., and A. Newall, 'Rowntree revisited: poverty in Britain, 1900', *Explorations in Economic History*, 37 (2000).

Gazeley, I., 'The levelling of pay in Britain during the Second World War', *European Review of Economic History*, 10 (2006).

Gilbert, A., 'Fit work for women: sweated homeworkers in Glasgow, *c.*1875–1914', in E. Gordon (ed.), *The World is Ill-Divided: Women's Work in Scotland in the Nineteenth and Early Twentieth Centuries* (Edinburgh, 1990).

Goldman, L., 'Ruskin, Oxford, and the British labour movement, 1880–1914', in D. Birch (ed.), *Ruskin and the Dawn of the Modern* (Oxford, 1999).

Gospel, H., 'Labour markets and skill formation in theory and practice: a reply to Charles More', *Historical Studies in Industrial Relations,* 4 (1997).

Gowers, R., and T. Hatton, 'The origins and early impact of the minimum wage in agriculture', *Economic History Review*, 50 (1997).

Griffiths, J., '"Give my regards to Uncle Billy…": the rites and rituals of company life at Lever Brothers, c. 1900–c. 1990', *Business History*, 37 (1995).

Grover, C., 'Living wages and the "making work pay" strategy', *Critical Social Policy*, 25 (2005).

Gurney, P., 'An appropriated space: the Great Exhibition, the Crystal Palace and the working class', in L. Purbrick (ed.), *The Great Exhibition of 1851: New Interdisciplinary Essays* (Manchester, 2001).

Harris, B., 'All that glitters is not gold: the show-shop and the Victorian seamstress', in Harris, *Famine and Fashion.*

Harris, J., 'The Webbs, the Charity Organisation Society and the Ratan Tata Foundation: Social policy from the perspective of 1912', in M. Bulmer, J. Lewis and D. Piachaud (eds), *The Goals of Social Policy* (1989).

Harris, J., 'Ruskin and social reform', in D. Birch, *Ruskin and the Dawn of the Modern.*

Harrison, R., 'Sidney and Beatrice Webb', in Carl Levy (ed.), *Socialism and the Intelligentsia, 1880–1914* (1987).

Hatton, T., 'Trade boards and minimum wages, 1909–39', *Economic Affairs*, 17 (1997).

Hay, J.R., 'Employers and social policy in Britain: the evolution of welfare legislation, 1905–14', *Social History*, 4 (1977).

Hay, J.R., 'Employers' attitudes to social policy and the concept of social control, 1890–1920', in P. Thane (ed.), *The Origins of British Social Policy* (1978).

Haywood, I., 'The retailoring of Dickens: *Christmas Shadows*, radicalism, and the needlewoman myth', in Harris, *Famine and Fashion.*

Hennock, E.P., 'Poverty and social theory in England: the experience of the eighteen eighties', *Social History*, 1 (1976).

Hennock, E.P., ' The measurement of urban poverty: from the metropolis to the nation, 1880–1920', *Economic History Review*, 40 (1987).

Hennock, E.P., 'Concepts of poverty in the British social surveys from Charles Booth to Arthur Bowley', in M. Bulmer, K. Bales, and K. Sklar (eds), *The Social Survey in Historical Perspective, 1880–1940* (Cambridge, 1991).

Henriques, U.R.Q., 'The Jewish emancipation controversy in nineteenth-century Britain', *Past and Present*, 40 (1986).

Horrell, S., and J. Humphries, 'The origins and expansion of the male breadwinner family: the case of nineteenth-century Britain', *International Review of Social History*, 42, Supplement 5 (1997).

Howells, G., '"On account of their disreputable characters": parish assisted emigration from rural England, 1834–1860', *History*, 88 (2003).

James, K., '"Unregulated and suicidal competition": Irish rural industrial labour and Scottish anti-sweating campaigns in the early twentieth century', *Labour History Review*, 70 (2005).

Jeremy, D., 'The enlightened paternalist in action: William Hesketh Lever at Port Sunlight before 1914', *Business History*, 33 (1990).

Jones, S., 'Trade union policy between the wars: the case of holidays with pay in Britain', *International Review of Social History*, 31 (1986).

Kahn-Freund, O., 'Minimum wage legislation in Great Britain', *University of Pennsylvania Law Review*, 97 (1948–1949).

Keevash, S., 'Wages councils: an examination of trade union and Conservative Government misconceptions about the effect of statutory wage fixing', *Industrial Law Journal*, 14 (1985).

Klingberg, F.J., 'Harriet Beecher Stowe and social reform in England', *American Historical Review*, 43 (1938).

Lal, D., 'The minimum wage: no way to help the poor', *Institute of Economic Affairs Occasional Paper*, 95 (1995).

Ledger, S., 'Chartist aesthetics in the mid-nineteenth century: Ernest Jones, a novelist of the people', *Nineteenth-Century Literature*, 57 (2002).

Lee, A., 'Aspects of the working-class response to the Jews in Britain, 1880–1914', in Lunn, *Hosts, Immigrants and Minorities.*

Lowe, R., 'The Ministry of Labour, 1916–1924: a graveyard of social reform?', *Public Administration*, 52 (1974).

Lowe, R., 'The erosion of state intervention in Britain, 1917–24', *Economic History Review*, 31 (1978).

Lowe, R., 'The failure of consensus in Britain: the national industrial conference, 1919–21', *Historical Journal*, 21 (1978).

Machin, S., and C. Meghir, 'Does crime pay better?', *Centrepiece*, 4 (1999).

McKinlay, A., and J. Zeitlin, 'The meanings of managerial prerogative: industrial relations and the organisation of work in British engineering, 1880–1939', in C. Harvey and J. Turner (eds), *Labour and Business in Modern Britain* (1989).

McWilliam, R., 'The melodramatic seamstress: interpreting a Victorian penny dreadful,' in Harris, *Famine and Fashion*.

Maitles, H., 'Jewish trade unionists in Glasgow', *Immigrants and Minorities*, 10 (1991).

Mappen, E.,'Strategies for change: socialist-feminist approaches to the problems of women's work', in John, *Unequal Opportunities*.

Marwick, A., 'Middle opinion in the thirties: planning, progress and political "agreement"', *English Historical Review*, 79 (1964).

Matthew, H.C.G., 'Hobson, Ruskin and Cobden', in M. Freeden (ed.), *Reappraising J.A. Hobson: Humanism and Welfare* (1990).

Melling, J., 'Employers, industrial housing and the evolution of company welfare policies in Britain's heavy industry: West Scotland, 1870–1920', *International Review of Social History*, 26 (1981).

Melling, J., 'Employers, industrial welfare and the struggle for workplace control in British industry, 1880–1921', in H.F. Gospel, and C.R. Littler (eds), *Managerial Strategies and Industrial Relations: An Historical and Comparative Study* (1981).

Metcalf, D., 'The British national minimum wage', *British Journal of Industrial Relations*, 37 (1999).

Metcalf, D., 'The Low Pay Commission and the national minimum wage', *Economic Journal*, 109 (1999).

Moore, R., 'Can't unions do more?', in F. Field (ed.), *Are Low Wages Inevitable?* (Nottingham, 1977).

More, C., 'Reskilling and labour markets in Britain c.1890–1940', *Historical Studies in Industrial Relations*, 2 (1996).

Morris, J., 'The characteristics of sweating: the late nineteenth-century London and Leeds tailoring trade', in John, *Unequal Opportunities*.

Neumark, D., and W. Wascher, 'The effects of New Jersey's minimum wage on fast food employment: a re-evaluation using payroll data', National Bureau of Economic Research, *Working Paper*, 5224 (1995).

Nyland, C., and G. Ramia, 'The Webbs and the rights of women', in P. Beilharz and C. Nyland (eds), *The Webbs, Fabianism and Feminism* (Aldershot, 1998).

O' Day, R., 'Interviews and investigations: Charles Booth and the making of the Religious Influences survey', in Englander and O' Day, *Retrieved Riches*.

O' Day, R., 'Women and social investigation: Clara Collet and Beatrice Potter', in Englander and O'Day, *Retrieved Riches*.

Pearson, R., 'Thackeray and Punch at the Great Exhibition: authority and ambivalence in verbal and visual caricatures', in Purbrick, *Great Exhibition*.

Pellew, J., 'The Home Office and the Aliens Act', *Historical Journal*, 32 (1989).

Pelling, H., 'Trade unions, workers and the law', in H. Pelling, *Popular Politics in Late-Victorian Britain* (1968).

Pond, C., 'Wages councils, the unorganised and the low paid', in G.S. Bain (ed.), *Industrial Relations in Britain* (Oxford, 1983).

Pullin, N., '"A heavy bill to settle with humanity": the representation and invisibility of London's principal milliners and dressmakers', in Harris, *Famine and Fashion*.

Rickard, J., 'The anti-sweating movement in Britain and Victoria: the politics of empire and social reform', *Historical Studies*, 18 (1979).

Riddell, N., '"The Age of Cole?" G.D.H. Cole and the British labour movement, 1929–1933', *Historical Journal*, 38 (1995).

Roberts, H., 'Marriage, redundancy or sin', in M. Vicinus (ed.), *Suffer and Be Still* (1980; first published 1972).

Roberts, S., 'Thomas Cooper', in J. Bellamy and J. Saville (eds), *Dictionary of Labour Biography Volume 9* (London, 1993).

Rogers, H., '"The good are not always powerful nor the powerful always good": the politics of women's needlework in mid-Victorian London', *Victorian Studies*, 40 (1997).

Rubery, J., 'The low paid and the unorganized', in P. Edwards (ed.) *Industrial Relations: Theory and Practice in Britain* (Oxford, 1995).

Savage, G., 'Friend to the worker: social policy at the Ministry of Agriculture between the wars', *Albion*, 19 (1987).

Saville, J., 'The Christian Socialists of 1848', in J. Saville (ed.), *Democracy and the Labour Movement* (1954).

Saville, J., 'The ideology of labourism', in R. Benewick, R. Berki, and R. Parekh (eds), *Knowledge and Belief in Politics: The Problem of Ideology* (1973).

Searle, G.R., 'Introduction,' in A. White, *Efficiency and Empire* (Sussex, 1973; first published 1901).

Searle, G., 'Arnold White', in H.C.G. Mathews and B. Harrison, (eds), *Dictionary of National Biography, Volume 58* (Oxford, 2004).

Simpson, B., 'Implementing the national minimum wage: the 1999 regulations', *Industrial Law Journal*, 28 (1999).

Simpson, B., 'A milestone in the legal regulation of pay: the National Minimum Wage Act 1998', *Industrial Law Journal*, 28 (1999).

Simpson, B., 'The national minimum wage five years on: reflections on some general issues', *Industrial Law Journal*, 33 (2004).

Simpson, L., and I. Paterson, 'A national minimum wage for Britain?' *Economics*, 28 (1992).

Smith, P., 'The road haulage industry, 1918–1940: the process of unionisation, employers' control and statutory regulation', *Historical Studies in Industrial Relations*, 3 (1997).

Stevenson, J., 'Pivot or pilot? The role of the independent members of wages councils', *Journal of Social Policy*, 9 (1980).

Taylor, E., 'A craft society in the age of general unions', *West Midland Studies*, 5 (1972).

Thane, P., 'Women and the Poor Law in Victorian and Edwardian England', *History Workshop Journal*, 6 (1978).

Thane, P., 'Towards equal opportunities? Women in Britain since 1945', in T. Gourvish and A. O'Day (eds), *Britain Since 1945* (1991).

Thom, D., 'Free from chains? The image of women's labour in London, 1900–20', in Feldman and Stedman Jones, *Metropolis London.*

Thompson, E.P., 'Mayhew and the *Morning Chronicle*', in E.P. Thompson and E. Yeo (eds), *The Unknown Mayhew* (1971).

Tomlinson, J., 'The limits of Tawney's ethical socialism: a historical perspective on the Labour Party and the market', *Contemporary British History*, 16 (2002).

Vinson, A., 'The Edwardians and poverty: towards a minimum wage?', in D. Reid (ed.), *Edwardian England* (1982).

Williams, B., 'The beginnings of Jewish trade unionism in Manchester, 1889–1891', in Lunn, *Hosts, immigrants and Minorities.*

Winter, J., 'R.H. Tawney's early political thought', *Past and Present*, 47 (1970).

Winter, J., 'The Webbs and the non-white world: a case of socialist racialism', *Journal of Contemporary History*, 9 (1974).

Winyard, S., 'Low Pay', in D. Bell, (ed.), *The Conservative Government, 1979–84: An Interim Report* (1985).

Wohl, A.S., 'The bitter cry of outcast London', *International Review of Social History*, 13 (1968).

Wright, A., 'Tawneyism revisited: equality, welfare and socialism', in B. Pimlott (ed.), *Fabian Essays* (1984).

Theses and dissertations

Atherton, J.R., 'R.H. Tawney as a Christian Socialist moralist', Ph.D., University of Manchester, 1979.

Blackburn, S., 'Sweated labour and the minimum wage: a case study of the women chainmakers of Cradley Heath, South Staffordshire, 1850–1950', Ph.D., University of London, 1984.

Boyaval, P., 'La lutte contre le sweating system: le minimum légal de salaire l'example de l'Australiasie et de l'Angleterre', Ph.D., University of Paris, 1911.

Brown, J., 'Ideas concerning social policy and their influence on legislation in Britain, 1902–11', Ph.D., University of London, 1964.

Davidson, R., 'Sir Hubert Llewellyn Smith and labour policy, 1886–1916', Ph.D., University of Cambridge, 1971.

Mallin, K., 'N. Hingley and Sons Limited: Black Country anchor smith and chain cable maker', Ph.D., University of Warwick, 1996.

Index

Note: illustrations are denoted by italics.